Contents

Volume 6   Numbers 1 & 2   200[...]

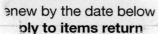

Associated Reviewers

JMM – The International Journal on Media Management

Editors' Note

Dear Readers,

Welcome to the first issue of the *International Journal on Media Management* of this year, a double issue devoted to the theme "Traditional Media and the Internet: The Search for Viable Business Models." We hope that our focus theme provides you with a deeper understanding of how the Internet has changed the nature of traditional media industries and that we can give you a preliminary view of things to come.

Our invited Guest Editor, Sylvia M. Chan-Olmsted from the University of Florida, is a distinguished scholar in the field of telecommunication management, media, and strategy. We would like to express our gratitude for her support and contribution throughout the whole cycle of this issue's preparation. In her guest editorial, Chan-Olmsted introduces all articles accepted for publication and provides the general context of this interesting special issue.

This double issue is the first result of our cooperation with Lawrence Erlbaum Associates, Publishers, as announced in the last issue. Our loyal readers will notice some changes to the layout like the new two-column format and the new typesetting style, but our scope and content remains the same. We hope you like our new look and feel. Apart from the production side of the journal, we also had some changes in the editorial team: Co-Editor Andreas Herrmann stepped down from this position. His function and additional support in the continuous improvement and development of the journal will be shared by two new Associate Co-Editors: Joachim Haes of the University of Lugano, who works on the economics of information goods and communication management, and Bozena I. Mierzejewska from the University of St. Gallen, who works on media management research and the publishing industry. She also used to serve as Executive Editor of this journal. Bozena and Joachim are very enthusiastic to work and serve the community of media management researchers, and they welcome suggestions, comments, and new ideas.

The final section of this issue is devoted to book reviews that spotlight policy issues in media management and a conference calendar.

Beat F. Schmid
Peter Glotz
Joachim Haes
Bozena I. Mierzejewska
Yingzi Xu

Introduction: Traditional Media and the Internet: The Search for Viable Business Models

Sylvia M. Chan-Olmsted

The arrival of the Internet has changed the rules of competition in many industry sectors. In the realm of media markets, the Internet's bona fide role as the newest mass medium and its unique characteristics of interactivity and personalization present tremendous challenges as well as potentials in the formulation of innovative business models, both from the existing media incumbents who wish to compete with and to leverage the Internet's popularity and from the new online ventures that attempt to take a bigger share of the revenue pie from media advertisers and consumers.

An important body of literature has emerged to address the changes and values that the Internet brought to a conventional marketplace. Many media scholars have begun to study the factors that might impact a firm's Internet strategy and proposed a range of Internet business models. Most literature suggests that the Internet has improved the effectiveness and efficiency of coordination in the value chain, become a source of competitive advantage by providing companies with new ways to outperform their competitors, encouraged direct interaction between producers and consumers, allowed businesses to access global markets, developed better business intelligence, and enhanced customer communication and service. Additionally, the Internet provides a tremendous opportunity for the Web retailing of digital multimedia goods.

It is evident that different media sectors and firms have approached the Internet with various emphases and intensities. Literatures suggest that these differences might be due to the nature of the product or service and its target market, the degree of organizational competency in integrating the existing business with the Internet, the degree of changes required from the organization to adopt the Internet, a firm's dependency on the Internet for revenue, and the size and age of an organization.

Address correspondence to Sylvia M. Chan-Olmsted, Department of Telecommunication, College of Journalism and Communications, P.O. Box 118400, University of Florida, Gainesville, FL 32611–8400. E-mail: chanolmsted@jou.ufl.edu

As the Internet increases its presence in average households, all traditional media have, in their own ways, embraced the Internet. Nevertheless, even as many Internet ventures are being launched by media firms, many are being scaled down or eliminated because of the lack of evident benefits and resources. The development of an appropriate business model is especially critical, as well as intricate, as the Internet offers an alternative distribution channel for traditional media's products and strengthens the existing media's position with their readers and audiences and at the same time competes with the traditional media for consumer attention and resources.

This issue of the *International Journal on Media Management (IJMM)* addresses the very topic of Internet business models from the perspective of the traditional media sectors. The 11 theme articles tackle the issues of online content delivery business models, the relation between online and offline media products, the Internet's impact on a media value chain, online marketing of music products, Internet content strategies, and comparative studies of Web content and strategies in different countries. From theoretical discussions to empirical investigations, the authors successfully examine the traditional media incumbents' efforts in developing business strategies that leverage their online competencies and suggest the factors that might play a role in this process.

Specifically, to provide a structured method of comparing business models between firms within or between industries with a goal of identifying key profit drivers, Fetscherin and Knolmayer propose five components that any business model for content delivery should include. Using the print industry as an example, they find that the most important key profit driver is still the product, followed by revenue and price. Also using the print media sector in their exploratory case study, Schulze, Hess, and Eggers analyze how the Internet affects publishers' content utilization practices. The authors find that although the Internet has various degrees of impact on the composition of publishers' content utilization chains, it has not delivered extra revenues. In fact, the Internet-based content utilization windows have not been adequately explored and are relatively dependent on their relations with the print-based ones. In the next article, Kolo and Vogt propose a list of key issues that account for the success of online spin-offs in the media industry. Based on empirical data pertaining to the German market, the authors conclude that the management of online spin-offs has played a more significant role than the offline reach, such as the brand equity of the offline product, in the success of its online spin-offs. The findings in these three articles are quite interesting, as they point to the essential role of the online product and its revenues in driving profitability, at the same time confirming the traditional media's inability to strategically capitalize on the unique characteristics of this new medium.

The next two articles examine the online business strategies of music and video products. Chang, Lee, and Lee taxonomically link the economic properties of video products to their Internet distribution strategies, and Vaccaro and Cohn use a services marketing framework to show how music products might be distributed and marketed online with a true consumer orientation. The same strategic focus was evident in Stahl, Schäfer, and Maass's work in selling paid content on print media Web sites. The authors here empirically test the strategy of selling bundled and unbundled content on newspaper and magazine Web sites and discover that cannibalization does occur when little strategic care is present in the bundling process (i.e., selling the same info goods offline and online simultaneously). Beyers's article in online dayparting strategy further demonstrates the importance of strategic competency in this uncharted online world. Some of these articles also suggest that traditional media do have a certain degree of competitive edge in the online arena because of their existing relationship and experience with media consumers.

Comparative media studies have always been fruitful in identifying the various exogenous conditions that influence the development of media products. Through the content analysis of top Web sites in the United States and South Korea, Ha and Ganahl's article succinctly identifies two general Webcasting business models and the cultural determinants that might impact the success of these models. Moving to the region of the European Union, Arampatzis compares the business models of online news publishers in Greece and the United Kingdom by differentiating their content emphases and ownership types. From a different perspective in viewing the online news product, in the following article, Bucy suggests that online news sites should be evaluated based on their nonmonetary rather than profit–loss contributions. Finally, Edge's work concluded our special theme section with an extensive case study of a failed ambitious Internet venture in Singapore, demonstrating the complexity of the Internet business environment.

In the general articles section, this issue has two interesting contributions from Calder and Malthouse addressing the qualitative media measurement of newspapers and from Albarran and Loomis tackling the regulatory changes and media management practices in the United States. I hope you will find the work in this special issue interesting and inspiring. I would also like to thank all of the reviewers who took the time to help us advance the scholarship in our field. Special thanks should go to the editorial team at *IJMM* and the authors who contributed to this issue. I know the revision time frame was almost impossible, but you did it. Thank you all for the privilege of editing your work.

Sylvia M. Chan-Olmsted
chanolmsted@jou.ufl.edu

is an Associate Professor in the Department of Telecommunication at the University of Florida. Her research interests include new media and its impacts on market competition and telecommunication brand/strategic management.

FOCUS THEME ARTICLES

Business Models for Content Delivery: An Empirical Analysis of the Newspaper and Magazine Industry

Marc Fetscherin and Gerhard Knolmayer
University of Bern, Switzerland

Although there have been efforts to define, describe, and classify business models, current literature does not provide a structured method of comparing business models between companies within or between industries. This article outlines a conceptual business model and proposes 5 components that a business model for content delivery should include: the product, the consumer, the revenue, the price, and the delivery. By using the newspaper and magazine industry as an example, we empirically test the impact of these 5 components on profit. Furthermore, we address 2 key issues content providers are confronted with when selling digital content: First, how much of the digital content is available free or at cost, and second, is the digital product as complementary or a substitute to the physical product. Finally, we assess the risk of cannibalizing the physical product with the digital one by a multiple regression analysis.

The Internet provides new opportunities to traditional methods of selling content as it gives content providers a new distribution channel that may increase their sales. Threats of selling digital content are that content providers have to compete against free offers of content (e.g., at news portals) and that the digital product may cannibalize their own physical product. So far, selling digital content has not resulted in the expected return on investment for many content providers from the music, film, and print industry. With the emergence of new technologies such as digital rights management systems (DRMS) and the introduction of new bills such as the Consumer Broadband and Digital Television Act and the Peer-to-Peer Piracy Prevention Act, some content providers believe that appropriate tools to protect and sell their digital content will be available soon.

To sell digital content to consumers, not only technological and legal solutions are required, but also attractive business models have to be established. Furthermore, the judicious selection of a business model may significantly reduce the need for technological or legal protection. This is especially true in the short term, as DRMS still have

some limitations and are missing broad consumer acceptance and as legislation may take several years to become operative. Despite efforts to sell digital content via the Internet, content providers have not come up with a viable business model.

There is an extensive amount of literature available about business models, the pricing of information goods, and digital content economics. However, despite an enormous effort to define and classify business models, currently no sound theoretical basis for evaluating business models in the content industry exists. Furthermore, very few empirical studies try to analyze business models of content providers, especially those operating in the newspaper and magazine industry.

The aim of this article is twofold: First, it investigates and analyzes current literature about business models. Despite the wide usage of this term in practice, we find a confusing spectrum of definitions and classifications. This article proposes to distinguish five key components of business models and to discuss the key profit drivers. The second part of the article empirically discusses two key issues newspaper and magazine editors are currently facing. First, we analyze how much of the digital content is provided free or at cost. Second, we provide evidence as to whether content providers are positioning the digital product as a complement to or a substitute for the physi-

Address correspondence to Marc Fetscherin, Institute of Information Systems, University of Bern, Engehaldestrassen 8, 3012 Bern, Switzerland. E-mail: fetscherin@iwi.unibe.ch

cal product. Finally, this article assesses the risk of cannibalizing the physical product by the digital one using a multiple regression analysis.

Business Model

Components of Business Models

We agree with Rappa (2000), who stated that business models may be the most discussed and least understood aspect of the Web. Despite the widespread usage in the contemporary business world and some parts of the literature, a rather confusing picture of the scope and dimensions of business models, especially for digital content, remains. As Alt and Zimmermann (2001) argued, current publications present a broad spectrum of understandings, interpreting auctions, business-to-business (B2B) or business-to-consumer (B2C), a revenue model, or a vertical portal as a business model. These models may be implemented in a variety of ways and a firm may combine different business models in its e-commerce strategy (Rappa, 2000).

A generally accepted definition and classification of business models does not exist. One of the established definitions is from Slywotzky (1996), who defined a business model as the totality of how a company selects its customers, defines and differentiates its offerings, defines the tasks it will perform itself and those it will outsource, configures its resources, goes to market, creates utility for customers, and captures profits. It is the entire system for delivering utility to customers and earning a profit from that activity. Timmers (1998) perceived a business model as the architecture for product, service, and information flows. This includes a description of the various business actors and their roles, the potential benefits for the various business actors, and the sources of revenues. Trombly (2000) defined an e-business model as an approach for conducting electronic business through which a company can sustain itself and generate profitable revenue growth. Mahadevan (2000) interpreted a business model as a unique blend of various streams.

Current literature provides a wide range of business model classifications (Äijö & Saarinen, 2001; Geoffrion, 1998; Rao, 1999; Rappa, 2000; Timmers, 1998; Trombly, 2000). Other publications focus on specific components of a business model, such as the revenue models by Novak and Hoffmann (2001) and Bhattacharjee, Gopal, Lertwachara, and Marsden (2003), the pricing models of information goods by Varian (1995) and Chen (1998), or models about economics of digital content by Choi, Stahl, and Whinston (1997) and Poddar (2002). Although these works provide a conceptual basis, they do not completely satisfy our need, as they most often focus on business

models for physical products, such as selling books or CDs via the Internet, rather than digital products, such as digital downloads or e-books.

Geoffrion (1998) distinguished 11 "pure" business models for electronic commerce on the Web, such as the storefront model, the mall model, and the customer service model. Timmers (1998) classified 10 different business models such as the e-shop, e-procurement, e-auction, and virtual communities along two dimensions. Rappa (2000) identified 29 types of business models divided into nine categories such as brokerage, advertising, informediary, and utility. Martinez (2000) distinguished five categories: offline facilitator, context provider, commerce destination, online exchange, and gateway. Trombly (2000) presented the widely accepted distinction into B2B, B2C, business-to-government (B2G), and e-marketplaces as a classification of business models. In a similar way Rao (1999) presented three major forms of online commerce (B2C, B2B, consumer-to-consumer [C2C]), along seven dimensions, such as market potential, value drivers, and revenue streams. Turban, Lee, King, and Viehland (2002) mentioned several types of Internet business models including "name your price," online auctions, customization, and electronic marketplaces.

Very little similarity can be found between the classifications just outlined. Because all nomenclatures describe the same phenomenon (i.e., business on the Internet), the mismatch and noncompatibility comes from different viewpoints and methodologies the authors have used when developing their models and classification schemes (Wang & Chan, 2003). Furthermore, only a few authors justify their classification by well-defined criteria. For example, Timmers (1998) backed up his classification by functional integration and degree of innovation, and Martinez (2000) used two dimensions, market primary focus and market scope. Rappa (2000) argued that his classification is based on case studies and observation (Wang & Chan, 2003).

We agree with Wang and Chan (2003), who argued that most authors do not explicitly explain the rules and criteria they use to classify business models. This raises the question of whether classifying business models is an appropriate approach for identifying profit drivers. Recently, Mahadevan (2000), Afuah and Tucci (2001), Amit and Zott (2001), Eisenmann (2002), and Rayport and Jaworski (2001) recognized this shortcoming and considered business models from a different perspective by discussing their key components. The value stream, the revenue stream, and the logistical stream are perceived as main components by Mahadevan (2000). Afuah and Tucci (2001) argued that a business model is defined by the value a firm offers its customers, its target customer segment, the scope of products and services it offers to different customer segments, its sources of revenue, its price–value ratio, the activities it must complete to offer that value, the capabilities these activities are based on, what a firm must do to sustain its advantages, and how well it can implement the elements of the business model. Amit and Zott (2001) presented three components of e-business models: content (exchanged goods and information), structure (the links between transaction stakeholders), and governance of transactions (the control of the flows of goods, information, and resources). Eisenmann (2002) stated that a business model consists of a company's profits in the long run, what a company will sell, to whom it will sell that product, how the company will collect revenues, what technologies it will employ, when it will rely on partners, and how its costs will increase with growth. Rayport and Jaworski (2001) argued that to develop an online business model, senior management must define four components of the model: first, a value proposition or value cluster for the targeted customer; second, an online offering, which could be a product, a service, information, or some combination of them; third, a unique, defendable resource system; and finally a revenue model. Table 1 summarizes the various components of a business model for each of the articles just mentioned. The column on the right presents the five key components emerging from this article.

There are three components mentioned by the majority of authors (cf. Table 1), namely the product, the consumer, and the revenue. Because, according to Varian (1995), the pricing of information goods is an important factor, we do not believe that it should be included in the revenue as proposed by Mahadevan (2000), Eisenmann (2002), or Rayport and Jaworski (2001), but that it deserves its own place in the business model. A content provider may obtain revenues from different sources (e.g., direct sales, advertising, or syndication); thus, we distinguish prices and revenues as different components. The component's technology, resource systems, activities necessary, capabilities of activities, im-

plementation, structure, governance of transaction, and logistical stream proposed by various authors are covered by the term *delivery*, which includes how digital content is delivered to the customer; with what kind of resources; and by what activities, technologies, and capabilities. The component "cooperation/partner" proposed by Eisenmann (2002) is not taken into account as it is in our opinion not a component of a business model but more concerned with the strategic direction of a company. It should be noted that the business model per se is not what makes a company successful and profitable, but rather the way the company utilizes the various components.

Research Method

The sample for the empirical study was selected in two steps. In the first step we used the following selection criteria: We identified daily newspapers and weekly magazines operating either in the European or U.S. consumer market. The content provider had to offer a physical product and be present on the Internet with at least a home page. In the second step we selected those companies that provided an online archive (subscription or free) or payable downloads (e.g., payable articles). Questionnaires were sent to the companies selected and the responses were analyzed.

The research was carried out in 2003. In the first step, 153 companies were identified (Hügli, 2003). After the second step we were left with 75 companies. A questionnaire was sent to them; 24 companies returned the questionnaire. Of those, 19 completed the questionnaire accurately, which represents a return rate of more than 25%. Among the respondents were Computer Zeitung, Financial Times Germany, *PCWorld*, *Salon*, *Stern*, and the *Wall Street Journal*. Fifty-eight percent of the respondents publish newspapers and 42% publish magazines.

Table 1. Components of Business Models

Mahadevan (2000)	Afuah & Tucci (2001)	Amit & Zott (2001)	Eisenmann (2002)	Rayport & Jaworski (2002)	Fetscherin & Knolmayer (this article)
Value stream (product)	Value offered (product)	Content (product)	What to sell (product)	Value proposition to customer (customer)	Product
Revenue stream (Revenue model)	Consumer segment	Structure	To whom (customer)		Consumer
Logistical stream	Scope of products (product)	Governance of transactions (resources, information)	How to collect revenues (revenue model)	On-line offering (product)	Revenue
	Revenue sources/model		What technology	Resource system	Pricing
	Pricing		Which cooperation/ partners	Revenue Model	Delivery
	Resources				
	Activities necessary				
	Capabilities of activities				
	Implementation				

Empirical Results

Three main analyses are presented in this article. First, we assess the importance of the five key components defined previously as key profit drivers of a business model. Second, we focus on two key questions content providers are struggling with: How much of the digital content is provided for free or at cost and whether content providers position the digital products as complements to or substitutes for their physical products. These two questions lead to our third analysis, which evaluates the risk of cannibalizing the physical product through the digital product.

Determine Key Profit Drivers

In this section we analyze which of the five business model components introduced earlier has the highest impact on profitability. The respondents have been asked to rate certain profit drivers on a scale with points at 1 (*not important*), 2 (*important*), and 3 (*very important*). Product was identified as the most important driver, receiving a mean value of 2.9, followed by revenue and pricing, both rated by the mean value of 2.1. The remaining components, consumer and delivery, were given ratings below 2.

To evaluate the leading position of the product component, we test whether the differences between the mean values 2.9 and 2.1 are statistically significant at level $\alpha = .05$.

H_0: $\mu_D = 0$, there is no significant difference between the mean values.

H_1: $\mu_D > 0$, there is a significant difference between the mean values.

The parameter of interest is the mean of the population of differences, which we label μ_D. For the mean values of product and revenue we obtain $t = 7.320$, for product and $t = 6.096$ for price. For a Student t distribution with $df = 18$ we obtain a rejection region $t > t(.05, 18) = 1.734$, provided that the differences are normally distributed. Therefore, we reject the null hypothesis. The difference between the mean values is statistically significant, which strengthens the dominant position of the product component.

Free Versus Fee-Based Content

Among the most controversial topics discussed when selling digital content on the Internet are which fraction of the offering should be made available free or at cost and whether the digital content should be offered as complement to or substitute for the physical product.

Digital content access for consumers can be offered in three ways: content that is provided free, free after regis-

tration, or for which the consumer must pay. Respondents were asked to assign their offerings of digital content into these three groups. In very few cases the respondents provided content free after registration. Therefore, we added the number of these responses to those of the free offerings. Figure 1 illustrates the percentage of the overall digital content offered free.

Figure 1 indicates that the majority of the respondents follow one of two basic strategies: They either offer most content free (respondents 1–11) or at cost (respondents 16–19). This finding can be related to Porter's (1998) widely referenced generic strategies cost leadership, differentiation, and focus. A cost leadership strategy is one in which a firm strives to have the lowest costs (and prices) in the industry; in our case this strategy seems to be followed by respondents 1 to 11 because providing content free does not need any additional prerequisites. A firm that follows a differentiation strategy offers products or services with unique features that customers value. The value added by this uniqueness allows the firm to demand a premium price; in our case this strategy seems to be followed by respondents 16 to 19. The focus strategy can be combined with either a cost leadership or a differentiation strategy and may be aimed toward a broad or narrow market. Figure 2 outlines the resulting strategies and the corresponding number of respondents.

As mentioned earlier, the concept of free access after registration is not used very often. A possible explanation can also be derived from the "stuck in the middle" phenomenon (Porter, 1998). Either content providers follow the cost leadership strategy and offer content free, do not demand any explicit information, and do not ask for registration from the consumer, or they follow a differentiation strategy because they have a unique product and de-

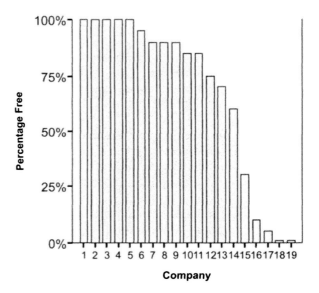

Figure 1. Percentage of free content provided.

Competitive Advantage

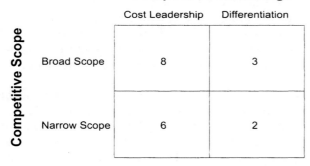

Figure 2. Generic strategies followed by respondents.

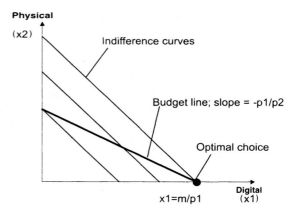

Figure 3. Optimal choice for perfect substitutes.

mand registration information, which is often seen as an obstacle by consumers.

Complement Versus Substitute

The relation between the digital and physical products can either be complementary or substitutive. The respondents were therefore asked how much of their entire content is available exclusively in digital format, how much exclusively in physical format, and how much in both formats. According to their responses, 64% of the content is provided simultaneously in a physical and a digital format, 20% of the content is provided exclusively physically, and only 16% is provided exclusively in a digital format. The relatively high percentage of content provided simultaneously in both formats indicates that in many cases the digital product may in principle substitute for the physical product.

We therefore test the hypothesis of whether companies in the newspaper and magazine industries position their digital products as complements to their physical products or as substitutes. We define a digital offering as a complement if the percentage of the digital content provided exclusively in digital format is higher than the percentage provided in both formats.

- H_0: $\mu_D \geq 0$, the digital product is positioned as a complement to the physical product.
- H_1: $\mu_D < 0$, the digital product is not positioned as a complement to the physical product.

In this test μ_D is the mean value of the differences between the percentage of content provided exclusively in a digital format and the percentage provided simultaneously in both formats. The t value corresponding to significance level .05 is 1.734; for the data analyzed we obtain t = 5.160. We therefore reject the null hypothesis. We conclude that newspapers and magazines are typically not positioning the digital product primarily as a complement to

the physical product but provide much content in both formats. Therefore they are exposed to the risk of cannibalizing the sales of their own physical product. Cannibalization means the reduction in the sales volume, revenue, or market share of one product (in our case the physical product) as a result of the introduction of a new product (in our case the digital product) by the same company.

If the majority of content is provided in both formats and if consumers were indifferent between them, we would have perfect substitution, in which the indifference curves are straight lines with a slope of -1 and the marginal rate of substitution equals $| 1 |$ (Varian, 2003).

Three cases have to be distinguished. Let x_1 be the quantity of the digital product and x_2 the quantity of the physical product sold at corresponding prices, p_1 and p_2, respectively. For $p_2 > p_1$, the slope of the budget line is flatter than the slope of the indifference curves (Figure 3). In this case the consumer spends the budget m on the digital product x_1. If $p_1 > p_2$, the consumer purchases only the physical product. Finally, for $p_1 = p_2$ any quantities of Products 1 and 2 that equal the budget constraint m are optimal.

In the case of perfect substitution, the optimal choice for a given budget will typically concentrate on one of the two products. The demand function of the digital product (x_1) is

$$
x_1 = \begin{cases} m/p_1 & \text{if } p_1 < p_2 \\ \text{any number between 0 and } m/p_1 & \text{if } p_1 = p_2 \\ 0 & \text{if } p_1 > p_2 \end{cases}
$$

Figure 4 illustrates the demand curve for the digital product x_1 in the case of perfect substitution.

Risk of Cannibalization

So far, the article has outlined for each respondent how much of its content is provided free or at cost and has as-

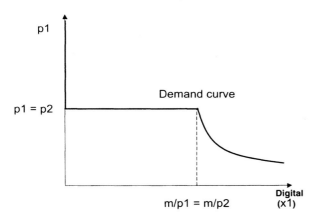

Figure 4. Demand curve for perfect substitutes.

sessed the risk of substituting the physical product with the digital one. However, we have not discussed which variables explain the risk of cannibalization. We describe this risk by the equation

$$y = \beta_0 + \beta_1 \, x_1 + \beta_2 \, x_2 + \beta_3 \, x_3 + \ldots + \beta_k \, x_k + \varepsilon$$

where y is the risk of cannibalization, $x_1, x_2, \ldots, x_k$ are the independent variables with corresponding coefficients β_0, $\beta_1, \ldots, \beta_k$, and ε is the error variable. The dependent variable was captured by asking the respondents why they invested in the online business. The statement "because there is a positive effect on the sales of our physical product" was rated on a 5-point Likert scale varying from 0 (*highly disagree*) to 4 (*highly agree*). Likert scales are either ordinal or interval. If well constructed and the distances between all neighboring values are equal, the Likert scales resemble an interval scale and therefore a multiple regression analysis may be applied.

This article has so far outlined two possible variables explaining the risk of cannibalization: the percentage of free digital content (FREE) and the percentage of content provided simultaneously in physical and digital format (SIM). We consider two additional variables that may be relevant in explaining the risk of cannibalization (RISK): Whether the content is general or specific (CONTENT) and whether the geographical focus of the content provider is local, national, or international (GEO). Therefore, one could formulate the following additive regression model:

$$RISK = \beta_0 + \beta_1 \, FREE + \beta_2 \, SIM + \beta_3 \, CONTENT + \beta_4 \, GEO + \varepsilon$$

However, a risk of cannibalization exists only if both variables FREE and SIM have positive values; the regression model just shown is not compatible with this property. For instance, if no content is provided in both formats and the digital content is provided entirely free (SIM = 0 and FREE = 100), the cannibalization risk is 0, whereas the re-

Table 2. Results of Regression Analysis

Model	Unstandardized Coefficients		t Values	Significance
	β	SE		
(Constant)	−.044	.765	−0.058	.955
FREESIM	.036	.007	5.328	.000
CONTENT	−.249	.464	−0.538	.599
GEO	.267	.340	0.784	.446

gression model would predict a positive risk. We therefore multiply the percentages FREE and SIM and use FREESIM = FREE*SIM / 100 as an independent variable. This leads to the regression model

$$RISK = \beta_0 + \beta_1 \, FREESIM + \beta_2 \, CONTENT + \beta_3 \, GEO + \varepsilon$$

Table 2 shows the resulting regression coefficients, their standard errors, and the t values for the significance level .05. The variables CONTENT and GEO, as well as the constant, are not significant but the product of FREE and SIM is. Thus, we obtain RISK = 0.036 FREESIM. In the example with SIM = 0 and FREE = 100 this equation predicts the risk of cannibalization as 0, which is a plausible result.

The overall usefulness of the regression model can be evaluated by an analysis of variance. The F value 10.54 is far higher than the corresponding critical value $F(3, 14) = 3.34, p = .05$, and we conclude that the model is useful. The coefficient of determination R^2 equals .693; thus, 69% of the variation of risk of cannibalization is explained by the product of the percentages of free digital content and content provided simultaneously in both formats.

Discussion and Conclusion

Current literature does not provide a clear understanding of business models for digital content and the picture remains insufficient with respect to identifying the key profit drivers. Many authors tried to establish different frameworks and classification criteria, but these efforts did not result in a common perception. We suggest another way to look at business models, structuring them into the five key components of product, consumer, price, revenue, and delivery. This approach allows a more consistent way to compare business models of companies to identify key profit drivers. Our results show that the most important key profit driver is the product, followed by revenue and price.

This article then addresses two key questions content providers are struggling with: how much of their digital content should be provided free or at cost and whether the digital product should be positioned as a complement to or substitute for the physical product. Our results indicate that most content providers follow either a differentiation or cost leadership strategy, where the majority is following the latter by providing most of their digital content free. It further shows that many newspapers and magazines are using, intentionally or not, the digital product as a substitute for the physical one. They therefore risk cannibalization of their own physical product. Finally, we assessed this risk and showed that the risk is mainly explained by two factors: the percentage of free digital content and the percentage of simultaneously provided physical and digital content. We perform a regression analysis in which these two factors are multiplied because risk exists only if both variables are positive.

One limitation of this study is that our empirical results are based on a rather small number of responses. More extensive replication of the study would be of interest. Furthermore, to fully understand the scale and scope of risk of cannibalization, one should not only tackle this issue from the supply side of content but also from its demand side. This would lead to studies that investigate whether consumers perceive digital products as a complement to or substitute for the corresponding physical products.

Acknowledgments

We would like to thank Salome Hügli (2003) for providing us with the data that allowed us to conduct the analyses in the empirical part of this article. The data were collected as part of a master's thesis submitted at the Institute of Information Systems, University of Bern.

Marc Fetscherin
(fetscherin@iwi.unibe.ch)

is a Research and Teaching Assistant at the Institute of Information Systems at the University of Bern, Switzerland. His research focuses on e-commerce, digital content distribution, and digital rights management.

Gerhard Knolmayer
(knolmayer@iwi.unibe.ch)

is a Professor and Director of the Institute of Information Systems, University of Bern, Switzerland. His research focuses on strategic issues in information systems, supply chain management, and e-learning.

References

Afuah, A., & Tucci, C. (2001). *Internet business models and strategies: Text and cases.* New York: McGraw-Hill/Irwin.

Äijö, T., & Saarinen, K. (2001). *Business models conceptual analysis.* Retrieved February 15, 2004, from http://www.tbrc.fi/pubfilet/TBRC_10042.pdf

Alt, R., & Zimmermann, H.-D. (2001). Preface: Introduction to special section—Business models. *Electronic Markets, 11*, 3–9.

Amit, R., & Zott, R. (2001). Value creation in e-business. *Strategic Management Journal, 22*, 493–520.

Bhattacharjee, S., Gopal, R., Lertwachara, K., & Marsden, J. (2003, January). *No more shadow boxing with online music piracy: Strategic business models to enhance revenues.* Paper presented at the 36th Annual Hawaii International Conference on System Sciences, Big Island, Hawaii.

Chen, P.-Y. (1998). *Pricing strategies for digital information goods and online services on the Internet.* Retrieved February 15, 2004, from http://www.mba.ntu.edu.tw/~jtchiang/StrategyEC/eec/report1/report1.htm

Choi, S.-Y., Stahl, D., & Whinston, A. (1997). *The economics of electronic commerce.* Indianapolis, IN: Macmillan Technical.

Eisenmann, T. (2002). *Internet business models: Texts and cases.* New York: McGraw-Hill/Irwin.

Geoffrion, A. M. (1998). *Business models for electronic commerce.* Retrieved February 15, 2004, from http://www.anderson.ucla.edu/faculty/art.geoffrion/home/ec1/businessmodels1198.htm

Hügli, S. (2003). Vergleich von Geschäftsmodellen in der Printindustrie [Comparison of business models in the print industry]. Unpublished master's thesis, Institute of Information Systems, University Bern, Switzerland.

Mahadevan, B. (2000). Business models for Internet-based e-commerce—An anatomy. *California Management Review, 42*(4), 55–69.

Martinez, P. (2000). *Models made "e": What business are you in?* Retrieved February 15, 2004, from http://www1.ibm.com/services/innovation/ gsee510160000f.pdf

Novak, T., & Hoffmann, D. (2001). *Profitability on the Web: Business models and revenue streams.* Retrieved February 15, 2004, from http://elab.vanderbilt.edu/research/papers/pdf/manuscripts/ProfitabiltyOnTheWebJan2001.pdf

Poddar, S. (2002). *Economics of software piracy and its global impact.* Retrieved February 15, 2004, from http://www.eco.rug.nl/SOM/SomSemC/Papers2002/16mei.pdf

Porter, M. (1998). *Competitive strategy: Techniques for analyzing industries and competitors.* New York: Free Press.

Rao, B. (1999). *Emerging business models in online commerce.* Retrieved February 15, 2004, from http://www.ite.poly.edu/people/brao/RT99.pdf

Rappa, M. (2000). *Business models on the Web.* Retrieved February 15, 2004, from http://digitalenterprise.org/models/models.pdf

Rayport, J., & Jaworski, B. (2001). *Introduction to e-commerce.* New York: McGraw-Hill/Irwin.

Slywotzky, A. J. (1996). *Value migration: How to think several moves ahead of the competition.* Boston: Harvard Business School Press.

Timmers, P. (1998). Business models for electronic markets. *Electronic Markets, 8*(2), 3–8.

Trombly, R. (2000). E-business models. *Computerworld, 34*(49), 61–62.

Turban, E., Lee, J. K., King, D., & Viehland, D. (2002). *Electronic commerce: A managerial perspective.* Upper Saddle River, NJ: Prentice Hall.

Varian, H. R. (1995, May). *Pricing information goods.* Paper presented at the Symposium on Scholarship in the New Information Environment, Harvard Law School, Cambridge, MA.

Varian, H. R. (2003). *Intermediate microeconomics* (6th ed.). New York: Norton.

Wang, C.-P., & Chan, K. (2003). *Analyzing the taxonomy of Internet business models using graphs.* Retrieved February 15, 2004, from http://www.firstmonday.dk/ issues/issue8_6/wang/

The Internet's Impact on Content Utilization Chains: An Exploratory Case Study on Leading Publishers in Germany

Bernd Schulze and Thomas Hess
Munich School of Management, Germany

Bernd Eggers
Hanover University, Germany

The market-side utilization of content is affected by the prevalence of the Internet. However, it is not clear in this context how and to what extent it has changed in detail. Aiming to reveal and evaluate the Internet's impact in the print media industries, we examine the latest enhancement of publishers' content utilization chains. For this purpose, we conduct an exploratory case study and apply time-series analysis as well as cross-case synthesis to analyze the data collected. As unit of analysis, we focus on 3 publishers whose content utilization practices represent best practice in the German newspaper, magazine, and book publishing industries, respectively.

Based on the results of the case study, we conclude that the Internet has an impact on the composition of publishers' content utilization chains but to a varying extent. However, because Internet-based content utilization windows hardly generate extra revenues or cannibalize existing ones, publishers' revenue models have not changed significantly so far. Besides, we state that the arrangement of Internet-based content utilization windows, which mostly constitute direct-channel distribution, decisively depends on their relation with print-based ones. Hence, we are able to show that the Internet's impact on publishers' content utilization chains manifests itself in various ways.

Background and Subject

The prevalence of the Internet has established new media markets that create additional opportunities for the utilization of content. Seeking to exploit extra sales potentials and hedge against sales revenue reallocation, many print media companies have seized these opportunities by integrating Internet-based content utilization windows into their content utilization chains (Doyle, 2002; Eierhoff, 2002). Basically, content utilization chains can—in conjunction with the content production chains—be understood as part of print media companies' value chains. The economic relevance and theoretical impact makes the Internet-driven enhancement of publishers' original content utilization chains worthy of researchers' attention.

Publishers' content utilization practice has been affected by the Internet, which provides a new platform for the distribution of content. However, it is not clear how and to what extent it has changed in detail. Aiming to reveal and evaluate the Internet's impact in the various print media industries, we examine the latest enhancement of original content utilization chains. For this purpose, we conduct an exploratory case study and apply time-series analysis as well as cross-case synthesis to analyze the data collected. As unit of analysis, we focus on three leading publishers whose content utilization practices represent best practice in the German newspaper, magazine, and book publishing industries, respectively. The case study results and corresponding conclusions might be useful both for media management researchers and practitioners because they put the enhancement of

Address correspondence to Bernd Schulze, Munich School of Management, Institute for Information Systems and New Media, Ludwigstrasse 28, 80539 Munich, Germany. E-mail: schulze@bwl.uni-muenchen.de

publishers' content utilization chains driven by the Internet into new perspective.

Concept and Related Research

Basically, media companies utilize content by offering media products in consumer and, where applicable, in advertising markets to generate revenues. Making media products available to consumers goes beyond their media-related distribution often highlighted by related literature (Picard, 2002). In our understanding, there are other aspects to be considered, such as pricing and promotion. As a consequence, we interpret the media companies' utilization of content as an overall approach to media markets that manifests itself in the definition of individual content utilization chains (Owen & Wildman, 1992). These content utilization chains usually consist of various content utilization windows, each providing a framework for the market-side utilization of content. The previously mentioned framework is determined by a set of technologically and economically consistent conditions for media products offered in a certain media market at one specific time (Brack, 2003). Hence, varying conditions for media products manifest themselves in different content utilization windows. The differentiation of Web- and print-based offerings provides an example for these varying conditions.

The definition of content utilization chains emanates from decision making regarding place-, product-, promotion- and price-related aspects that, in all, represent the media companies' marketing mix (McCarthy, 1964). Product- and place-related decision making refer to the basic selection and time-based assignment of content uti-

lization windows as well as their logical arrangement and institutional coverage, respectively. As a result, they determine the design of content utilization chains that manifests itself in the organization of the content utilization windows. The commercialization of media products in the narrow sense that takes place in these content utilization windows goes in line with promotion- and price-related decision making, referring to content announcing and branding as well as pricing and revenue sharing, respectively. Figure 1 illustrates the definition of content utilization chains as a result of decision making with respect to the various aspects of the marketing mix.

This understanding paves the way for analyzing the Internet's impact on the design of publishers' original content utilization chains in detail. However, before turning to the various print media industries, we first take a look at the film industry where the utilization of content has been initially discussed. Based on an oversimplified design of the film companies' common content utilization chain, related research in that area has focused on the maximization of revenues by determining the optimal product entry date and offering period for content utilization windows (Lehmann & Weinberg, 2000; Prasad, Bronnenberg, & Mahajan, 2004). Furthermore, some papers have also been dealing with the impact of revenue sharing, advertising expenditures and word-of-mouth promotion on revenues and profits generated alongside content utilization chains (Henning-Thurau, Houston, & Walsh, 2003; Litman, 2000; Mortimer, 2002). However, lacking a clear understanding, effectively assigned content utilization windows have hardly been distinguished accurately in this research. As a consequence, strategic complexity in content utilization practice has not been

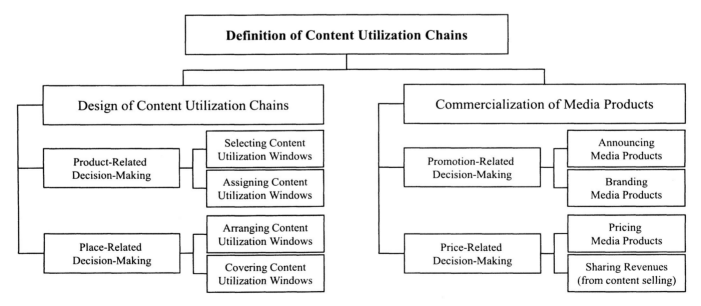

Figure 1. Framework for the definition of content utilization chains.

properly taken into account. Against this background, it is not surprising that the usefulness of derived management recommendations that mainly refer to the optimization of content utilization practice in real life seems to be rather limited.

Up to now, neither on a strategic nor on an operational level have content utilization chains been discussed in the newspaper, magazine, and book publishing industries. However, due to the emergence of new business opportunities that go back to the prevalence of the Internet, their design's change has been presumed in many cases. An example is the utilization of online- and e-papers (Bucher, Büffel, & Wollscheid, 2003; Saksena & Hollifeld, 2002), personal digital assistant offerings and electronic program guides (Handel, 2002; Riedel & Schoo, 2002), and e-books and books-on-demand (Hess & Tzouvaras, 2001; Ziv, 2002). However, instead of analyzing the Internet's impact on publishers' original content utilization chains, thus far related research has limited its focus to the general interrelation between online- and offline markets. The change of recipients' consumption behavior patterns in the Internet age and its impact on publishers' revenue models has been a special matter of researchers' interest (Doyle, 2002; Glotz & Meyer-Lucht, 2003; Picard & Grönlund, 2002). By applying the concept of content utilization chains to the various print media industries, we expect that deepening insights and some more useful recommendations can be generated because it puts publishers' current approaches to Internet-based media markets into new perspective.

Research Aim and Design

Aiming to reveal and evaluate the Internet's impact on the market-side utilization of content in detail, we first model the current design of content utilization chains in the various print media industries. Then, we work out its enhancement driven by the Internet between July 2000 and July 2003. Because of the design focus, the investigation merely deals with product- and place-related decision making that determines the basic selection and time-based assignment as well as the logical arrangement and institutional coverage of content utilization windows, respectively. As a consequence, the market-side commercialization of media products in the narrow sense that—as mentioned before—premises promotion- and price-related decision making is not explicitly covered by the investigation.

According to Yin (2003), adequate research methods for the investigation might be historians, case studies, and experiments. However, because we deal with a complex phenomenon within a real-time context, experiments are not applicable as a research method. They require control over behavioral events that cannot be guaranteed in the frame of the investigation. In addition, because of the contemporary nature and the lack of records concerning the research focus, historians do not seem to be a suitable basis for the investigation, either. Instead, historians are usually applied if there is virtually no access both to the phenomenon itself and relevant persons to be interviewed. As a consequence, we have chosen the case study approach as the underlying research method to analyze a contemporary phenomenon within its real-time context without the boundaries between the two being clearly evident (Yin, 2003).

Based on a holistic, multiple-case design we subsequently analyze the Internet's impact on original content utilization chains in the various print media industries. As unit of analysis, we examine three leading publishers whose content utilization practices represent best practice in the German newspaper, magazine, and book publishing industries, respectively. Due to varying industry affiliations, theoretical replication logic is applied (i.e., contrasting results can be expected for predictable reasons). Strictly speaking, the various types of content are likely to come along with different content utilization practices. Regarding the available types of content, it has to be stated that the newspaper and book publishing companies almost exclusively provide information- and entertainment-based content, respectively. An equal mix of both can be assumed for the magazine publishing company. Taking different content characteristics into account we suppose that the Internet's impact on publishers' original content utilization chains might vary significantly between the individual cases (Hass, 2002). Assuming that the Internet promotes timeliness-driven product offerings, our first proposition is that the integration of underlying content utilization windows is especially relevant for publishers who mainly utilize information-based content. Particularly, this may be the case for the newspaper publishing company. Second, corresponding to high time elasticity of demand in media markets, we propose that Internet-based content utilization windows—once integrated into publishers' content utilization chains—are usually arranged in the first stages.

To ensure the highest possible validity of the research design, we make use of various data collection and data analysis techniques. As data collection techniques, we have chosen and applied half-structured interviews with commercial top-level managers, real-time observations, and document screening between July and September 2003. The data collected are edited in individual case reports, with each being reviewed and approved by the interviewees. Based on these case reports, we make use of time-series analysis and cross-case synthesis to reveal and evaluate the Internet's impact on publishers' content utilization chains in detail. The investigation is restricted to a time period of 3 years ranging from July 2000 until July 2003.

Results of the Case Study

Subsequently, we focus our investigation on Frankfurter Allgemeine Zeitung (FAZ), Heinrich Bauer Group (HBG) and Random House Group (RHG). The reason for selecting these publishers is that their content utilization practices represent best practice in the German newspaper, magazine, and book publishing industries, respectively. Against this background, we expect the results and corresponding conclusions to be trendsetting for other players as well.

Newspaper Publishing Industry: The FAZ Case

FAZ is one of the biggest and best known newspaper publishing companies in Germany. Among others, it publishes the *Frankfurter Allgemeine Zeitung* with a daily circulation of approximately 400,000 copies. Analyzing the market-side utilization of content, traditional newspaper publishing companies such as FAZ have started to develop and assign print-based content utilization windows. Meanwhile, FAZ has supplemented its original content utilization chain by 12 non-print-based content utilization windows; 7 of them have been integrated since July 2000. Among these recently integrated content utilization windows, six are Internet based.

Due to the latest enhancement of FAZ's original content utilization chain, we have been able to distinguish 15 content utilization windows in July 2003. Ten of them are Internet-based windows, comprising various Web, download, and e-mail offerings. Their assignment is temporally limited except for the case of archival products. Despite generating direct revenues in advertising markets, the accumulated share of direct revenues generated by the Internet-based content utilization windows is only marginal up to now. Actually, by far the biggest share of direct revenues can be traced back to FAZ's print offerings, particularly to the daily and to a much smaller extent to the Sunday newspaper offering.

The integration of Internet-based content utilization windows between July 2000 and July 2003 constitutes both vertical and horizontal differentiation of FAZ's original content utilization chain. As a consequence, the print-based core product *Frankfurter Allgemeine Zeitung* is supplemented by timeliness-driven and archival product offerings. The latter are arranged previously, parallel and subsequently to the newspaper offering. Because all media products are being made up of almost the same content elements, the large-scale differentiation of the con-

tent utilization chain is mainly caused by varying media connections and product entry dates. Apart from product portfolio diversification, it also comes along with an extension of the overall content utilization period that is manifested by the development and offering of digitized media products. Finally, we can state that the differentiation of the content utilization chain also constitutes an expansion of direct access to consumers. E-mail offerings must be highlighted in this context because they allow FAZ and other publishers to build up more intensive relations. Figure 2 illustrates the previously mentioned comments on FAZ's content utilization chain and its enhancement.

Magazine Publishing Industry: The HBG Case

HBG is the leading magazine publishing group in Europe. Among others, it covers 55% of the German program press market with titles such as *TV Movie, tv Hören und Sehen, TV Klar, Fernsehwoche, auf einen blick, TV pur,* and *tv14.* Because of technologically and economically consistent conditions with respect to the market-side utilization of content, this range of print-based TV guides can be attached to only one content utilization window. Apart from the range of TV guides, HBG also makes use of information other than entertainment-based content to provide a multitude of non-print-based media products. Due to the differentiation of its product portfolio, HBG has supplemented its original content utilization chain with five non-print-based content utilization windows. Two of them have been integrated since July 2000 but only one can be classified as Internet based.

By July 2003, we were able to distinguish seven content utilization windows in all. Three of them are Internet based, comprising Web, e-mail, and download offerings. Apart from print- and Internet-based media products, TV-based teletext/nexTView, and electronic program guide (EPG) offerings constitute further content utilization windows, with each being temporally limited. Even though four out of five non-print-based content utilization windows generate direct revenues, the accumulated share of direct revenues generated by them is only marginal up to now. At present, by far the biggest share of direct revenues can still be traced back to HBG's print offerings (i.e., its TV and to a much smaller extent its movie guides).

Boosting vertical differentiation on the second stage of HBG's content utilization chain, the download offering constitutes the one and only Internet-based content utilization window integrated between July 2000 and July 2003. The non-print-based content utilization windows comprise timeliness-driven products that are arranged not previously but subsequently to HBG's

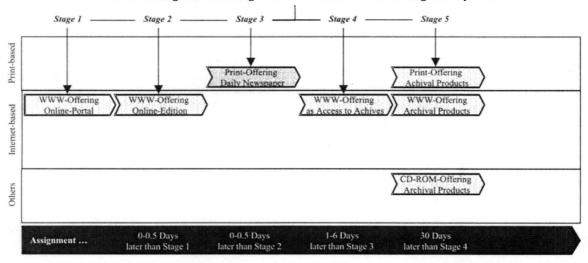

Frankfurter Allgemeine Zeitung's Content Utilization Chain: Design in July 2000

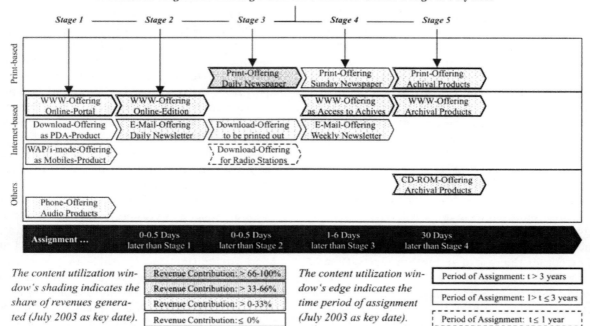

Frankfurter Allgemeine Zeitung's Content Utilization Chain: Design in July 2003

The content utilization window's shading indicates the share of revenues generated (July 2003 as key date).

| Revenue Contribution: > 66-100% |
| Revenue Contribution: > 33-66% |
| Revenue Contribution: > 0-33% |
| Revenue Contribution: ≤ 0% |

The content utilization window's edge indicates the time period of assignment (July 2003 as key date).

| Period of Assignment: t > 3 years |
| Period of Assignment: 1 > t ≤ 3 years |
| Period of Assignment: t ≤ 1 year |

Figure 2. Frankfurter Allgemeine Zeitung's content utilization chain and its enhancement driven by the Internet between July 2000 and July 2003.

print-based core products. Strictly speaking, print-based TV and movie guides are followed by Internet-based Web and e-mail as well as TV-based teletext-/nexTView, and EPG offerings. Because of downstream arrangement, HBG can update program information already provided by print-based offerings. As a consequence, the placement of media products in Internet- and TV-based content utilization windows allows reacting to short-term program reallocations. These remarks are illustrated by Figure 3.

Book Publishing Industry: The RHG Case

Bertelsmann's RHG represents the biggest book publishing group worldwide, presently comprising more than 100 independently operating publishing units in 16 different countries. Analyzing the market-side utilization of content, we focus our investigation on the German division. Initially, its publishing units have developed and assigned print-based content utilization windows like any other traditional book publishing company. Mean-

B. Schulze, T. Hess, and B. Eggers

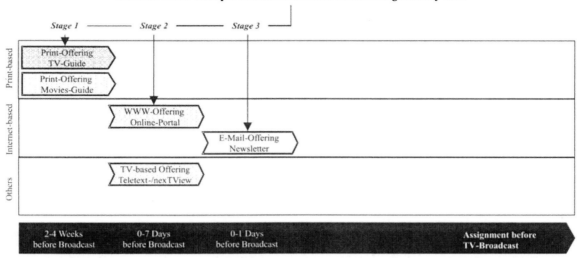

Heinrich Bauer Group's Content Utilization Chain: Design in July 2000

Heinrich Bauer Group's Content Utilization Chain: Design in July 2003

The content utilization window's shading indicates the share of revenues generated (July 2003 as key date).	Revenue Contribution: > 66-100%
	Revenue Contribution: > 33-66%
	Revenue Contribution: > 0-33%
	Revenue Contribution: ≤ 0%

The content utilization window's edge indicates the time period of assignment (July 2003 as key date).	Period of Assignment: t > 3 years
	Period of Assignment: 1> t ≤ 3 years
	Period of Assignment: t ≤ 1 year

Figure 3. Heinrich Bauer Group's content utilization chain and its enhancement driven by the Internet between July 2000 and July 2003.

while, RHG has supplemented its content utilization chain with four non-print-based content utilization windows, three of them integrated since July 2000. All are Internet based, which clearly indicates RHG's orientation toward the enhancement of its content utilization chain.

By July 2003, RHG's content utilization chain was made up of 10 content utilization windows in all. Three of them are Internet based, comprising Web offerings for extract reading and extract listing, as well as e-books that can be

understood as download offerings to be consumed electronically. All are characterized by a temporally unlimited utilization period. Because only e-books are sold in comparatively small quantities at present, the accumulated share of direct revenues generated by Internet-based content utilization windows is only marginal up to now. Actually, by far the biggest share of direct revenues can be traced back to RHG's print offerings. Differentiated by cover design, pricing, and targeted customers, these print offerings are published as hardcover, paperback, and an-

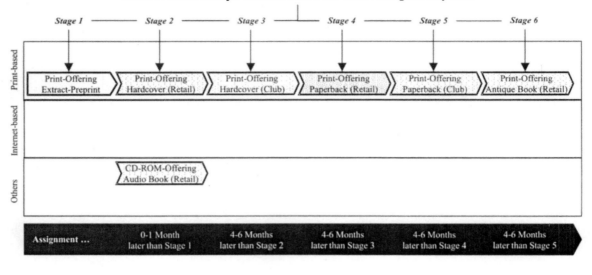

Random House Group's Content Utilization Chain: Design in July 2000

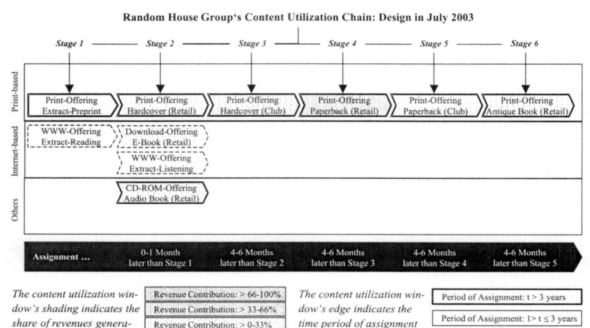

Random House Group's Content Utilization Chain: Design in July 2003

The content utilization window's shading indicates the share of revenues generated (July 2003 as key date).

| Revenue Contribution: > 66-100% |
| Revenue Contribution: > 33-66% |
| Revenue Contribution: > 0-33% |
| Revenue Contribution: ≤ 0% |

The content utilization window's edge indicates the time period of assignment (July 2003 as key date).

| Period of Assignment: t > 3 years |
| Period of Assignment: 1 > t ≤ 3 years |
| Period of Assignment: t ≤ 1 year |

Figure 4. Random House Group's content utilization chain and its enhancement driven by the Internet between July 2000 and July 2003.

tique books. Apart from retail distribution, they are also sold in book club markets that can only be accessed by preregistered book club members.

The integration of Internet-based content utilization windows between July 2000 and July 2003 constitutes vertical differentiation of RHG's content utilization chain on the first two stages. Due to the enhancement of the content utilization chain, print offerings are now supplemented by Web-based extract offerings and e-books, all consisting of similar content elements. Compared with print offerings,

e-books are characterized by technologically different conditions. As a consequence, RHG is able to activate new consumer segments, particularly in the science fiction and erotic genre. Apart from product portfolio diversification, the differentiation of RHG's content utilization chain also comes along with an extension of the content utilization period. Because of their digital nature, e-books can be offered without warehousing costs, which usually limit the offering period of physical products. Figure 4 illustrates these comments on RHG's content utilization chain.

Lessons Learned From the Case Study

Applying time-series analysis and cross-case synthesis, we can derive some lessons from the results of the case study. First, we conclude that the composition of publishers' content utilization chains has changed due to the integration of Internet-based content utilization windows. However, as our results suggest, the extent of the changes varies among the individual cases. Subsequently, we illustrate this point by comparing the number of Internet-based content utilization windows with the sum of all actually assigned and the sum of all recently integrated ones. Figure 5 reveals the varying extent to which the Internet has changed the composition of publishers' original content utilization chains in the cases of FAZ, HBG, and RHG.

As related research suggests, the composition of all three publishers' content utilization chains has changed due to the integration of Internet-based content utilization windows (Riedel & Schoo, 2002; Saksena & Hollifeld, 2002; Ziv, 2002). However, the extent varies significantly among the cases, reflecting different consumption preferences for new media products in the various print media industries. Because information-seeking recipients tend to consume online, it is not surprising that FAZ's content utilization chain is characterized by the highest comparative share of Internet-based content utilization windows (Meyer-Lucht, 2003). However, analyzing the latest changes we did not expect the Internet's impact on RHG's content utilization chain to be more intensive than in the case of FAZ. Surprisingly, all recently integrated content utilization windows are Internet based in this case, clearly indicating the Internet's late recognition and its increased relevance in the book publishing industry.

Apart from the composition of content utilization chains, we have also been dealing with the Internet's impact on publishers' revenue models. According to the results of the case study, Internet-based content utilization windows hardly generate extra revenues or cannibalize existing ones now. As related research suggests, the limited extent to which they generate extra revenues is caused by a lack of financially strong demand in advertising and particularly in consumer markets for respective media products (Riedel & Schoo, 2002). For this reason, the three publishers largely forego generating direct revenues by pricing Internet-based media products or exclusively focusing on advertising markets as revenue sources.

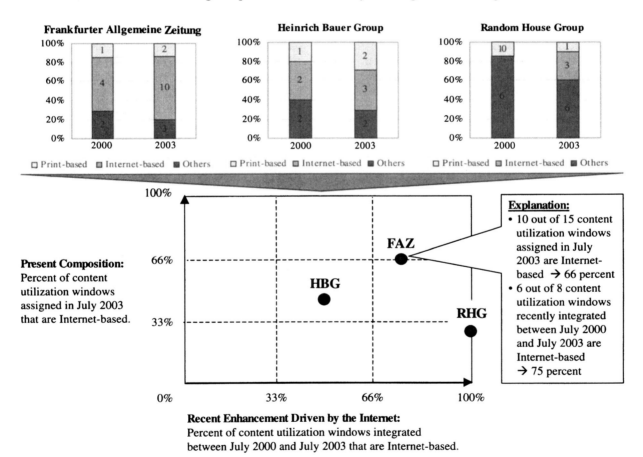

Figure 5. The composition of publishers' content utilization chains and their change driven by the Internet between July 2000 and July 2003.

Apart from ancillary selling in terms of content syndication, FAZ's archival products and RHG's e-books represent the only exceptions. Against this background, our second conclusion is that the integration of Internet-based content utilization windows has not changed publishers' revenue models significantly up to now.

After discussing the Internet's impact on product-related aspects of publishers' content utilization chains, we now turn to place-related decision making that refers to both the arrangement and coverage of content utilization windows. Based on the results of the case study, we assume that the arrangement of Internet-based content utilization windows decisively depends on their relation with print-based ones. Basically, this relation is substituting, neutral, or complementary coming along with negative cannibalization and positive stimulation effects, respectively (Litman, 2000; Owen & Wildman, 1992). Other than a substituting relation that usually implies subsequent arrangement, a complementary or at least neutral one does not correspond to a definite pattern (Bhatia, Gay, & Honey, 2001). Furthermore, not even the underlying product types clearly determine it. An example for this can be seen in the set of HBG's timeliness-driven new media products. Other than expected, these are arranged not in the first but in the last stages of the content utilization chain. The subsequent arrangement allows HBG to ensure an ongoing actuality of program information already provided by print offerings. As a consequence, our third conclusion is that there is no definite pattern regarding the general arrangement of Internet-based content utilization windows.

Other than print-based ones, Internet-based content utilization windows mostly constitute direct-channel distribution (i.e., media products are delivered without sales agents and intermediaries being involved). Because of direct-channel distribution paving the way for immediate interaction with consumers, Internet-based content utilization windows allow traditional publishers to build up learning relationships with them. According to related research in the field of mass customization, the build-up of learning relationships by immediate interaction provides a basis for the individualized configuration of media products (Zipkin, 2001). However, as the results of the case study suggest, our fourth conclusion is that these potentials have not yet been totally exploited by the examined publishers. At present, only FAZ has undertaken the first steps in this direction by providing e-mail newsletter offerings that can be customized according to recipients' consumption preferences.

Implications for Media Management

Even though their validity needs to be approved and sanctioned by further empirical research, the results of the case study and corresponding conclusions allow us to derive some implications for media management. From the researchers' point of view, the concept of content utilization chains has proved to be an adequate basis for analyzing the Internet's impact on publishers' content utilization chains in detail. As a consequence, related work can be reclassified and discussed within a broader context (Bucher et al., 2003; Handel, 2002; Hess & Tzouvaras, 2001; Riedel & Schoo, 2002; Saksena & Hollifeld, 2002; Ziv, 2002). In addition, new research questions can be derived. Focusing on new opportunities for the market-side utilization of content and increasing revenues and profits by integrating additional content utilization windows might become a special matter of researchers' interest. Aiming to ex ante evaluate economic consequences, subsequent research might result in development of a model that supports media companies to make equitable decisions regarding the enhancement of content utilization chains. Furthermore, there is also a need for decision support with respect to already integrated content utilization windows that refers to the coordination of media products' timing and pricing in particular. Based on the understanding of the concept, already existing management support systems for the market-side utilization of content could be enhanced to provide effective decision support alongside the entire content utilization chain (Eliashberg, Jonker, Sawhney, & Wierenga, 2000; Wierenga & Van Bruggen, 2001).

From the practitioners' point of view, we believe that the concept of content utilization chains promotes strategic thinking with respect to the production and utilization of content. Particularly, it raises questions regarding the optimal planning and coordination of product portfolios. The concept of content utilization chains allows print media companies, for example, to search for new opportunities regarding the market-side utilization of media products in a more elaborate fashion. Furthermore, by pointing out negative cannibalization and positive stimulation effects between content utilization windows, they are also able to discuss the economic consequences of providing additional media products in a broader context (Henning-Thurau et al., 2003; Lehmann & Weinberg, 2000; Prasad et al., 2004). Because of their effect on the economic attractiveness of media products, production costs have to be considered, too. Aiming to minimize them, media companies increasingly reuse the same content to produce various media products. Apart from cost-related effects, multiple usage of content is likely to go in line with revenue-relevant effects if the diversity between product offerings decreases (Desai, Kekre, Radhakrishnan, & Srinivasan, 2001). As a consequence, balanced action with respect to the production and utilization side seems to be crucial for print media companies to manage content successfully.

Bernd Schulze

(schulze@bwl.uni-muenchen.de)

is a Research Assistant and PhD student at the Munich School of Management, University of Munich, Germany.

Thomas Hess

(thess@bwl.uni-muenchen.de)

is a Professor for Information Systems and New Media at the Munich School of Management, University of Munich, Germany. Their research is focused on the impact of new technologies on media companies' business models.

Bernd Eggers

(eggers@eggers-partner.de)

is an Assistant Professor at the Hanover University, Germany. His research is focused on the strategic management in and transformation of publishing companies.

References

Bhatia, G. K., Gay, R. C., & Honey, W. R. (2001). Windows into the future: How lessons from Hollywood will shape the music industry. Retrieved May 10, 2004, from http://www.bah.de/content/downloads/insights/5J_Windowsi.pdf

Brack, A. (2003). Das strategische Management von Inhalten in der Medienbranche: Synergien und Gestaltungsoptionen [The management of content in media industries: Synergies and strategic implications]. Wiesbaden, Germany: Gabler.

Bucher, H.-J., Büffel, S., & Wollscheid, J. (2003). Digitale Zeitungen als ePaper: echt Online oder echt Print? [Digital newspapers as epaper: Purely online or purely print?]. Media Perspektiven, 21, 434–444.

Desai, P., Kekre, S., Radhakrishnan, S., & Srinivasan, K. (2001). Product differentiation and commonality in design: Balancing revenue and cost drivers. Management Science, 47(1), 37–51.

Doyle, G. (2002). Understanding media economics. London: Sage.

Eierhoff, K. (2002). Medienprodukte über alle Kanäle für mehr Kunden – die Click-and-Mortar-Strategie der Bertelsmann AG [Increasing the customer base through the multi-channel distribution of media products: Bertelsmann's click-and-mortar strategy]. In M. Schögel, T. Tomczak, & C. Belz (Eds.), Roadm@p to E-business—Wie Unternehmen das Internet erfolgreich nutzen (pp. 344–360). St. Gallen, Switzerland: Thexis.

Eliashberg, J., Jonker, J. J., Sawhney, M. S., & Wierenga, B. (2000). MOVIEMOD: An implementable decision-support system for prelease market evaluations of motion pictures. Marketing Science, 19, 226–243.

Glotz, P., & Meyer-Lucht, R. (2003). Zentrale Ergebnisse der St. Galler Delphi-Studie [Key results of St. Gallen's Delphi Study]. Retrieved May 10, 2004, from http://www.unisg.ch/org/mcm/web.nsf/df7 6d44a9ef44c6cc12568e400393eb2/1edd7fba517b0f6bc1256c0 9004beefb/$FILE/ZentraleErgebnisse.pdf

Handel, U. (2002). Die Multimedialisierung hat längst begonnen: Crossmediale Markenstrategien der Axel Springer AG [The multimedia age has already begun: Axel Springer's cross-media-brand strategy]. Zeitschrift für Medienwirtschaft und Medienmanagement, 1(1), 5–7.

Hass, B. H. (2002). Geschäftsmodelle von Medienunternehmen: Ökonomische Grundlagen und Veränderungen durch neue Informations- und Kommunikationstechnik [Media companies' business models: Economic foundations and transformations due to the emergence of new information and communication technologies]. Wiesbaden, Germany: Gabler.

Henning-Thurau, T., Houston, M. B., & Walsh, G. J. (2003). The differing role of success drivers across sequential channels (Working Paper No. 3/2003). Weimar, Germany: Bauhaus-University of Weimar, Institute for Marketing and Media Research.

Hess, T., & Tzouvaras, A. (2001). Keyword: Print-on-demand. International Journal on Media Management, 3(1), 39–41.

Lehmann, D. R., & Weinberg, C. B. (2000). Sales through sequential distribution channels: An application to movies and videos. Journal of Marketing, 64(3), 18–33.

Litman, B. R. (2000). The structure of the film industry—Windows of exhibition. In A. N. Greco (Ed.), The media and entertainment industries: Reading in mass communications (pp. 99–121). Boston: Allyn & Bacon.

McCarthy, J. E. (1964). Basic marketing: A managerial approach. Homewood, IL: Irwin.

Meyer-Lucht, R. (2003). Sinkende Auflagen, Einbrüche im Anzeigengeschäft, Konkurrent Internet: Die Krise auf dem deutschen Tageszeitungsmarkt [Decreasing issues, collapse of advertisement, competition by the Internet: The crisis on the German market for daily newspapers] (Working Paper No. 9/2003). Friedrich-Ebert-Association for Information Society. Retrieved May 10, 2004, from http://www.berlin-institut.de/Krise-Tageszeitungsmarkt.pdf

Mortimer, J. H. (2002). The effects of revenue-sharing contracts on welfare in vertically-separated markets: Evidence from the video rental industry (Working Paper). Cambridge, MA: Harvard University, Department of Economics. Retrieved May 10, 2004, from http://post.economics.harvard.edu/faculty/mortimer/papers/02jmp070.pdf

Owen, B. S., & Wildman, S. S. (1992). Video economics. Cambridge, MA: Harvard University Press.

Picard, R. G. (2002). The economics and financing of media companies. New York: Fordham University Press.

Picard, R. G., & Grönlund, M. (2002, June). The impact of the Internet on European media advertising expenditures. Paper presented to the COST A20 Impact of the Internet on the Mass Media Conference, Tromsø, Norway. Retrieved May 10, 2004, from http://www.tukkk.fi/media/Picard/Publication%20and%20Paper%20Files/Internet%20and %20Media%20Ad%20Expenditures.pdf

Prasad, A., Bronnenberg, B., & Mahajan, V. (2004). Product entry timing in dual distribution channels: The case of the movie industry. Review of Marketing Science, 2(4), 1–18. Retrieved April 10, 2004, from http://www.bepress.com/romsjournal/vol2/iss1/art4

Riedel, H. H., & Schoo, A. (2002). Cross-Media Management im Medienverbund von Print und Online: Das Beispiel TV Movie [Cross-media management for print and online: The TV movie case]. In B. Müller-Kalthoff (Ed.), Cross-Media Management: Content-Strategien erfolgreich umsetzen (pp. 139–165). Berlin, Germany: Springer.

Saksena, S., & Hollifeld, C. A. (2002). U.S. newspapers and the development of online editions. *International Journal on Media Management, 4*(2), 75–84.

Wierenga, B., & Van Bruggen, G. H. (2001). Developing a customized decision support system for brand managers. *Interfaces, 31*, 128–145.

Yin, R. (2003). *Case study research: Design and methods* (3rd ed.). Thousand Oaks, CA: Sage.

Zipkin, P. (2001). The limits of mass customization. *Sloan Management Review, 42*(1), 81–87.

Ziv, N. D. (2002). New media as catalysts for change in the transformation of the book publishing industry. *International Journal on Media Management, 4*(2), 89–99.

Traditional Media and Their Internet Spin-Offs: An Explorative Study on Key Levers for Online Success and the Impact of Offline Reach

Castulus Kolo and Patrick Vogt
University of St. Gallen, Switzerland

This study examines factors that account for the success of traditional media's Internet spin-offs in terms of attracted users and the page impressions they generate. Based on empirical data pertaining to the German market, we derive a model explaining online success through the reach of the parent offline medium regarded as given, and the varying degrees to which 5 key levers are employed by the Web site management. The analysis demonstrates that differences in offline reach, considered as one of the main assets of traditional media to leverage online, account for only about a third of the differences in the number of users and for about a tenth of the differences in page impressions. Although the argument for the importance of offline reach (i.e., the brand equity to be leveraged online) is theoretically convincing, this analysis illustrates that the large differences in page impressions and the number of users still are predominantly due to the considerable disparities in manageable levers, inherently independent of offline reach. By benchmarking these levers, the analysis elucidates that managers of online spin-offs are far from maximizing online success.

Traditional media companies have played an important role in the online world since the emergence of the Internet. The online efforts of traditional media have been considered offensively and defensively. From an offensive perspective, the Internet has been understood as a new enabler to generate additional revenues and profits, chiefly due to its synergistic benefit of leveraging the assets of traditional media companies on the Internet. Unlike pure players, traditional media companies started their online ventures with an existing offline customer base or more abstractly, with a well-known brand. An established and recognized brand has been regarded as the most important asset to leverage in an online world. O'Reilly (1996), for example, argued that brand names and trademarks are key elements of differentiation, especially in light of the abundant content consumption opportunities now available. Advertising space and content present traditional media with additional resources to capture online opportunities. Furthermore, online spin-offs were initiated to introduce new distribution channels for traditional media products. They have the potential to increase brand awareness by extending the total customer base across both the online and the offline world.

Defensively, the Internet has been considered a threat to traditional media, prompting traditional media players to invest online to defend their core business. To a large extent, traditional media companies invested in related businesses, such as business-to-consumer Internet. These were predominantly content-driven Internet ventures, such as online portals and online spin-offs, offering equivalent benefits to offline.[1] However, even though adhering to ventures relating closely to the core business, traditional media companies rarely succeeded on the Internet, particularly when defined in financial terms. According to an empirical study done in the U.S. market, traditional media companies owning separate Internet entities are (at least so far) no more profitable than traditional media companies without such diversification (Kolo & Vogt, 2003).

However, is not the offline customer base, the essence of the brand of a traditional medium, a distinctive asset in an online world? What are the manageable levers that online spin-offs can pull? What are the levers that are most effectively pulled by online managers, and do online man-

Address correspondence to Castulus Kolo, Lucile-Grahn-Str. 27, 81675 Munich, Germany. E-mail: castulus.kolo@web.de

agers really pull them? These questions refer to two related research issues:

1. The relative importance of offline reach for the success of online ventures at the time being as compared to other, manageable factors.
2. The extent to which these factors are exploited by the management over time and across different Web sites.

To tackle these issues we first outline the conceptual framework relating online success to measurable, comparable, and accessible indicators. We then trace back the success of online spin-offs of traditional media companies to the offline reach and a number of additional factors, which provide manageable levers and do not inherently depend on the offline reach. For that reason we derive a model based on empirical data. The article proceeds with a discussion of the resultant limited influence of offline reach on online success. Furthermore the article investigates the managerial implications related to pulling the different levers and concludes with an outline of the limitations of the applied methodology and of issues warranting further research.

Conceptual Framework

The analysis is focused on traditional consumer offline media and ranges from general interest to special interest and from newspaper and magazine publishers to TV broadcasters. Media companies adapt various business models for these online ventures. This has been widely researched (Alt & Zimmermann, 2001; Goldman, 1995; Picard, 2000; Stähler, 2001; Timmers, 1998), particularly with reference to different business models and revenue sources for online spin-offs of newspapers (Chyi & Lasorsa, 2002; Chyi & Sylvie, 1998; Ihlström & Palmer, 2002). Three different revenue sources are observed for Web sites focusing on editorial content (Madsen, 1996), although in practice, a combination of them is often applied: paid content (be it charge-per-use or subscription), transaction-based revenues (e.g., e-commerce), and advertising-based revenues (e.g., banner ads). Today, most media sites still depend largely on the latter (Frey, Klein, & Koch, 2003; Glotz & Meyer-Lucht, 2004; Pauwels & Dans, 2000), the concept being to offer content for free, thereby maximizing audience enticement. These audiences may then be sold on to advertisers (Chyi & Lasorsa, 2002).

Ideally, the success of an online business model would be assessed utilizing financial data. However, this kind of data is, in most cases, neither publicly available nor available on request. Most traditional media companies do not publish profit-and-loss statements per business unit, particularly not if they display large losses such as may be the case with their online ventures. Additionally, some Internet ventures may not be run as an organizationally separate business unit and precise financial figures may therefore not even be accurately known internally. Hence, any discussion of success will have to be indirect and based on indicators.

To derive indicators for online success we take a closer look at the factors driving the revenue. The pricing models for online advertising as the prevailing revenue source are still dominated by the sale of a certain amount of page impressions (PIs), which we will synonymously refer to as traffic, at a fixed price, typically per 1,000 PI. This is due to the fact that advertisers are interested in maximizing exposure to their ads, which depends on the number of pages read. Furthermore this number can be measured fairly easy in terms of purely technical, automatic procedures and therefore provides a reliable standard for advertisers to compare the overall exposure of Web sites to their audience.

Although earnings are therefore mainly driven by the overall traffic, the quality and quantity of users play an important role, too, when advertisers consider the allocation of their budgets. Online sites with a high number of users and a specific or particularly coherent sociodemographic profile[2] are more likely to be considered. This in turn leads to higher yields in sold traffic and higher prices per 1,000 PIs. Advertisers increasingly try to shift this model from sheer volume in terms of traffic to alternative models more based on the number of people actually attracted by the advertising (e.g., the click-through).[3] Furthermore, revenue based on paid content is gaining importance. Also in this case, the number of users is a relevant indicator. However, because we would expect that the more impact the site has on a user, the more he or she is attracted by the content and is therefore willing to pay, the traffic the users generate remains of relevance in this respect.

This leads us to conclude that in the absence of comparable financial data for a sufficiently large sample, the success of Web sites with a focus on editorial content can be understood as ultimately determined by the size of the audience in terms of numbers of users and the overall exposure of this audience to the Web site in terms of traffic or PIs. Both measures are therefore taken as success indicators. Although these indicators are no guarantee for economic success, they nevertheless can be considered a currency convertible into revenues. Obviously they vary in their relative weight according to the specific mix of revenue sources of a Web site, but it can be generally assumed (for both of them equally) that the higher the value the more likely a success in terms of revenues would be achieved.

We employ these two indicators, although we are aware that high values indicating potentially high revenues reflect only one side of the coin. Traffic and the number of users may be achieved at high costs (e.g., by a large number of editorial staff creating premium content or by high marketing spending). Nevertheless, as is the case with the reach for consumer offline media, a large and intensively interacting audience and in turn substantial revenue are also necessary prerequisites for the sustainable profitability of a Web site.

Data Sample

To compare the audience or demand-side characteristics of online spin-offs of traditional media brands, we collected data for 34 Web sites, all providing editorial content, that are similar in brand to the offline parent medium and of national relevance in Germany.[4] The sample comprises the spin-offs of five TV channels, 22 magazines, and seven newspapers. Although most of these sites offer some form of pay-per-use or subscriptions (e.g., for archive services), the majority of the content and services are free of charge and, at least currently, none of the Web sites explicitly follows a business model predominantly based on paid content. Table 1 provides a summary of the online sites and some of their characteristics considered in the analysis.

This selection of online sites was obtained by taking into account the availability of online data (on the traffic and the number of visits on the Web site) as well as offline data (on the number of Internet users among readers[5] and

Table 1. Characteristics of Online Spin-Offs of Traditional Media

URL: http://www. ...	Traditional media background (content focus)	T	i	f	o	y	N	N_{new}/N	R
bild.de	Ne (News, tabloid)	252	14.43	5.26	0.47	0.22	3.31	0.73	8.43
handelsblatt.com	Ne (News, business)	14	4.51	2.53	0.86	0.24	1.22	0.92	0.49
ftd.de	Ne (News, business)	10	3.94	2.61	0.88	0.29	0.98	0.94	0.24
sueddeutsche.de	Ne (News, general interest)	29	7.65	2.13	0.72	0.29	1.79	0.87	1.14
welt.de	Ne (News, general interest)	20	5.69	2.37	0.77	0.20	1.48	0.94	0.60
faz.net	Ne (News, general interest)	15	6.78	2.37	0.78	0.12	0.92	0.91	0.89
zeit.de	Ne (News, general interest)	9	6.35	0.82	0.77	0.22	1.64	0.84	1.55
manager-magazin.de	Ma (Business)	10	2.93	6.62	0.89	0.17	0.49	0.84	0.53
boerse-online.de	Ma (Business)	5	6.25	0.48	0.82	0.46	1.75	0.90	0.45
wiwo.de	Ma (Business)	2	5.88	0.41	0.82	0.22	1.01	0.87	0.71
autobild.de	Ma (Cars)	15	13.18	0.62	0.63	0.19	1.81	0.83	2.60
cinema.de	Ma (Cinema)	6	8.78	0.47	0.75	0.21	1.54	0.82	1.67
gamestar.de	Ma (Computer games)	19	6.91	3.09	0.91	0.35	0.89	0.70	0.86
pcgames.de	Ma (Computer games)	11	6.48	1.21	0.89	0.34	1.41	0.73	1.26
tomorrow.de	Ma (Multimedia)	10	8.55	1.31	0.92	0.19	0.87	0.83	0.86
chip.de	Ma (Computers)	73	6.70	4.95	0.95	0.48	2.20	0.68	1.55
pcwelt.de	Ma (Computers)	32	6.58	3.26	0.94	0.29	1.51	0.68	1.77
max.de	Ma (Lifestyle)	9	9.74	1.91	0.73	0.08	0.47	0.85	1.13
fitforfun.de	Ma (Fitness)	3	6.62	0.47	0.72	0.16	1.04	0.77	2.04
spiegel.de	Ma (News, general interest)	149	5.24	8.90	0.73	0.24	3.20	0.68	5.79
focus.de	Ma (News, general interest)	104	8.57	3.94	0.71	0.21	3.08	0.76	4.92
stern.de	Ma (News, tabloid)	45	9.36	1.66	0.66	0.19	2.91	0.68	7.52
kicker.de	Ma (Sports)	29	7.23	2.00	0.61	0.38	1.99	0.74	2.24
tvtoday.de	Ma (TV program)	7	6.29	1.26	0.66	0.07	0.82	0.84	2.66
tvspielfilm.de	Ma (TV program)	6	7.39	0.75	0.63	0.08	1.09	0.63	7.59
tvmovie.de	Ma (TV program)	5	5.39	0.91	0.66	0.09	1.02	0.64	6.36
brigitte.de	Ma (Women)	13	15.31	0.98	0.56	0.14	0.87	0.68	3.56
freundin.de	Ma (Women)	3	7.32	0.60	0.56	0.09	0.70	0.80	2.80
amica.de	Ma (Young women)	10	9.74	2.20	0.74	0.06	0.45	0.89	1.07
rtl.de	TV (Entertainment)	266	18.06	4.22	0.54	0.16	3.49	0.43	22.84
sat1.de	TV (Entertainment)	166	35.20	1.84	0.54	0.12	2.56	0.55	17.85
prosieben.de	TV (Entertainment)	54	14.85	1.51	0.59	0.14	2.39	0.56	13.17
mtv.de	TV (Music)	10	4.96	0.87	0.70	0.26	2.43	0.58	5.65
n-tv.de	TV (News)	58	6.40	4.33	0.66	0.17	2.09	0.60	7.58
Minimum		2	2.93	0.41	0.47	0.06	0.45	0.43	0.24
Maximum		266	35.20	8.90	0.95	0.48	3.49	0.94	22.84
Mean		43	8.80	2.32	0.73	0.21	1.63	0.76	4.13
Relative spread in %		156	66	84	18	50	87	17	124

Note. Ne = newspaper spin-offs; Ma = magazine spin-offs; TV = spin-offs of TV channels; T = page impressions per month (millions); i = page impressions per visit; f = visits per user per month; o = ratio of readers/viewers online to all readers/viewers; y = yield; N = number of users per month (millions); N_{new}/N = share of newly acquired users among users; R = offline reach in readers or viewers per copy per day (millions). Web sites consituting the subsample are printed in bold.

the number of readers of the traditional medium). Because both sets of data are provided by different organizations and their samples differ slightly, not all online spin-offs of traditional media brands could be included. In terms of traffic, however, our collection of online sites comprises the largest sites in their category (referring to the editorial focus of the content; e.g., business, news, politics, computers, etc.).

Among the 50 largest Web sites, in terms of traffic, in Germany, we cover 86% of the sites with editorial content, a similar offline brand, and national importance. Seventy percent of the total traffic derived from such online spin-offs with certified traffic measurements is included in the sample.[6] We conclude from these facts that the results for our sample are representative for all Web sites in Germany with the same properties.[7]

For each Web site the following data were collected offline (termed offline data): users per month, readers per copy (newspapers and magazines), and viewers per day (TV channels); Internet users who are also readers; and the users per month of the online spin-off who are concurrently readers of the traditional offline medium. These data are provided every year by the Allensbacher Computer- und Technik-Analyse (ACTA), conducted by the Institut für Demoskopie Allensbach on the basis of an offline survey among more than 10,000 people[8] representing the German population between 14 and 64 years old (ACTA, 2003). As a service of several publishers the data are freely accessible online (Spiegel Media, 2003). The raw data for 2003 were accumulated through personal interviews during a field period between January and August. Unlike anonymous online measurements, these means of data acquisition take into account the actual number of users (or, more specifically, unique users) behind the number of visits and PIs (see later).

Online data (i.e., on PIs and visits) were obtained from the Informationsgesellschaft zur Feststellung der Verbreitung von Werbeträgern (IVW).[9] The values for both variables are tracked automatically by purely technical and standardized procedures and published in monthly intervals on a freely accessible Web site (IVW Online, 2003). To arrive at values also comparable to the offline data, we considered the monthly averages between January and August 2003.

We first conducted our analysis on the basis of the entire data set, which we then compared to the analysis of 10 online spin-offs from news media with a print background, thus providing a more homogeneous subsegment.[10] For the brands of this subsample we also collected offline and online data for the years 2000, 2001, and 2002 (ACTA, 2003; IVW Online, 2003) with the intention to analyze the overall changes of the variables' absolute values (given by the sample mean for each variable) and their relative spreads (given by the standard deviation

in relation to the sample mean) over time. The Web sites constituting the subsample are printed in bold in Table 1.

Model and Variables

Established companies in the realm of traditional media have a long way to go to achieve effective leverage from their offline endeavors and to subsequently generate PIs. First of all, to attract readers to the online site, the reader has to be a current Internet user and as observed in this study on the German market, there are large differences across the audiences of traditional media offerings in terms of Internet usage[11] (see Table 1). The discrepancies further extend to the percentage of Internet users among readers who are eventually gained as users of the related Web site and the number of additional users newly attracted to the brand by the online spin-off (see also Chyi & Lasorsa, 2002). On the other hand, attracting users is not enough. The users should come frequently to the site and interact intensively to eventually create a substantial number of visits and PIs.

On the one hand, there are several studies focusing on the usage patterns of online and offline editions under a common brand, based on survey data (i.e., offline data; ACTA, 2003; Chyi & Lasorsa, 2002). On the other hand there are studies based on online data of Web site traffic (e.g., Pauwels & Dans, 2000). To obtain a more comprehensive picture of how offline reach is linked to online traffic via several steps, we think it is necessary to combine both perspectives and subsequently both kinds of data. Each step requires different management means to be successful. By comparing just the first one—offline reach—with the last one—Web site traffic—as, for example, in Pauwels and Dans (2000), only a net effect is summarized. The effect of good online site management is thereby omitted and the question remains unanswered as to whether or not a high volume of traffic is achieved because there are many users, because a rather small number of users visit very frequently, or through the high level of interactivity induced by the site; a combination of the latter factors; or through other means.

In the first step we decompose Web site traffic into its constituent factors. In a second step, we model the number of users as a function of offline reach and other parameters independent of offline reach.

Decomposition of the Web Site Traffic

The number of PIs (or the Web site traffic, termed T) is a result of the number of users the site attracts in a given period of time (termed N), as well as the impact they have, or the number of pages they read (or rather click) in a given period of time. The latter can be further separated into a factor describing the frequency of use (termed f), or the number of visits per user in a given period of time, and a factor describing the intensity of use (termed i), when they are visiting the Web site (i.e., the number of PIs per visit):

$$T = i \cdot f \cdot N \quad \text{or} \quad PI = \frac{PI}{visits} \cdot \frac{visits}{user} \cdot \text{number of users} \quad (1)$$

The two factors i and f do not inherently depend on the offline reach of the traditional medium and are manageable levers.[12] Both factors show considerable differences across the sites compiled in Table 1. The intensity of use ranges from about 3 pages per visit to more than 35, resulting in an overall relative spread of the values around their mean at 66% (standard deviation in relation to the sample mean). Even more varied are the values for f, or the number of visits to the site the users undertake per month. They range between approximately one visit every second month to almost nine per month, resulting in an overall relative spread of the values at 84%. For this reason, the traffic on the sites exhibits a far higher relative spread (156%)[13] than the relative spread in the number of users (87%) would lead us to expect.

The number of users (N) comprises the users also being readers of the traditional medium (termed N_{old}) and the users who were newly attracted to the online site (termed N_{new}). The former (N_{old}) can be factorized as a product of the number of Internet users among offline readers (i.e., the online affinity, termed o, of the offline readers), the number of users of the spin-off per number of all Internet users among readers (i.e., the yield, termed y), and finally the number of readers or offline reach (termed R). Again, the two factors o and y are manageable levers in principle:

$$N_{old} = y \cdot o \cdot R$$

or

$$N_{old} = \frac{\text{user of own site}}{\text{readers online}} \cdot \frac{\text{readers online}}{\text{readers}} \cdot \text{readers} \quad (2)$$

Online affinity exhibits a relative spread of 18% around the mean value (see Table 1) and the values for the individual sites range from .47 to .95; that is, 47% to 95% of the readers are Internet users. The latter value is achieved by a Web site from a computer magazine. Unsurprisingly, 95% of its readers are online. When compared with the online affinity of the German population between 14 and 64 years old at 56 % (ACTA, 2003), the average online affinity of consumers of traditional media at 73% in our sample appears fairly advanced.

A higher relative spread than in online affinity can be observed in the yield among readers online (y), however still a lot less than for the impact factors frequency (f) and

intensity (i) as seen earlier. The yields range from only 6 out of 100 Internet users among readers who are converted to the related Web site, to almost half of them, resulting in an overall relative spread of the values at 50% (standard deviation in relation the sample mean). Although the influence of the management on the online affinity is rather limited, evidently a lot more can be done in terms of attracting the Internet users among the readers to the Web site, although with varying levels of success, as the differences in the yields depict.

A general observation among the Web sites in our sample is that the overlap of users of the online spin-off and the readers of the related traditional medium is rather low[14] (24% with regard to all users of the Web site and 9% with regard to all readers). From an advertiser's point of view a small overlap is an advantage because otherwise the online product would largely deliver a less-than-unique audience. However, this small overlap may question the positioning of many Web sites as companion sites to the offline medium. According to the numbers obtained in our analysis most sites appear instead as destination sites; that is, sites navigated to in their own right and not because of strong references from the traditional parent medium.

Finally, the combination of Equations 1 and 2 leads to a representation of the traffic (T) as a function of several constituents:

$$T = i \cdot f \cdot N = i \cdot f \cdot (N_{old} + N_{new}) = i \cdot f \cdot (y \cdot o \cdot R + N_{new}) \quad (3)$$

For N_{new}, however, there is no equivalent "natural" decomposition into a set of measurable variables, as is the case for T or N_{old}. We therefore have to explore a possible dependence of N_{new} on the number of readers empirically. With a model for N_{new} as a function of R, the offline reach, and possibly additional parameters, we can then compare the actual values of N_{new} with the ones we could anticipate in accordance with the model. It is evident that there are a number of sites that attract more users than the model would suggest and others that lag in this respect. This leads us to the final manageable lever for online success, the excess (termed e), referring to actual newly acquired users in relation to the number we would expect, in accordance with the model:[15]

$$N_{new}^{measured} = e \cdot N_{new}^{model} \quad (4)$$

Modeling the Dependence on Offline Reach

The two components (N_{old} and N_{new}) of the total number of users will depend, in different ways, on the offline reach (R). From the decomposition in Equation 2 it is clear that N_{old} is a function of the latter and with the two additional factors online affinity (o) and yield (y) not being correlated[16] with R, we would expect in a diagram depicting the values of N_{old} and R to see a distribution of data points around a straight line intercepting the origin.[17] Indeed, this is the case, as is illustrated in Figure 1 (upper left and lower left).

For N_{new} the situation is different. Table 1 (column N_{new}/N) shows first of all that the contribution of N_{new} to the overall number of users N varies considerably among online sites, from 43% up to 94%, therefore providing a larger percentage to N than N_{old}, for most Web sites. On average roughly 75% of Web site users are not concurrent readers.[18] From these numbers the argument for a strong traditional brand pushing forward the success of a Web site appears reverted. We observe that most Web sites attract a large number of entirely new people to the brand. In this respect the online endeavors actively promote a media brand rather than only benefitting from the existing brand of the traditional offline medium, profiting from the existing brand equity in terms of the number of readers of the traditional parent medium.

N_{new} could be a function of the offline reach (R), but also of N_{old}, of both, or of neither of them. It could be argued that R is a measure for brand awareness and the higher the brand awareness, which comprises a larger set of people than the number of readers alone, the higher the number of newly attracted users. In this case N_{new} should be a function of R. Likewise it could be reasoned

that users of a Web site who are concurrently readers of the related offline product have a particularly strong affinity to the brand and wield a powerful influence as multipliers by attracting entirely new users to the brand. Such multiplying effects are well known from studies on the diffusion of innovations (Rogers, 1971). In this case N_{new} should be a function of N_{old}. Of course, the number of new users could also result from a superposition of both effects. Additionally, there may be a number of new users achieved regardless of R and N_{old}, but due to marketing activities, such as advertising in print media (other than the one belonging to the brand) or traffic partnerships.

We tested three models: a multilinear model with R and N_{old} as independent variables and a constant representing possible marketing effects not related to existing reach of the brand, and two further models with either only R or only N_{old} as independent variable plus a constant. Applying the F test to assess and to compare the goodness of fit given the different degrees of freedom of the models we derive that the number of new users N_{new} can best[19] be described by:

$$N_{new} = a^{reg} \cdot N_{old} + b^{reg}, \qquad (5)$$

whereby a^{reg} and b^{reg} are the coefficients given by the linear regression analysis.[20] The addition of the offline reach as an independent variable and therefore of a further regression coefficient does not increase the goodness of the

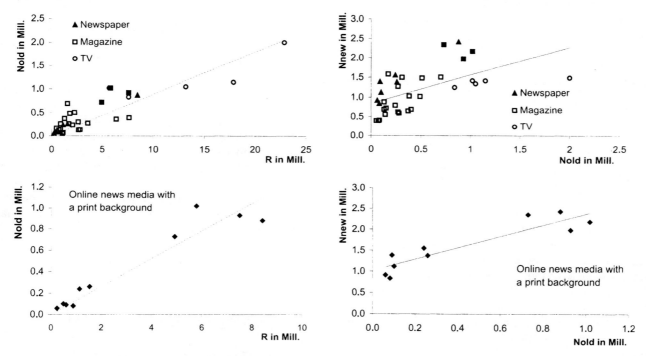

Figure 1. Dependence of the number of users on the reach of the offline medium.

The diagrams exhibit the functional dependence of the number of users also reading the traditional medium (N_{old}) on the number of readers (R, upper left) and the regression model for the number of newly acquired users (N_{new}) depending on the number of users of both media (N_{old}, upper right) for all Web sites. Among them the subsample of news sites with a print background is highlighted with solid symbols. The latter are displayed exclusively in the lower two figures.

fit, nor does a model with offline reach as the single independent variable lead to a better description of the values for the dependent variable. On the contrary, in the full sample of online sites there is not even a significant correlation between N_{new} and R. This leads us to conclude that N_{new} does not directly depend on the offline reach (R). It is only connected to R via N_{old} (see Equation 2).

Figure 1 (upper right and lower right) depicts the results from the regression analysis and shows that a certain amount of N_{new} is dependent on N_{old}, whereas there is an additional offset. Given our model for the different factors that influence the number of all users N, we can now represent the latter as the sum of three contributions:[21]

$$N = N_{old} + a^{reg} \cdot N_{old} + b^{reg}. \qquad (6)$$

$a^{reg} \cdot N_{old}$ can be understood as the number of new users acquired via the multiplier effects already mentioned; that is, via the influence of readers also using the online spin-off on new users across their individual communication networks. The value for a^{reg} ranges from 0.72 in the case of the total sample to 1.34 in the case of online news sites. This denotes that 100 users, also reading the traditional medium, are attracting a further 72 and 134 users, respectively, via such networks of recommendation and communication. Apparently the strength of such multiplier effects is greater for the subsample of news sites than for the total sample; that is, the average of all sites.

b^{reg} can be considered as a contribution of new users, which is independent of any measure of reach (neither N_{old} nor R) achieved by marketing activities not based on media products of the brand.[22] The value for b^{reg} ranges from 0.84 in the case of the total sample to 1.03 in the case of online news sites. This means that an average of .84 million users per month or 1.03 million users per month, respectively, are attracted in this way. Comparing these numbers to the average number of all users for both samples we derive that for all Web sites, 52% of all users and for online news sites 50% of all users can be attributed to marketing activities outside the realm of the brand.

In summary we arrive at the following average contributions of N_{old}, $a^{reg} \cdot N_{old}$, and b^{reg} to N (see also Equation 6): 28%, 20%, and 52% for the complete data set and 21%, 29%, and 50% for online news media. Otherwise stated, for online news media, 50% of the number of users (given by the contribution of b^{reg} in relation to N) is independent of any measure related to offline reach (52% for the full sample). With respect to the other half of the users ($N_{old} + a^{reg} \cdot N_{old}$), the offline reach is an important factor, because the latter determines, together with the online affinity and the yield, the number of concurrent users of both media: $N_{old} + a^{reg} \cdot N_{old} = (1 + a^{reg}) \cdot y \cdot o \cdot R$. The model can now also be used to analyze whether a specific site is better than the average site, with regards to acquiring new users and therefore to calculate the excess in the number of new users (e).[23]

Discussion of Results and Management Implications

We are now able to discuss the relative importance of the offline reach for online success; that is, how the large differences in traffic and in the number of users can be explained and how much of these differences is due to the power of the offline brand. Furthermore, we discuss to what extent the different values given for the manageable factors for each spin-off contribute to the differences in traffic and the number of users; that is, the individual ways the levers are pulled by the Web site management.

Offline Reach and Online Success: The Importance of the Brand

We have seen in the earlier section on the modeling of the empirical data that the large relative spread in traffic can be attributed only to a small degree to the relative spread in the number of users (which vary at a considerably lower level than other factors; see also Table 1). For all Web sites, we calculate the contributions[24] of the intensity of use (i), the frequency of use (f), and the number of users (N) to the traffic (T) as 33%, 41%, and 26%, respectively. For the subsegment of news sites we get a slightly higher contribution of N at 29% and f at 45%. The factor i with 26% plays a less important role in this case. Among all three factors determining the traffic level, we can conclude from these results that the frequency of use (f) is generally the one factor most accountable. Frequent use implies strong user retention, or user loyalty. This is in line with strategies applied by successful Web sites, such as building loyalty, being acknowledged as the "most important strategic objective" and retention as the "key measure in deepening ... (the) user relationships" by the chief executive officer of New York Times Digital (Nisenholz, 2003), one of the most successful Web sites with a newspaper background in the United States.

From our model we deduced that about half of the number of users (N) can be accounted for by new users acquired via marketing measures independently of any variable related to reach (52% for all Web sites and 50% for the subsample of news sites), the balance being given by $N_{old} + a^{reg} \cdot N_{old} = (1 + a^{reg}) \cdot y \cdot o \cdot R$. However, the latter contribution to the total number of users is not only dependent on offline reach (R) but also on the online affinity (o) and the yield (y). Using the same procedure as we used to compute the individual contributions of differences (i.e., the relative spread) in the values for i, f, and N to the relative spread in the traffic T, we can now calculate how the relative spread of the size-dependent component of N among the Web sites is explained by the relative spread in o, y, and R. As a result we get the contributions of o, y, and R as 9%,

26%, and 65%, respectively, for all Web sites, and 11%, 17%, and 72%, respectively, for news sites with a print background. This leads to an overall influence of R to N of 31% for all Web sites ($0.48 \cdot 0.65 = 31\%$) and 36% for news media with print background ($0.50 \cdot 0.72 = 36\%$). Given the contribution of N on differences in the traffic (T) on the order of 26% for all Web sites and 29% for news media with a print background we arrive at an overall contribution of R to the relative spread of T of 8% and 10%, respectively. The propagation of differences in the offline reach to the actually observed differences in Web site traffic for online news sites is summarized in Figure 2.

Both measures, the number of users and the number of PIs, were argued for as indicators for online success. Although online advertising is mainly based on PIs, the number of users matters more when revenues are based on paid content and transactions. The specific dependence of online success on offline reach therefore depends on the mix of revenue sources, which varies from site to site. Nevertheless, given our results, we can generally conclude that differences in offline reach only account for between about one third to one tenth of the differences in online success (depending on the measure taken). The larger the share of paid-content- or transaction-based revenues the more relevant are differences in offline reach. It should be kept in mind, however, that the limited influence of the brand reflects only the situation of Web sites up to now, which is characterized by large differences in the extent to which the discussed management levers are pulled. With differences in these factors decreasing to zero, the offline reach and the brand would remain as the single source of differences in online success. We discuss such changes over time later.

Pulling the Levers for Online Success

Apart from the offline reach, which we regard as externally given, management can work on several independent levers to increase traffic. We have identified the intensity of use (i), the frequency of use (f), the online affinity (o), the yield among readers (y), and the excess in the number of new users (e) as manageable levers. A benchmark can now be provided by the maximum value achieved for each of them. Because the Web sites included in the full sample have very different means to pull the levers, we discuss the results among the subsample of news sites.[25]

Table 2 shows the performance for online news media along the five dimensions, the levers independent of offline reach. As Table 2 illustrates, none of the news sites in our sample outperforms consistently and managers are still far from maximizing their online success given the number of readers of the traditional medium as a starting point.

We did not systematically survey and analyze concrete management measures (e.g., how the management tried to increase the frequency of use or its intensity), but focused our article on an explorative analysis of quantitative data of the Web sites in our sample. Nevertheless, we discuss a few observations of practical relevance in the following paragraphs.

Using bild.de as an example, we observe that the site outperforms its peers in both the intensity of use (i) and the frequency of use (f), as well as in the excess in the number of newly acquired users (e). The site performs on average concerning the yield (y). However, the online affinity (o) of readers of the German tabloid *Bild* is extremely low. Although online affinity is certainly difficult to influ-

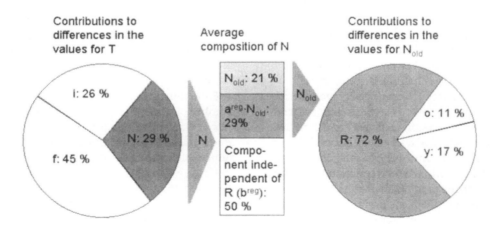

Figure 2. Relative impact of offline reach on Web site traffic.

All numbers are given for the sample of online news sites with a print background. The percentages are computed for a Web site with a traditional parent medium of average reach (R). Only 29% of the differences in the values for traffic (T) are caused by differences in the number of users (N). According to our model, N is to 50% independent of the offline reach. Differences in the size-dependent component of N ($1 + a^{reg}$) are to 72% due to differences in the offline reach. In total, roughly 10% of the variations in traffic are related to differences in offline reach.

Table 2. Performance Matrix for Players in the Domain of Online News Sites

Site	Intensity of Use (i)	Frequency of Use (f)	Online affinity of Readers (o)	Yield Among Readers Online (y)	Excess in Number of New Users (e)
bild.de	++	++	- -	o	+
faz.net	o	-	o	- -	-
ftd.de	- -	-	+	++	-
handelsblatt.com	- -	-	+	o	o
sueddeutsche.de	o	- -	o	++	+
welt.de	-	-	o	-	+
zeit.de	-	- -	o	o	o
focus.de	+	+	o	o	+
spiegel.de	-	++	o	o	o
stern.de	+	- -	-	-	-

Note. ++ = more than 30% above mean; + = between 10% and 30% above mean; o = between mean ± 10%; - and - - = analogous.

ence, a medium can nevertheless aspire to increase the online affinity of its readers by producing relevant content on online topics in the offline medium or by promoting the purchase of computers with Internet connections. The latter method is extensively practiced by *Bild,* which makes sense, because online affinity is, as outlined earlier, the lever where bild.de can probably most efficiently drive the number of its users and its traffic.

The levers are obviously easier to pull for the management of a specific site when there is a large relative spread among the individual values for the competitors and the value for the site under consideration is comparatively low.[26] Although there is a large relative spread in the values for the frequency of use (f) and intensity of use (i) at 71% and 42%, respectively, the relative spreads of the values for online affinity (o), yield (y), and excess in number of new users (e) are considerably lower (15%, 21%, and 16%, respectively). Apparently the major differences in most Web sites exist in their inventiveness of how to increase the frequency of use, followed by their means to stimulate the intensity of use.

However, the differences among Web sites in their success to push the intensity of use (i) can partly be understood by the differences in their editorial focus and do therefore not only reflect management capabilities. It is clear that Web sites with a large portion of tabloid content or pertaining to a parent medium with such properties have less difficulties achieving high interaction rates (e.g., by providing a large number of enticing photo galleries). Sites pertaining to high-quality newspapers or news magazines usually provide longer text elements and fewer topics are addressed that are suited for extensive photographic coverage. Indeed, we observe in our sample that the more elements of tabloid journalism, the higher the intensity of use, being lowest for the business news sites ftd.de and handelsblatt.com and peaking at bild.de. An explanation of the differences among Web sites in terms of the frequency of use (f) achieved is less obvious than for the intensity of use. It

requires, we think, an analysis of the values over time, which we do later.

As the third lever contributing to differences of online success, the yield (y) deserves to be mentioned, because two Web sites stand out in this respect: the site of *Süddeutsche Zeitung* and the site of the German edition of the *Financial Times* (sueddeutsche.de and ftd.de). They both achieve the highest yields in our sample; that is, they reach the largest fraction of onliners among the readers of the parent medium. We attribute this to the fact that the Web sites offer a significant added value for the readers of the parent medium, more than the other sites in the sample. Without a survey among their users and readers we can only mark some observations analyzing their online and offline offerings. In both cases the Web site is not only promoted in the print medium but explicitly referred to as comprising part of the editorial output under the brand (e.g., a box on page 1 of *Süddeutsche Zeitung* referring to topics exclusively covered by the online subsidiary sueddeutsche.de). Further, articles in the print edition frequently point to additional information on the Web site and some services on the Web site specifically enhance the information given in print. In the case of ftd.de, this additional information includes real-time data on financial markets as well as continuously updated news on business issues. In the case of sueddeutsche.de this is up-to-date information on events and activities in and around Munich, the city where a large fraction of readers lives. Although *Süddeutsche Zeitung* is considered as a national newspaper, it nevertheless has a strong regional and even local aspect in terms of content as well as in its geographical distribution. In a systematic study on the role of geography in online newspaper markets, Chyi and Sylvie (2001) showed that there are significant differences in the overlap of online and offline audiences for national, metropolitan, and community newspapers, the overlap being larger the more local the newspaper market is.

The mean values for the levers as well as the relative spread of the individual values around their means were not always as they are today, but changed over time. We should anticipate the relative spreads in the values for the levers to decrease and their mean values to increase. This would result if managers gained collective experience, became more aware of their peers' strategic moves, and copied the most effective ones. Consequently the differences in traffic or in the number of users would depend less on differences in how the levers are pulled and increasingly on the differences in the offline reach of the parent medium. Ultimately the latter would remain as the only source of difference if the levers converged. However, this will most probably not be the case, as Web sites, as well as the traditional media, will never fully simulate each other to achieve excellence in all of the levers.

So far, only the differences in the individual values for online affinity (o) and the excess in the number of new users (e) have continuously decreased since 2000 (Figure 3, left), but slowly and at relatively low levels. The relative spread of the yields (y) did not change substantially either. We attribute this to the fact that Web site managers did not work heavily on improving the performance of their sites on these three dimensions. Most sites in the sample rather developed "naturally" together with the evolving patterns of Internet usage. However, for the frequency of use (f) and the intensity of use (i), we observe substantial change.

Coinciding with several relaunches during 2001 (Glotz & Meyer-Lucht, 2004; Vogel, 2001) and increasing professionalism in Web site operations, the relative spread in the intensity of use (i) more than doubled as did its mean value, which is reflected in a substantial rise in overall traffic above the number of users (see Figure 3, right). More recently the relative spread of values for the intensity of use decreased, meaning that fewer sites stand out in inducing interactivity and the numbers of PIs generated per visit on each of them got closer to each other. From this it can be concluded that all managers nowadays increasingly know how to drive PIs.

From all levers, the frequency of use (f) stands out when regarding the differences among Web sites. Although a number of measures have been proposed to keep users attracted to the site (e.g., Schlegel, 2002), for most of the sites in our sample the frequency of use (f) in absolute terms remained fairly equal. With only some raising their frequency of use and the others basically stagnating, it is clear that the overall differences (i.e., the relative spread) will rise. A potential explanation for this phenomenon is that the online news market exhibits a "winner takes it all" dynamic; that is, for specific user segments only a few Web sites, if not just one, achieve to become the counterpart of the daily newspaper, whereas other Web sites are visited for specific or additional information needs. In our subsample only spiegel.de and bild.de managed to substantially increase their user retention (i.e., their frequency of use). Both Web sites serve a large but almost mutually exclusive audience resulting from their different editorial focuses. These focuses are a natural extrapolation to the online world of the focuses of the parent media (one being a news magazine targeting readers with a relatively high formal education level and the other a tabloid newspaper).

The fact that levers were pulled differently over time can also be seen when the developments in the number of PIs (T), the number of visits ($f \cdot N$), the number of users (N) and its component N_{old}, and finally in the number of readers (R) are compared, as shown in Figure 3 (right). Whereas the number of readers (R) stayed approximately the same,[27] we see that the average number of users (N) more than doubled from 2000 to 2003, as did the number of visits ($f \cdot N$). The average values for the traffic (T), however rose even faster, in particular from 2001 to 2002, due to the fact that all Web sites achieved a substantial rise in the intensity of use (i), or the number of PIs generated per visit.[28] This rise was fueled by an increasing number of interactive elements on the Web sites in the course of the professionalization of traditional media's Internet ven-

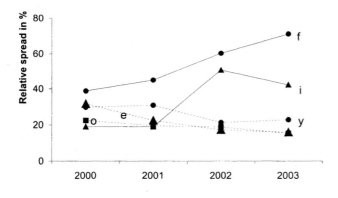 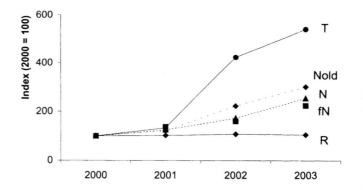

Figure 3. Relative spread in the levers for online success and growth characteristics for different measures of the size of the audience.

The figure shows the relative spread in the manageable levers for online success of news sites with a print background over time (left) and the development of the mean values for numbers of all users (N), readers of the traditional medium among them (N_{old}), visits ($f \cdot N$), page impressions (T), and offline reach (R) (right) for the same sample.

tures. Managers learned through collective experience how to induce repetitive interactions of the user with their Web site (e.g., by photo galleries, games, or frequently updated live reports on sports events).

Suggestions for Further Research

This analysis was conducted focusing on quantitative offline and online data on users and readers as well as on the traffic and the visits the users generate. Thorough insight was gained on the extent to which the management of individual sites pulls the levers (i.e., the values for the levers the management achieved to improve online success). Nevertheless, the chosen approach has some shortcomings, limiting the conclusions that can be drawn. However, these shortcomings point at the same time to future research needs when additional data will eventually be accessible and can be included in the analysis.

The shortcomings of this analysis due to missing financial data could be overcome once the initial furtiveness of online site operators gives way to a policy of more open publication of results. The number of users and the traffic, as indicators of online success, could then be replaced or enhanced with financial data. This would also allow for the examination of a possible relation between the number of newly acquired users and individual marketing spending.

Additionally, a systematic qualitative analysis of the Web sites in the sample could elucidate what concrete measures are undertaken to work on the levers and which of them work most effectively. Information on the overlap of online and offline content would shed some light on the specific value both channels deliver under the same brand and the share of paid content on the Web site on the incurred costs relative to print. Currently paid content plays only a minor role, this may change in the near future.

A further aspect limiting the conclusions to be drawn from this study is the concept of brand value or importance of the brand, which we operationalized by the single variable of offline reach. Brand value, however, resides not only in the size of the audience but also in its awareness by nonusers or nonreaders and its reputation for delivering high-quality, reliable, and unique content. A more complete picture of the importance of the brand to online success could be achieved by including such factors in the analysis.

The relation of the online site and the offline medium will also influence future changes in the numbers of readers and users (as well as their overlap). In this respect the success of an online spin-off is not necessarily beneficial for the parent medium. It could also lead to substantial cannibalization. Actually, there is an indication of a negative correlation in the number of copies of newspapers

sold (IVW Print, 2003) in our sample and the success of the related Web sites. However, the occurrence of cannibalization would be an unjustified conclusion without analyzing other factors possibly leading to this decrease (e.g., demographic change, general economic development). Additionally, the overlap between online and offline audience as well as the share of paid content on the Web site should be accounted for in a sound analysis of cannibalization effects. However, even studies in the United States (Chyi & Lasorsa, 2002), where Internet usage is more widespread than in Germany, are still inconclusive about cannibalization, which may be compensated for by new subscribers acquired via the Web site.

Castulus Kolo
(castulus.kolo@web.de)

is a consultant and a visiting research fellow at the Institute for Media and Communications Management at the University of St.Gallen, Switzerland. His research focuses on strategy and innovation management in the area of media as well as information and communication systems. Previously, he was member of the management board at the online subsidiary of a large German publishing house.

Patrick Vogt
(patrick_vogt@gmx.ch)

is a consultant, lecturer, and researcher in the fields of strategy, media, and communications. He lectures on, among others topics, strategy and media management at the Executive MBA in Media and Communication at the University of St.Gallen, Switzerland. Previously, he was a consultant with a leading strategy consultancy, a manager, and a journalist in several media companies.

Endnotes

1. Investments in businesses in the area of technology, telecommunication, or like Bertelsmann with its investment in America Online (AOL) and AOL Europe in the Internet service provider business were scarce and often divested soon after.
2. Usually the number of users with a certain sociodemographic profile is compared when deciding on the allocation of advertising expenditures.
3. Advertisers in the United States still go further and view not even the click-through as the main measure of success. Their goal is to finally track directly to sales (Nisenholz, 2003). In this case, the number of users will be the most important success factor on the demand side.
4. We did not consider online sites with an affiliation to a traditional publisher but launched under a differing brand. Regional media were also not considered.

5. We simplify by using the term *readers* for readers and viewers.

6. The sites not included in the sample represent to a large degree adult content sites.

7. An alternative approach, namely to generate the data in field research (i.e., a survey among Web sites) rather than relying on secondary research, would not have resulted in a better database, because Web sites not being included in both statistics (ACTA, 2003; IVW Online, 2003) undertake their own measurements in one or the other variable (if they measure them at all). Therefore, such an approach would neither provide comparable nor more complete data as in our set.

8. The survey was conducted among 10,424 people between 14 and 64 years old (ACTA, 2003).

9. This agency is managed by shared responsibility by representatives of the media and the advertising industry. Formerly reporting the circulations and audiences of traditional media (e.g., magazines and newspapers), since 1997, the IVW also certifies the measurements of Web site audiences of its members. The IVW in this respect is the counterpart of the Audit Bureau of Circulations for the United States and Canada, both being members of the International Federation of Audit Bureaux of Circulations.

10. A subdivision according to the traditional media background makes only limited sense, because on the Internet, for example, news-oriented spin-offs of magazines or newspapers are competing as fiercely for the attention of the consumer (see also Chyi & Sylvie, 1998). On the other hand the cross-promotion potential (e.g., the possibilities to share content) and the timeliness vary across exactly these categories. Therefore, the influence of the audience from the Web site on the audience of the traditional medium and vice versa possibly varies, too. As a compromise we compared the results for all media in the sample to the results for 10 online spin-offs from news media with a print background. The latter sample gives us a focus in terms of content, requirements on timeliness, and category of the parent medium.

11. Such differences are still observed also in countries where the general diffusion of Internet usage is further advanced than in Germany; see for example Chyi and Lasorsa (2002) for newspapers in the United States.

12. However, it is possible that Web sites of strong offline brands are given better means (e.g., in terms of technology and staff) to push the frequency and intensity of use, for example, by better or more actual content and services. This in turn would lead to a correlation of i or f with the offline reach, and indeed we observe a significant correlation of i and R (correlation coefficient of .72 at a significance of 3%) but none between f and R.

13. Additionally, the distribution of the values for T is skewed with a tail to high values.

14. Chyi and Sylvie (2000) also reported small overlaps with regard to all users of the Web sites of national newspapers (e.g., of about 10% for *USA Today*), but a completely different pattern for local newspapers (e.g., the *Austin American Statesman*) with up to more than 80%.

15. Obviously, by doing this we treat the abilities to attract new users to the site as a kind of "black box." The reasons why a certain Web site is better than another in this respect may be manifold and actually based on several levers resulting in a value for the excess (e) as a net effect.

16. Unless otherwise stated we use for all correlation measurements the coefficient after Pearson. This measure is valid for normally distributed variables, which we proved by the application of a Kolmogorov–Smirnov test.

17. For the whole sample we get a correlation coefficient of .84 at a significance < 0.1% and for the online news sites a correlation coefficient of .96 at a significance < 0.1%. A straight line fit intercepting the origin explains 72% of the variance ($R^2 = .72$) for all Web sites and 90% for the online news sites ($R^2 = .90$).

18. This is a higher number than the approximately 50% obtained in the United States (Chyi & Lasorsa 2002), which might be due to differences in marketing intensity for the spin-offs and Internet penetration.

19. As measures for the goodness of fit we summarize here the explained variance (R^2), the value of F according to the F test statistics, and the corresponding confidence level (c). The indexes N_{old}, R, and R/N_{old} shall denote the results for the three models: the model with N_{old} as the independent variable plus a constant, the multilinear model with R and N_{old} as independent variables plus a constant, and the model with R as the independent variable plus a constant. We obtain for the full data set: $R^2_{N_{old}} = 0.334$, $F_{N_{old}} = 17.0$, $c_{N_{old}} = 0.001$; $R^2_{R,N_{old}} = 0.486$, $F_{R,N_{old}} = 15.6$, $c_{R,N_{old}} = 0.001$; $R^2_R = 0.104$, $F_R = 4.0$, $c_R = 0.055$ and for the subsample of news media with a print background: $R^2_{N_{old}} = 0.831$, $F_{N_{old}} = 39.3$, $c_{N_{old}} = 0.001$; $R^2_{R,N_{old}} = 0.834$, $F_{R,N_{old}} = 17.6$, $c_{R,N_{old}} = 0.002$; $R^2_R = 0.786$, $F_R = 29.3$, $c_R = 0.001$.

20. The regression analysis gives for all Web sites as well as for the subset of online news sites a significance of a_{reg} and b_{reg} at a level below 0.1% (failure to reject the null hypothesis).

21. Unfortunately the model only gives us the values of a and b as an average across the samples. However we would expect that Web sites differ in how effective they are in attracting new users via "multiplier effects" (given by the parameter a) and how large their component of new users acquired independent of an measure of reach is. If we assumed that multiplier effects are equal for all sites and titles and cannot be influenced by management measures (i.e., that the coefficient a is equal for all Web sites) then we could compute the resulting number of new users attributable to this effect as $a^{reg} \cdot N_{old}$. The reach-independent part of N_{new} could then be calculated as ($N_{new} - a^{reg} \cdot N_{old}$), within which would lie the influence of management decisions on N_{new} driven by marketing measures. ($N_{new} - a^{reg} \cdot N_{old}$) is not correlated with R. We expect, however, that it would be correlated with marketing expenditures.

22. Going back in the short history of online news media, we observe that b^{reg} (i.e., the offset in the N_{new} versus N_{old} diagram) was close to zero in 2000 and grew every year to the number reached today. Of course, the more users of online news services in general, the more users of a particular site can be attracted via marketing measures. Indeed, as reported by ACTA (2003), the number of users of news sites grew considerably within recent years, exceeding the overall growth in Internet usage.

23. The lever we introduced to account for the apparent differences in the number of new users regardless of how these differences are achieved.

24. To calculate the contribution of each of the factors in Equation 1 to the spread in traffic we refer to the following approximation:

$$DT \approx \frac{\partial T}{\partial i} \cdot Di + \frac{\partial T}{\partial f} \cdot Df + \frac{\partial T}{\partial N} \cdot DN = f \cdot N \cdot Di + i \cdot N \cdot Df + i \cdot f \cdot DN$$

whereby $\partial T/\partial i$ is the partial derivation of T to i, and Δi the standard deviation of the values for i (for f and N analogous). This approximation was originally formulated by Gauss for the propagation of errors in the independent variable to the error of the dependent variable in a given formula. The approximation gives an estimate of the propagation of differences in the variables to the overall spread. As a result we get the contributions given in the text.

25. Of course, the Web sites included in the subsample also differ in their means to work on the levers. After all, the subsample comprises spin-offs from a tabloid via business newspapers and magazines. We think however, that the comparison gives a useful hint about whether there is room for improvements. The same procedure could be applied in principle on any choice of peers considered relevant from the perspective of a specific site.

26. In this respect there may be differences in countries with differing patterns of Internet usage or Internet penetration. We would expect a much lower relative spread, for example, in the values for the online affinity of offline readers (o) where the diffusion of Internet usage is relatively advanced and has almost reached saturation.

27. Actually, there is a decrease on the order of a few percent.

28. The fact that visits and PIs rose at different rates was also observed by Pauwels and Dans (2000) for newspaper sites in Spain.

References

ACTA. (2003). *Allensbacher Computer- und Technik-Analyse*. Allensbach am Bodensee, Germany: Institut für Demoskopie Allensbach, Allensbach am Bodensee.

Alt, R., & Zimmermann, H. D. (2001). Guest editors note. *Electronic Markets, 11*, 5–14. Retrieved September 2, 2003, from http://www.electronicmarkets.org/modules/pub/view.php/electronicmarkets-110

Chyi, H. I., & Lasorsa, D. L. (2002). An explorative study on the market relation between online and print newspapers. *Journal of Media Economics, 15*(2), 91–106.

Chyi, H. I., & Sylvie, G. (1998). Competing with whom? Where? And how? A structural analysis of the electronic newspaper market. *Journal of Media Economics, 11*(2), 1–18.

Chyi, H. I., & Sylvie, G. (2000). Online newspapers in the U.S.—Perceptions of markets, products, revenue, and competition. *International Journal on Media Management, 2*(2), 69–77.

Chyi, H. I., & Sylvie, G. (2001). The medium is global the content is not: The role of geography in online newspaper markets. *The Journal of Media Economics, 14*(4), 231–248.

Frey, L. G., Klein, H., & Koch, A. (2003). *Zeitungsverlage im Umbruch – Stimmungen und Perspektiven* [Changing framework conditions for newspaper publishers - Tendencies and perspectives]. Eschborn, Germany: Ernst & Young.

Glotz, P., & Meyer-Lucht, R. (2004). *Online gegen Print - Zeitung und Zeitschrift im Wandel* [Online versus print - Newspapers and magazines in times of change]. Konstanz, Germany: UVK.

Goldman, E. (1995). *Generating revenue from websites.* Retrieved October 25, 2003, from http://eric_goldman.tripod.com/articles/generatingrevenuesarticle.htm

Ihlström, C., & Palmer, J. (2002). Revenues for online newspapers: Owner and user perceptions. *Electronic Markets, 12*, 228–236.

IVW Online. (2003). [Home page of IVW Online]. Retrieved October 12, 2003, from http://www.ivw-online.de

IVW Print. (2003). [Home page of the IVW]. Retrieved December 3, 2003, from http://www.ivw.de

Kolo, C., & Vogt, P. (2003). Strategies for growth in the media and communication industry: Does size really matter? *International Journal on Media Management, 5*, 252–262.

Madsen, H. (1996). Reclaim the deadzone. *Wired, 4*(12), 206–220.

Nisenholz, M. (2003). *Keynote at the Editor & Publisher and Mediaweek Interactive Media Conference and Trade Show.* Retrieved February 12, 2003, from http://www.nytco.com/investors-presentations-20030508.html

O'Reilly, T. (1996). Publishing models for Internet commerce. *Communications of the ACM, 39*(6), 79–86.

Pauwels, K., & Dans, E. (2000). Internet marketing the news: Leveraging brand equity from market place to market space. *Journal of Brand Management, 8*(4–5), 303–314.

Picard, R. G. (2000). Changing business models of online content services—Their implications for multimedia and other content producers. *International Journal on Media Management, 2*(2), 60–68.

Rogers, E. M. (1971). *Diffusion of innovations.* New York: Free Press.

Schlegel, M. (2002). *Marketing-Instrumente für Online-Zeitungen* [Marketing instruments for online newspapers]. München, Germany: Fischer.

Spiegel Media. (2003). *ACTA 2003.* Retrieved October 12, 2003, from http://spiegel.zaehlservice.de/perl/index.pl?aid=0110022300

Stähler, P. (2001). *Geschäftsmodelle in der digitalen Ökonomie – Merkmale, Strategien und Auswirkungen* [Business models in the digital economy - Properties, strategies and consequences]. Lohmar, Germany: Eul.

Timmers, P. (1998). Business models for electronic markets. *Electronic Markets, 8*(2), 3–8.

Vogel, A. (2001). Onlinestrategien der Pressewirtschaft [Online strategies of print publishers]. *Media Perspektiven, 12*, 590–601.

Devising Video Distribution Strategies via the Internet: Focusing on Economic Properties of Video Products

Byeng-Hee Chang, Seung-Eun Lee, and Yang-Hwan Lee
University of Florida, USA

This article tries to link economic properties of video products to strategies that can be used by Internet-based video distributors. First, this study suggests 4 economic properties of video products: video as an experience good, returns to scale, video as a public good, and interdependency of willingness to pay. Second, based on economic attributes, this study synthesizes several strategies. Finally, this article uses a case study to compare theoretical strategies to actual strategies used by 2 Internet-based movie distributors. As a result of this study, we found that there are several possible strategies that are not yet being used in practice. It is expected that as the market becomes more mature through the development of technologies (e.g., digital rights management), more strategies will be adopted by online video distributors.

In a packed Washington congressional hearing, Michael Eisner, Chief Executive Officer of Walt Disney Corporation, accessed the Web and downloaded an unauthorized video clip from the Disney movie *Blackhawk Down* while Senate Commerce panel staffers and lobbyists watched. Moments later, he declared that Congress must act fast to protect the motion picture industry from Internet pirates (Clark &Vaida, 2002).

This demonstration shows how much Hollywood studios fear that the Internet could cannibalize their business profits through illegal copying. They are worried that distribution of their video products via the Internet might result in another "Napsterization." During the first half of 2001, music sales tumbled 6.7%, to $5.53 billion. The music industry blames piracy for this sales drop (Green, 2002), and Hollywood studios suspect that the same harmful effect of new technology experienced by the music industry could also expand into the movie and television industries (Schwartz, 2003).

Hollywood studios have encountered difficulty in deciding how and when to begin offering downloadable movies to Internet users, with unsettled issues such as technology and copyright protection still looming. There has been criticism about the failure of the recording industry to respond to the realities of the Internet and consumer demand. The recording industry has not been willing to sacrifice its big profit margins from CD sales in exchange for the untested business models of digital distribution. This unwillingness is not surprising. In fact, the movie industry has a long history of resistance to new technologies. When television first entered the market, the movie industry's initial response was to boycott the television industry (Balio, 1985). Movie studios refused to permit their creative personnel, who were under contract, to appear in television programs, nor would any of the large movie studios produce television series or license films from their libraries for television exhibition (Litman, 1998). They also tried to block the penetration of VCR use through lawsuits, such as *Sony v. Universal City Studios* (1984), but it was all in vain.

Despite their misgivings, major studios have begun to carefully recognize the Internet as a new outlet for distributing their video products. Recently, a few Internet-based video services such as MovieLink (www.movielink.com) and CinemaNow (www.cinemanow.com) have started to provide Internet users with both recent and classic movies produced by major studios. This cautious approach shows that the major studios recognize the growing market potential of the Internet, which they cannot ignore any longer as a new distribution channel.

This positive attitude toward using the Internet as a new revenue source is based on two recent technological developments: the rapid diffusion of broadband Internet services and the expansion of digital rights management (DRM) technologies. First, in the case of broadband infrastructures, the main issue has been whether the magni-

Address correspondence to Byeng-Hee Chang, College of Journalism and Communications, University of Florida, 2096 Weimer Hall, PO Box 118400, Gainesville, FL 32611. E-mail: changbye@ufl.edu

tude of broadband subscribers is sufficient to give video content producers and distributors incentives to invest in the Internet. Unlike the case of music, distributing video files via the Internet demands a stronger broadband infrastructure. If consumers with a dial-up connection, who make up the majority of the online population, watch video in *streaming* format, which is the transmission of audio and video in real time over the Internet, the quality of video is much inferior to that of over-the-air television. Even worse, if the same consumers attempt to download a video file, it takes much longer. Considering these technological constraints, the actual market for video on demand (VOD) via the Internet does not include the entire population of Internet users, but only the users of broadband Internet services such as cable modem and digital subscriber line (DSL). The growing number of broadband subscribers now provides video product producers and distributors with incentives to use the Internet as a new distribution channel. For example, at the beginning of 2000, the number of cable modem subscribers was 1.9 million, but as of September 2003, that number increased to 15 million (NCTA, 2003).

The other technological development that has created a positive attitude among movie studios is DRM. At first, VOD service providers only offered streaming video services. When employing streaming technology, no permanent copies are made on the user's system (Burk & Cohen, 2001). Therefore, copyright owners can entrust their music or video file to the streaming format because the risk of unauthorized reproduction or dissemination is considered to be lower than with those formats available for download (Pollack, 2000). Nevertheless, streaming has some fatal problems: Because of the general bandwidth of broadband, high-quality video cannot be secured and some fluctuation of signals is inevitable. Now, however, VOD service providers can offer their video products in streaming, as well as downloadable, format because DRM technologies make it possible to restrict unauthorized copying of the video product and prevent Internet users from watching the video program after a certain period by deactivating the downloaded file in the user's system.

Although the rapid diffusion of broadband and development of DRM technologies increase the potential of the Internet as a new distribution window for video programming, media executives themselves admit their companies do not have a formal review process to decide what strategies they can pursue to maximize revenue from online content distribution (KPMG, 2002). Based on this notion, we argue that it is necessary to use the Internet for video programming distribution. It is time for video program providers to develop specific strategies to build new revenue streams from Internet-based video distribution. Unfortunately, there are few research

that deal with strategies for VOD distribution via the Internet. Even though some researchers have discussed strategies for distributing information goods (Gallaugher, Auger, & BarNir, 2001; Shapiro & Varian, 1999), they do not specifically apply their logic into disseminating video programming via the Internet.

This article strives to explore and suggest a framework for strategies of digital video distribution via the Internet and focuses on economic characteristics of video products. As a form of information good, video products have peculiar characteristics differentiated from the other categories of products. Based on these different economic properties of information goods, this article suggests strategies for online video distributors, including providers of television programs and movies.

Specifically, this study proposes the following research questions:

RQ1: What kinds of strategies are appropriate, given the economic properties of video products, for video distributors to build new revenue streams for online video distribution?

RQ2: What kinds of strategies are actually adopted by current Internet-based video distributors?

To answer RQ1, this study adopts a theoretical approach for analyzing previous literature and synthesizes its theoretical reasoning. Given the current lack of literature on the economic properties of video products and related strategies, this study is exploratory in nature. Therefore, answering RQ1 could be somewhat subjective. A case study is utilized for RQ2, through which we analyze the strategies adopted by current major online video distributors.

Economic Properties of Video Products

It is useful to consider two aspects of the economic properties of video products in devising distribution strategies. First, in many cases it is certain that product characteristics may affect how the product should be distributed. For example, video products can be digitalized so that it is not necessary to physically deliver them. Second, we can easily and efficiently conceptualize and categorize several specific distribution strategies by considering the economic characteristics of video products.

Video products can be considered as a kind of *information good,* which refers to any product with content. In the context of the Internet, the content should be digitalized. The properties of information goods may include experience good, returns to scale, public good, and interdependency of willingness to pay (Ki & Chang, 2002; Varian, 1998).

Experience Goods

Video products are an experience good in that consumers choose and use the good solely to experience and enjoy it (Holbrook & Hirschman, 1982). Experience good also means that customers cannot estimate the quality of a product or expect satisfaction from consuming the product before they actually consume it (Varian, 1998). For example, before watching a new television program and getting a certain amount of information about the program, it is difficult for viewers to guess the expected satisfaction from watching the program. To overcome the problems caused by the experience good property, information good producers need to provide some high-credibility proxies for evaluating the information good. Varian (1998) suggested three kinds of strategies regarding the experience good property: previewing/browsing, reviews, and reputation.

In the case of *previewing/browsing,* information producers provide potential customers with opportunities to experience products before purchasing them. This strategy is generally observed in selling computer software; users can download a trial version and use it for a limited time period. Likewise, VOD service providers can give a potential buyer an opportunity to preview highlights of a video product.

The second strategy is for economic agents or third parties to specialize in *reviewing* products and provide these evaluations to other potential customers. Examples of this strategy are easily found in the media and entertainment industry, such as film and music reviews.

Producers of information goods can also overcome the experience good problem via *reputation.* For example, consumers may purchase an information good because they trust the ability of the producer based on previous experience and satisfaction with other products from the producer (Keller, 1998). In the entertainment industry, it is a common strategy to stress famous directors and actors for a video product.

Returns to Scale

Information is costly to produce, but cheap to reproduce (Shapiro & Varian, 1999). For example, it costs about $200 million to produce the movie *Titanic,* but less than $1 to reproduce a professional videotape containing the content. This cost structure—high fixed costs and low marginal costs—causes great difficulties for the competitive market (Varian, 1998). First, the high fixed costs can function as a sunk cost to producers of a video product (Gallaugher et al., 2001). If a film fails to attract a sufficient audience, the producer does not have another chance to recover the costs. Second, low marginal costs can eliminate incentives to produce video products in a competitive market because price is equal to marginal cost. The problem is that, in the case of information goods, the marginal cost is close to zero. If the price is zero, then producers will not produce the product.

Some of these problems can be solved by the market structure of the entertainment industry. First, in the entertainment industry, the return on investment is sometimes extremely high. Big hit movies can result in a profit of more than 10 times the initial investment. This structure can compensate for the high risk of investment failure. Proportionate to the high risk of failure, the entertainment industry enjoys a high expected return. Second, video products are not identical to each other. A competitive market assumes that producers produce similar products. In fact, the entertainment industry is not in a perfect competition, but rather, a monopolistic competition. This market structure can give producers the power to control prices within the market.

The remaining problems can be solved by price and quality discrimination. When the marginal cost equals zero, producers cannot set the price equal to marginal cost. In this case, producers set the price equal to the willingness of consumers to pay (or reservation price). Because each group of consumers has a different willingness to pay, the optimal strategy is to set different prices according to the varying willingness to pay. Windowing, a commonly adopted multistep distribution system in the entertainment industry, is based on this logic. According to different reservation prices for different groups of viewers, films are first released and shown in theaters, then on video, pay-per-view channels, pay channels, and so on.

Quality discrimination is closely related to price discrimination. Setting different prices for different consumers for the same product might result in legal problems. It might also decrease the incentives of consumer groups with higher reservation. So, when a producer uses a price discrimination strategy, it also uses a kind of quality discrimination. For example, Internet VOD service providers could use different image resolutions relative to different prices.

Public Good

Generally, a pure public good is both nonrival and nonexcludable (Samuelson, 1954). *Nonrivalry* means that one person's consumption does not diminish the amount available to other people, and *nonexcludability* means that one person cannot exclude another person from consuming the good. Classic examples of public goods are goods like national defense and TV broadcasts.

Nonrivalry is similar to the concept of returns to scale in that both assume that marginal cost is minimal. Nonrivalry means that an additional cost is not required to provide an information good to additional consumers. This shows that marginal cost is close to zero. Thus, we argue that returns to scale can be grouped in the same category as nonrivalry, and therefore the strategies based on nonrivalry will be the same as those based on returns to scale.

Varian (1998) argued that the two properties of a public good are quite different. Nonrivalry is a property of the good itself, whereas excludability is a bit different because it depends on the legal regime. That is, exclusion is not an inherent property of goods, public or private, but is rather a social choice.

To overcome the nonexcludability problem, two groups of strategies can be suggested: security technologies and legal solutions. Recent development of several DRM technologies has enabled Internet-based VOD providers to offer more video production in various formats, including streaming and downloading. In the case of legal solutions, two conflicting arguments can be suggested. One is to actively use law enforcement to defend video products as intellectual property. The other is to permit users to share video products, as long as trade can satisfy some conditions (e.g., each group has the same number of consumers; Bakos, Brynjolfsson, & Lichtman, 1999).

Interdependency of Willingness to Pay

Interdependency of willingness to pay means that one consumer's purchase of an information good can affect another consumer's willingness to pay (Ki & Chang, 2002). Suppose that a stock market analyst wrote a report to predict the future trend of stock prices. If we assume that the analyst's previous reports accurately predicted stock price trends, then we can also assume that stock investors will have a high willingness to pay for the report. Although the report has an attribute of returns to scale (i.e., marginal cost is close to zero), the pricing strategy is different from solutions based on returns to scale. When investors approach the analyst to buy the report, they demand that the analyst should not sell the report to other investors. So, the price for the report includes a new element of cost, which can be called *exclusion cost* (Berg, 1973).

Suggested Strategies and Tactics for Internet-Based VOD Providers

With the diffusion of the Internet among consumers, the commercial advantage of the Internet as a distribution channel has been recognized by many researchers. For example, Chircu and Kauffman (1999) argued that the emergence of new technologies for electronic commerce on the Internet made possible different ways of interacting for all the players in a market. Especially, Internet-based electronic marketplaces were expected to match buyers and sellers with increased effectiveness and lower transaction costs (Bakos, 1998). Based on this distributive advantage, content providers began to consider the Internet as a new window for selling their content (Dewan, Freimer, & Seidmann, 2000). Given the economic properties of video products, we suggest possible strategies for online VOD providers. The strategies are either based on theoretical analyses or found by observing the behaviors of current players in the entertainment industry.

Experience-good-based strategies. To overcome experience good problems, this article presents three kinds of strategies: preview/browsing, review, and reputation. First, in the case of preview/browsing, the main objective is to provide potential viewers with sufficient information for decision making. Specifically, the VOD provider can use visual promos, text descriptions, links to relevant Web sites, and free samples.

Through visual promos, the provider shows attractive scenes from the video products, and text description provides customers with sufficient background information. Through this strategy, the provider can explain the plot of a video product and introduce important elements such as directors and actors. Links to relevant Web sites can provide users with more diverse information. Another strategy is giving free samples to users. Although this tactic is not specific to individual video products, it provides potential users with information regarding the entire service. By providing free video products, the service provider can induce the user to experience the service itself.

Unlike preview/browsing, reviews can provide credible information to potential users. Possible tactics under the review strategy include user evaluation, expert evaluation, and e-mail referral function. User evaluation is provided by previous purchasers. Service providers also can use outside expert evaluation to provide credible information. Online book vendors such as Amazon.com and BN.com present good examples of this strategy. In the case of books, editorial reviews by leading magazines are provided by the company. For all products, customer reviews are available. Moreover, customers can rate each other's evaluations. A rating figure is placed with each review so that customers can decide whether to read it or not. An e-mail referral function induces users and purchasers to send information regarding a video product to other users or friends.

In the case of reputation building, two kinds of strategies can be used: celebrity endorsement and ingredient branding. Celebrity endorsement advertises the service by using the credibility and trustworthiness of a celebrity. Ingredient branding is a kind of brand-building strategy focused on elements incorporated into the video product (Aaker, 1991). For more specific tactics, service providers can stress big names, such as famous producers, actors, award-winning history (e.g., Academy Awards), and previous performances, such as box office records or television ratings.

Return to scale/nonrivalry-based strategies. Video products have near zero marginal cost and this property demands that VOD service providers maximize their profits by differentiating prices according to willingness to pay for each consumer group. Considering the difference in willingness to pay, two kinds of strategies can be used: price–quality discrimination and bundling.

Regarding quality discrimination (i.e., versioning), Shapiro and Varian (1999) introduced several specific strategies, including delay (i.e., windowing), user interface, convenience, image resolution, flexibility of use, capability, features and functions, and annoyance.

First, delay is the most frequently used strategy in the entertainment industry. Delay is identical to the previously discussed windowing strategy. Second, a user interface strategy provides different levels of search capabilities. For example, regarding the background information of a video product, the service provider can offer different search interfaces to long-term and short-term users. Third, convenience strategy restricts the time at which an information service is used. For instance, there are different time length plans in renting a video. Similarly, VOD service can set different time plans according to the characteristics of video products and user willingness to pay. Fourth, online VOD service providers also use visual resolution as a way of price–quality discrimination. The service providers can offer a high-resolution video (e.g., 700 kilobytes/sec) to customers with higher willingness to pay, and low-resolution video (e.g., 56 kilobytes/sec) to those with lower willingness to pay. Fifth, flexibility of use refers to giving different versions of video products to the buyers who have different willingness to pay in terms of their usage. For example, a low-priced version allows users to only watch streaming video, whereas a high-priced version permits users to enjoy watching streaming video, as well as download the video products. Sixth, capability strategy means that a high-priced version contains some special information that the low-priced version does not. A DVD usually contains more than the video product itself. For example, the *Monsters, Inc.* DVD has extra content including a game, a music video, interviews with the producers, abandoned story concepts, a tour of the Pixar animation studio, and a trailer for an upcoming animated film. For consumers, viewing the DVD means getting more than just a movie (Ahrnes, 2002). Given that in today's Hollywood the largest portion of revenue comes from sales and rentals of DVDs, a VOD service provider might need to leverage this capability strategy. Seventh, the features and function strategy is closely related to viewing environment. For example, with the help of a video-viewing program such as Microsoft Windows Media Player or RealOne Player, service providers can provide different levels of functions for high-priced and low-priced versions. Eighth, in the case of annoyance strategy, service providers can attach some commercial information in the video product of a low-priced version.

Another way to leverage users' different willingness to pay is bundling strategy. Bundling can be divided into three specific tactics: pure bundling, mixed bundling, and unbundling (Stremersch & Tellis, 2002). When pure bundling is adopted, only bundled products are sold, whereas the service providers with unbundling strategy can segment the original product into several parts and sell each part. In the case of mixed bundling, buyers can purchase products either by single product or by bundling, according to their preferences (Adams & Yellen, 1976). For example, when distributing a music CD via the Internet, sellers can sell the whole CD (bundling), or sell each song contained in the CD (unbundling).

Nonexcludability-based strategies. Regarding the nonexcludable property of information goods, two solutions were suggested in the previous section: technological solutions and legal solutions. In terms of technological solutions, service providers can use two specific strategies. One is to use DRM systems. DRM technologies ensure that only the people who have obtained the rights to use a specific piece of information or content can do so, and specify exactly how the content can be used. These mechanisms also have the ability to allow copies to be made on payment or to charge "micropayments" for each small use of the product. In this regard, DRM might allow a strong degree of price discrimination. The other strategy is to allow user video file sharing to some degree, based on DRM technologies. Bakos et al. (1999) argued that under some conditions (i.e., small-sized consumer group with similar number of members), sharing can increase the profits of information good distributors. In the case of music downloading, service providers allow consumers to make a limited number of copies of a song onto different computers. This type of strategy can be applied to video products. For example, video service providers can permit a limited number of consumers to share a video product for a higher price.

In the case of legal solutions, service providers prevent users from illegal copying by relying on law enforcement or legal complaints. Specifically, service providers can use two tactics: filing lawsuits or prior notices that warn of illegal copying or distribution. These tactics, however, are difficult to observe so this article does not analyze them.

Interdependency-of-willingness-to-pay-based strategies. Two types of strategies can be used to exploit interdependency of willingness to pay: personalization and privilege. Personalization means that video distributors provide consumers with customized services. For example, Amazon.com uses collaborative filtering and other personalization techniques to recommend books and music to users. The company retains the name of each customer, which allows the Web site to greet each returning individual as they log in. Then, when the user picks a book, the system recommends a few other books that may be of interest to the user. This kind of personalization strategy can be applied to online VOD service providers. In the case of privilege, consumers can enjoy exclusive access to a video product prior to mass distribution. In fact, this strategy is used when movie studios provide VIPs with special premieres before releasing their movies.

Case Study

Strategic Importance of the Internet as a Distribution Window

The Internet is a new window for distributing video products. As explained earlier, windowing is a strategy that distributes video products into different media in different time periods at different prices. Usually windowing is considered a type of price differentiation.

Before conducting the case study, it is useful to explore what kinds of business models are currently used to distribute video products over the Internet. We suggest two dimensions to categorize these business models: analog versus digital and rental versus purchase. Based on the two dimensions, we have four types of business models: analog rental, analog purchase, digital rental, and digital purchase. In analog rental, service providers rent video products over the Internet; however, the delivery is physically made. NetFlix (netflix.com) is included in this category. In analog purchase, retailers such as Wal-Mart sell video products using electronic commerce systems. In digital rental, distributors provide consumers with streaming or limited downloading services. Here, limited downloading services means that consumers may view downloaded video products within specific time periods. In digital purchase, consumers may download and permanently own video products. This article only focuses on digital rental and digital purchase categories in that they provide consumers with instant access to the products without having to wait for offline delivery (see Figure 1).

Case study of MovieLink and CinemaNow

To examine how Internet-based VOD service providers are actually using strategies based on economic properties of video products, we conducted a case study. Through this case study, this article compares the theoretically sug-

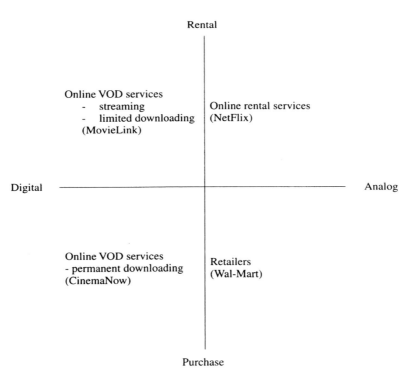

Figure 1. Business models of Internet-based video services.

gested strategies with actual tactics used by VOD service providers via the Internet.

Currently, only a few firms such as MovieLink.com, CinemaNow.com, Atomfilms.com, and SightSound.com provide VOD services via the Internet. Among these services, this article focuses on MovieLink and CinemaNow because they are exclusively distributing movies produced by major Hollywood studios. Other service providers, such as Atomfilms and SightSound, only deal with independent films. Since the demise of companies such as Movies.com and Intertainment.com, MovieLink and CinemaNow are duopolizing the online movie distribution market.

MovieLink was founded in 2001 as a joint venture by major Hollywood studios, including MGM Studios, Paramount Pictures, Sony Picture Entertainment, Universal, and Warner Brothers. MovieLink provides pay-per-view services that offer about 450 movies. Customers can download and enjoy movies on their computers for a limited time period. A typical service of MovieLink is to allow customers to rent videos for 30 days. Customers, however, can only watch the films within a 24-hr period that begins with their first viewing.

Unlike MovieLink, which is supported by major studios, CinemaNow was founded in 1999 by Lions Gate Entertainment and nonmovie media companies including Blockbuster and Microsoft. Featuring 1,200 movies, including 500 adult films, CinemaNow provides both subscription and pay-per-view services through streaming and downloading.

Applied to the dimensions of Figure 1, MovieLink is included in the digital rental model and CinemaNow belongs to both the digital rental and digital purchase models. MovieLink allows users to rent movies for only a limited time period. CinemaNow, however, provides users with two options: rental and download for permanent ownership.

Experience-good-based strategies. Of the four preview/browsing strategies, visual promos, text description, and free samples are currently used by both MovieLink and CinemaNow, and links to relevant Web sites are not used. Some photos and short trailers of a movie are generally used as promos and free samples. For text descriptions, the companies provide detailed information about a movie, synopsis, actors, directors, and credits.

Regarding review strategies, none of the three specific strategies, user evaluation, expert evaluation, and e-mail referral function, is adopted by MovieLink. CinemaNow, however, adopts user evaluation and e-mail referral function. By means of these two functions, users can more cautiously select movies and share information about movies with others. The lack of review strategies utilized by MovieLink might result in some loss of credibility attached to the video products. In practice, it would cost MovieLink little to add these evaluation features and e-mail referral functions to their Web site.

In light of ingredient branding with regard to reputation strategies, MovieLink and CinemaNow are not actively adopting these strategies. They seldom provide information about any award-winning history or the box office records for their movies; nor do they stress or utilize the brand image or power of actors or directors. Occasionally they use some celebrity (e.g., Larry King) endorsements, but not on a regular basis.

Returns to scale/nonrivalry-based strategies. In the previous section, we suggested eight specific strategies related to price–quality discrimination. In terms of delay, two kinds of windowing practice are possible; one is intermedia windowing and the other is intramedia windowing. For example, if a movie is released to video after its theatrical run, this can be referred to as intermedia windowing. On the other hand, after some period, while still in a video rental shop, if the price for renting a video is lowered, it can be considered as intramedia windowing. In terms of intermedia windowing, the release time for Internet VOD service is a little later than that of the video market, with its release sequence being approximately similar to pay-per-view (Pogue, 2003). In the case of intramedia windowing, the service sets different prices for video products based on the time period after release. MovieLink used delay strategy by differentiating prices based on release time.

In the case of user interface, we could not find any differentiation regarding search capabilities according to consumer willingness to pay.

In terms of convenience, customers can choose different time plans for their convenience. For example, a customer can rent a video product for 3 days or 5 days. MovieLink provides customers with a similar service. Customers can continue to rent a movie for an additional 24-hr viewing period for up to 30 days after the initial download, typically at a reduced price.

Regarding image resolution strategy, these companies do not apply different levels of image resolution to consumers with different willingness to pay.

This article defines flexibility of use as whether or not the service provided users with both streaming and downloading options. CinemaNow offers its movies in two ways, streaming and downloading, but MovieLink has only adopted the downloading method.

In terms of capability, as shown in by the DVD example, information good providers need to add extra value to existing products to leverage consumers' different willingness to pay. Some movies at MovieLink are provided with extras (i.e., promotional copy of soundtrack), but these may not be used as a price–quality discrimination.

Regarding features and functions, these services do not use different levels of play options, using viewing software such as Windows Media Player or RealOne.

Finally, the services do not use an annoyance strategy because they only adopt pay-per-view or subscription business models without advertising.

Another way to consider different levels of willingness to pay is to use a bundling strategy. MovieLink and CinemaNow do not use any of the three specific bundling strategies.

Nonexcludability-based strategies. Both companies use DRM technology to prevent users who download a digital product from sharing it with other users, and to make the downloaded video program expire automatically after some period. As another strategy, service providers can allow users to share movies with their colleagues under strict conditions. Only a limited number of copies should be allowed. Neither service, however, uses this strategy.

Interdependency-of-willingness-to-pay-based strategies. As to personalization strategy, neither service provides the explicit customizations that are evident on Internet vendors such as Amazon.com. In the case of privilege strategy, CinemaNow provides different levels of membership under which customers are required to pay different fees.

MovieLink, which sticks to the pay-per-view model, does not use this type of strategy.

Discussion

Generally, this study showed that the suggested four economic properties of video products could successfully categorize the strategies that were actually utilized or could theoretically be used by online video distributors (see Table 1). Most of the actual strategies that have been adopted by the services could be included and several unused strategies could be suggested.

Compared to the other properties, experience-good-based strategies have been actively used by online video services. Both MovieLink and CinemaNow have adopted some strategies such as visual promo, text description, and free samples. These strategies have been frequently used by traditional media and are not difficult to apply to an online situation. Unexpectedly, reputation strategies, which stress the importance of brand image of actors and directors or previous history (e.g., awards, box office record) of a movie have not been actively used. It seems that these strategies are too complex or more costly to conduct compared with preview/browsing or review strategies. For example, reputation-related data should be gathered and refined by service providers themselves, whereas preview/

Table I. Analysis of Distribution Strategies

Property	Strategy Category	Strategies & Tactics	MovieLink	CinemaNow
Experience good	Preview/browsing	Promo	O	O
		Text description	O	O
		Links to relevant Web sites	X	X
		Free samples	O	O
	Review	User evaluation	X	O
		Expert evaluation	X	X
		E-mail referral	X	O
	Reputation	Celebrity endorsing	X	O
		Actor/director/writer	X	X
		Award	X	X
		Previous performance	X	X
Returns to scale	Price/quality discrimination	Delay	O	X
		User interface	X	X
		Convenience	X	X
		Image resolution	X	X
		Flexibility of use	X	X
		Capability	X	X
		Features and functions	X	X
		Annoyance	X	X
	Bundling	Pure bundling	X	X
		Mixed bundling	X	X
		Unbundling	X	X
Nonexcludability	Technology	DRM	O	O
		Limited sharing	X	X
Interdependency of willingness to pay	Personalization	Personalization	X	X
	Privilege	Exclusive access	X	O

Note. Legal strategies are not analyzed because of unavailability of data. O = present; X = absent; DRM = digital rights management.

browsing or review-related data are easily obtained or provided free of charge.

Unlike expectation, most strategies related to the returns-to-scale property have not been actively used by online video services. Price–quality discrimination or bundling strategies are frequently observed in the information industry, which sells database or computer software. In the case of the entertainment industry, these strategies are not yet widely used. Complicated calculations regarding the responses of consumers need to be conducted prior to their implementation.

This study suggests that a possible strategy could be to allow customers to share video products based on the theoretical work of Bakos et al. (1999). With the help of DRM technologies, online video services can increase their revenues by allowing video product sharing. This suggestion is important in that online video services could face illegal copying problems without relying on legal solutions and take better advantage of file sharing among broadband users.

Strategies related to the property of interdependency of willingness to pay have not been actively used among online video services. This property is a little difficult to apply to the entertainment industry, although it is easily used in the decision-making situations that are frequently found in the information industry. However, the concept of exclusion cost can be similarly applied to both the entertainment and the information industries. We conclude that the lack of use by online video services is due to unfamiliarity with the concept.

This article suggests some managerial implications based on these findings. First, when devising strategies for online distribution of video products, service providers need to look at the big picture, rather than getting caught up in individual strategies, because in many cases, individual strategies are related to one another and are based on one of the product's properties. Second, price–quality discrimination and bundling strategies based on the returns-to-scale property need to be actively utilized by online video distributors. Although these strategies are unfamiliar, they may increase the revenues of online services simply by compiling user information and predicting responses based on that information. In addition, it is not costly to use these strategies. Third, it is recommended that online video services respond to illegal copying problems with positive approaches that utilize file sharing behaviors among broadband users, rather than try to prohibit them from copying.

This article primarily focused on movies as a video product. However, there are several types of video products. One important type is television programs. To increase more general use of the suggested framework, it is necessary to consider television programs for online distribution. Television programs are also a kind of information good in that they consist of contents that can be easily digitalized. Therefore, all the economic attributes applied to general video products can be applicable to television programs.

Television programs, however, have some peculiar characteristics different from general video products. First, the traditional television market has been assumed to be an oligopoly market, whereas the general video product market is assumed to be a monopolistic competition. This could be a theoretical explanation for why the current distribution of television programs via the Internet is minimal. Second, unlike general video products, television programs are shown for free to viewers at the initial stage. Thus, if television producers cannot add new values to television programs to satisfy viewers in the following windows, the viewers will not pay to watch television programs online. Third, compared to the movie industry, in which the first distributors in the windowing process are the same as the second window distributors, the television market will require different distributors for the television program in each window. Based on this observation, we can conclude that the incentives to distribute video products through the windowing process in the television market are less than those in other video product markets.

Conclusion

This article tried to link economic properties of video products to strategies that can be used by Internet-based video distributors. As a first step, considering video products as a kind of information good, this study suggested four economic properties: video as an experience good, returns to scale, video as a public good, and interdependency of willingness to pay. Second, based on these economic attributes, this study synthesized several strategies. Through a case study, this article compared theoretical strategies to actual strategies used by two Internet-based movie distributors. Based on the comparison, we can conclude that several possible strategies are not yet used in practice. This seems to result from the fact that Internet-based video distribution is currently at its initial stage. We expect that, as the market becomes more competitive, online distributors will adopt more strategies. Finally, this study discussed the kinds of problems service providers will face in distributing television programs via the Internet.

As this study is only exploratory, several suggestions made here require empirical examination. First, in terms of consumer perspectives, future research needs to examine how consumers will react to the suggested strategies in both experimental and real-world situations. Second, future research needs to observe and determine what kinds of strategies Internet-based video distributors will adopt as the industry grows.

Byeng-Hee Chang

(changbye@ufl.edu)

is a PhD student in the College of Journalism and Communications, University of Florida, Gainesville, Florida, USA.

Seung-Eun Lee

(leeseung@ufl.edu)

is a PhD candidate in the College of Journalism and Communications, University of Florida, Gainesville, Florida, USA.

Yang-Hwan Lee

(kneon3@ufl.edu)

is a MA student in the College of Journalism and Communications, University of Florida, Gainesville, Florida, USA.

References

Adams, W. J., & Yellen, J. L. (1976). Commodity bundling and the burden of monopoly. *Quarterly Journal of Economics, 90,* 475–498.

Aaker, D. A. (1991). *Managing brand equity.* New York: Free Press.

Ahrnes, F. (2002, October 7). Hollywood sees the big picture with DVD. *The Washington Post,* p. A1.

Bakos, Y. (1998). The emerging role of electronic marketplaces on the Internet. *Communications of the ACM, 41*(8), 35–42.

Bakos, Y., Brynjolfsson, E., & Lichtman, D. (1999). Shared information goods. *Journal of Law & Economics, 42*(1), 117–155.

Balio, T. (Ed.). (1985). *The American film industry.* Madison: University of Wisconsin Press.

Berg, S. V. (1973). Interdependent tastes and fashion behavior. *Quarterly Review of Economics & Business, 13*(2), 49–58.

Burk, D. L., & Cohen, J. E. (2001). Fair use infrastructure for right management systems. *Harvard Journal of Law & Technology, 15,* 41–83.

Chircu, A., & Kauffman, R. (1999). Strategies for Internet middlemen in the intermediation/disintermediation/reintermediation cycle. *Electronic Markets, 9,* 109–117.

Clark, D., & Vaida, B. (2002). Copyright issues: Digital divide. *National Journal's Technology Daily.* Retrieve February 14, 2004, from http://nationaljournal.com/about/technologydaily/

Dewan, R., Freimer, M., & Seidmann, A. (2000). Organizing distribution channels for information goods on the Internet. *Management Science, 46,* 483–496.

Gallaugher, J. M., Auger, P., & BarNir, A. (2001). Revenue streams and digital content providers: An empirical investigation. *Information & Management, 38,* 473–485.

Green, H. (2002, October 14). Digital media: Don't clamp down too hard. *Business Week, 3803,* 140–143.

Holbrook, M. B., & Hirschman, E. C. (1982). The experiential aspects of consumption: Consumer fantasies, feelings, and fun. *Journal of Consumer Research, 9,* 132–140.

Keller, L. K. (1998). *Strategic brand management.* Upper Saddle River, NJ: Prentice Hall.

Ki, E., & Chang, B. (2002). How does intellectual property law affect the value creation process and strategies of database companies. *International Journal on Media Management, 4*(3), 150–155.

KPMG. (2002). *The digital challenge.* Retrieved February 14, 2004, from www.kpmg.com/Rut2000_prod/Documents

Litman, B. R. (Ed.). (1998). *The motion picture mega industry.* Needham Heights, MA: Allyn & Bacon.

NCTA. (2003). *High speed Internet access via cable.* Retrieved February 14, 2004, from http://www.ncta.com

Pogue, D. (2003, May 15). Film rentals via the Internet: A studio cut. *The New York Times,* p. G1.

Pollack, W. M. (2000). Tuning in: The future of copyright protection for online music in the digital millennium. *Fordham Law Review, 68,* 2445–2488.

Samuelson, P. A. (1954). The pure theory of public expenditure. *Review of Economics and Statistics, 36,* 387–389.

Schwartz, J. (2003, December 25). In chasing movie pirates, Hollywood treads lightly. *New York Times,* p. C1.

Shapiro, C., & Varian, H. R. (1999). *Information rules.* Boston: Harvard Business School Press.

Sony Corp. v. Universal City Studios, 464 U.S. 417 (1984).

Stremersch, S., & Tellis, G. J. (2002). Strategic bundling of products and prices: A new synthesis for marketing. *Journal of Marketing, 66*(1), 55–72.

Varian, H. R. (1998). *Markets for information goods.* Working paper. Berkeley, CA: University of California.

The Evolution of Business Models and Marketing Strategies in the Music Industry

Valerie L. Vaccaro
State University of New York, USA

Deborah Y. Cohn
Yeshiva University, USA

This article provides a strategic analysis using a services marketing framework of 3 business models in the music industry: the traditional music industry; renegade peer-to-peer music file trading; and new, legitimate online downloading services. Key recommendations are made on how new, legitimate services can succeed using convergent marketing strategies. Finally, a conclusion is provided addressing the future of the music industry and other media-related industries.

Digital Distribution of Music

Since 1999, the Internet has drastically altered the production, distribution, and consumption of music (Molteni & Ordanini, 2003). Digital music distribution via unauthorized consumer peer-to-peer (P2P) file trading has become one of the most popular Internet activities throughout the world via the renegade pioneer Napster and now current unauthorized organizations such as the popular Kazaa. The term *unauthorized* refers to the fact that the music currently traded on P2P networks is not licensed by record labels and copyright holders, and under the law throughout the world, is illegal. (An explanation of this issue can be found at http://www.whatsthedownload.com/whats_the_controversy/faq/index.aspx#5.)

After 4 years of users being spoiled with access to unauthorized free music, file trading behavior has become part of global culture (Cohn & Vaccaro, 2002; Ewing & Green, 2003; Freedman, 2003; Hughes & Lang, 2003). As of June 2003, "The number of infringing music files at any one time on peer-to-peer services is now estimated at 1 billion, compared to 500 million in June 2002" (IFPI, 2003). From 1999 to 2002, annual global music sales declined by about $2 billion, which was attributed to unauthorized online P2P file trading, offline piracy (e.g., production

and sales of counterfeit CDs), a poor economy, and shifts in purchase priorities of young consumers from music to DVDs and video games (Strauss, 2003). Darwin's survival of the fittest and Levitt's marketing myopia indicate the power of new technologies to disrupt existing business models to adapt or become obsolete. Two major factors have contributed to this imperative: technology and consumer dissatisfaction with the traditional business model (Freedman, 2003).

Research on Digital Music Distribution

Previous research has examined major record labels' responses to the pirate culture of music downloading (e.g., via litigation and digital copyright protection technologies; Freedman, 2003). Other research has focused on the economic and social impacts of P2P and the shift in power from the record labels to independent artists and consumers (Hughes & Lang, 2003). A study on perceptions of P2P with consumers from nine nations found cross-cultural values are related to the adoption of file trading (Cohn & Vaccaro, 2002). Additional research on P2P identified consumer groups with distinct attitudes that have implications for market segmentation strategies (Molteni & Ordanini, 2003). Another study looked at how consumers' music purchasing behavior was influenced by P2P in regards to demographic, economic, and technological factors (Bhattacharjee, Gopal, & Sanders, 2003).

Address correspondence to Valerie L. Vaccaro, SUNY–College at Old Westbury, School of Business AV-D300, 223 Store Hill Road, Old Westbury, NY 11568, USA. E-mail: ValVaccaro@aol.com

Contribution of This Study

It has been recommended that record labels should shift their attention from lawsuits to promotion and marketing (Freedman, 2003). This study is a guide to point the music industry in that direction using a marketing perspective. As mentioned, earlier studies have already provided an analysis of the music industry's litigation strategy (e.g., Freedman, 2003). This article extends previous research by being the first to provide a detailed analysis of strategies related to each of three business models (traditional, renegade, and new) using a services marketing mix framework. Also, this is the first study to provide in-depth marketing recommendations on how firms in the music industry can succeed. Finally, a conclusion is provided that addresses the digital revolution's impact on the future of the music and other media-related industries.

Business Models and Marketing

A business model can be defined as "the method by which a firm builds and uses its resources to offer its customers better value than it competitors and to make money doing so" (Afuah & Tucci, 2003, p. 4). A good business model addresses these questions: (a) What does the customer value? (b) How does the business generate income? and (c) Who is the customer? (Magretta, 2002). This article addresses all three of these issues, from a marketing perspective, for three business models in the music industry: traditional, renegade, and new.

The Traditional Business Model

The traditional business model in the music industry includes the mass production and distribution of physical goods (Hughes & Lang, 2003). This model includes the record labels that manufacture the product (e.g., mainly CDs) and distribute it via bricks-and-mortar stores, direct mail clubs, and online e-tailers, as well as artists selling their CDs at concerts. The traditional model includes the history of the industry from the early 20th century through the present (Hull, 1997; Rivkin & Meier, 2002).

The Renegade Business Model

The renegade business model is based on illegal, unauthorized P2P music file trading (of digital MP3 files) via the Internet; this activity is enabled by organizations providing software that empowers millions of consumers to become unauthorized mass distributors of music for free. Between 1999 and 2000, the pioneer Napster was the first renegade organization to garner brand recognition and loyalty, with more than 60 million users worldwide, before it was shut down by the U.S. court system (Greenfeld, 2000). Because the record industry was bypassed and there was "no tollgate for collecting payments and royalties ... (it became) a runaway worldwide bazaar" (Maney, 2000, p. B2). Soon after, other unauthorized services entered the market (Richtel, 2001; Strauss, 2001). By 2003, Kazaa was the new renegade leader and like the pioneer Napster, it became a lawsuit target. In May 2003, more than 230 million users had downloaded Kazaa Media Desktop software, making it the most downloaded program on the Web ("Most Downloaded," 2003). The popularity of renegade P2P file trading continues to grow as part of the emerging trend on the Internet of self-organizing, emergent digital community networks (Hughes & Lang, 2003).

The renegade model can be considered a combination of two types of "native Internet" business models: freeware (i.e., free software) and information barter (i.e., exchange of information; Bambury, 1998). Organizations offering renegade services and content can be considered business models due to their contribution to economic value in the form of knowledge and content provided by the participants (Lechner & Hummel, 2002; Timmers, 1998). There are also legitimate free services such as tinyurl.com turning a profit by including Google's AdSense (i.e., contextual advertising) on their site. Like tinyurl.com, many companies offer free services and content with the hope of upselling consumers to premium paid services and content (Dean, 2004). At present, music industry "P2P services often support themselves by serving up unwanted ads—annoying pop-ups, spam and the like—to users" (Taylor, 2003, p. 34).

Currently, the renegade business model is in the early stages of development. Although the renegade approach offers content and services to consumers free of charge, the intention for these organizations is usually to find a way to generate income. For example, in October 2003, 2 years after it was shut down by the court system, Napster was reintroduced as a for-profit, legitimate business in the United States with plans to enter the European market.

The present renegade leader, Kazaa, has its headquarters in Australia, with offices in Denmark, Estonia, the Netherlands, Sweden, the West Indies, and Vanuatu (Levack, 2003). The Recording Industry Association of America (RIAA) has been trying to get Kazaa shut down by the U.S. court system. The senior vice president of Sharman Networks, the parent company of Kazaa, appeared at U.S. Senate hearings to answer questions about P2P software ("Top 50," 2003). In April 2003, Kazaa countersued the entertainment industry

for copyright misuse, monopolizing content, and deceptive acts and practices ... [which] is one of the largest cases of online copyright infringement. … Kazaa's future will depend on whether it can prove both the issue of monopolizing content and whether Kazaa can be used legally. … If Kazaa wins … it will set precedents the world over for online film and music distribution. (Levack, 2003, p. 16)

Another strategy Kazaa is pursuing to become a legitimate online music firm is to try to negotiate a deal with the major record labels, or get compulsory licensing approved. In November 2003, to promote its mission to turn legitimate, Kazaa spent $1 million on a marketing communications campaign ("Kazaa Launches," 2003). Kazaa's strategies are discussed in more detail later.

Meanwhile, Kazaa has numerous sources of revenue. The first source of revenue is from advertising software (e.g., adware) that is included with users' agreement in all free Kazaa downloads. Adware refers to software applications that display ads (e.g., banner and pop-up ads) while the programs are in operation. In addition, adware also may track consumers' Web browsing history to send targeted promotional messages to consumers who have installed the program on their personal computers. Adware has generated legal and industry controversy when it tracks users' personal information and passes it to third parties without the users' permission (in which case it is known as spyware). Some of Kazaa's advertising clients include Microsoft, NetFlix, and DirecTV ("Kazaa," 2004). In addition, promotional firms such as Claria and Cydoor (which claim high click-through rates) provide messages from their networks of advertisers to Kazaa users (Fadner, 2004). As a backlash to the adware, an unrelated organization introduced Kazaa Lite, a copy of the Kazaa software without the adware. In response, Kazaa offered for sale (at a price of U.S. $29.95) Kazaa Plus, a greatly enhanced version of the free program without adware (Lyman, 2003).

A third source of revenue is related to Kazaa's innovative attempt to establish a new model of advertising-supported television. Kazaa distributed to its 60 million registered users a free weekly hip-hop culture TV show hosted by rap star Ice T and produced by digital broadcaster Pseudo.com; soft-drink maker Red Bull was a paying sponsor of this show (Olsen, 2003). A fourth source of revenue is from paid content related to Kazaa's partnership with a firm called Altnet that promotes legally licensed content (e.g., music files, video games, videos, and other material; "Kazaa," 2004). In conjunction with Altnet, Kazaa has sold paid content associated with more than 15 million copy-protected files per month (Borland, 2003). Finally, a fifth source of revenue for Kazaa is from Altnet, which receives fees from selling more than 500,000 licenses per day to independent artists who pay $99 and up to post their content (Jesdanun, 2003; Hachman, 2003).

The New Business Model

The new business model includes legitimate online digital music services. By 2008, Forrester expects that approximately 33% of music sales will be from legitimate online downloads, and that CD sales will drop 30% from their peak in 1999 (Needham, 2003). Forrester currently estimates that by the end of 2004, online music sales may amount to $270 million, up from $89 million in 2003 (Legon, 2004).

Legitimate online music services are part of the native Internet business model category of digital products and digital delivery (e.g., including music) that often have strategic alliances with access providers (Bambury, 1998). The first legitimate online music services began to appear on the Internet in 1995, but none of the early services were very successful (e.g., Rivkin & Meier, 2002). When Apple Computers introduced its iTunes service in April 2003, it marked the first major success for this new business model; within its first 6 months of operation, a record number of 14 million songs were purchased for download. In July 2004, iTunes reached its 100 millionth download ("iTunes Tops," 2004).

In the European market, there are more than 30 legitimate online services that offer music either by pay-per-download or by subscription (IFPI, 2004). In May 2004, Napster 2.0 started its European market entry with its UK edition, and the following month Apple iTunes began service to Europe in the United Kingdom, Germany, and France ("iTunes Tops," 2004; Twist, 2004). In 2004, competition will intensify, as more than 10 Windows-based online music services will be introduced in the market (Legon, 2004). However, right now, the legitimate downloading of music is still just a drop in the bucket compared to the massive adoption and usage of file trading via unauthorized, illegal music services.

Services Marketing Strategies and the Three Music Industry Business Models

The American Marketing Association defines *marketing* as "the process of planning and executing the conception, pricing, promotion, and distribution of ideas, goods, and services to create exchanges that satisfy individual and organizational objectives" (*American Marketing Association Dictionary of Marketing Terms*, 2004). Thus, the marketing process is a means to implement a business model. Marketing strategists have asserted that for an organization to succeed, a marketing orientation using a customer focus must be a company-wide mandate, not just the responsibility of a functional department (e.g., Webster, 1992, 2002).

There are three main modern marketing management orientations that an organization may have: a production, sales, or marketing orientation (Keith, 1960; Kotler & Armstrong, 2004). These orientations are organizational philosophies that are part of corporate culture that become drivers of a firm's business model and strategies. A production orientation philosophy is implied when management decisions are made without taking into consideration consumer needs. A sales orientation philosophy is in place when an organization attributes its success to large-scale promotional efforts in the mass media. In contrast, a true marketing orientation is a business philosophy where the organization fully explores consumers' needs first, and then implements strategies to generate maximum customer satisfaction and profitability.

The traditional music industry is being forced to shift from the paradigm of a physical product manufacturer and distributor of music to a service provider. Therefore, an understanding of services marketing becomes essential to the development of successful strategies for all business models in the music industry. The following analysis uses the framework of the services marketing mix to compare strategies of the three business models (traditional, renegade, and new) and to make recommendations. The services marketing mix consists of eight Ps: the four Ps in the traditional marketing mix of product, price, place, and promotion, and four additional Ps of process, people, physical evidence, and productivity (Lovelock & Wright, 2002).

This services marketing mix framework analysis refers to the three modern marketing management orientations (Keith, 1960) and ties the eight Ps to six major reasons consumers desire to be online for product acquisition: convenience, choice, customization, communication, control, and cost (Kerin, Hartley, & Rudelius, 2003). The analysis also connects the six Cs of online motivations with five convergent marketing strategies. "Convergence ... means more than the fusion of different technologies (television, computers, wireless, PDAs) or the combination of channels (such as ... (a) bricks-and-clicks model) ... There is a more basic convergence within the consumer ... created by the technology and the enduring behaviors of human beings" (Wind & Mahajan, 2002, p. 68). Convergent consumers are those with both online and offline attitudes and behaviors. The five Cs of convergence marketing are community, customerization, choice tools, channel, and competitive value (Wind & Mahajan, 2002).

Productivity

In the services marketing literature, *productivity* is defined as how efficient and effective an organization is at using its resources and producing value for the customer. This is accomplished by implementing the other seven Ps in the services marketing mix in terms of issues such as cost control, which can lead to customer satisfaction and retention, as well as higher profits and larger market share (Lovelock & Wright, 2002).

Traditional business model and productivity. What have traditional business channel members done to improve productivity in the face of declining CD sales? As do many large production-oriented corporations in other industries, they have cut costs (e.g., laid off employees and dropped artists). The big labels have also been seeking mergers or strategic alliances to achieve economies of scale (Graves, 2004; Needham, 2003). In the United States, Tower Records filed for bankruptcy and restructured its debt, and other U.S. record chains such as Sam Goody have closed some stores ("Tower Records," 2004). In Australia, some retail chains have closed, and others have changed their merchandise assortments from an emphasis on CDs to DVDs (Donovan, 2003; Needham, 2003).

A number of costs contribute to the average retail price of a CD, which in 2000 was U.S.$16.98. A typical retail store cost structure included a gross margin of about $6.23 (because the wholesale price from the record labels was about $10.75); after store labor, rent, and distribution, the average operating profit per CD was $0.97. For major record labels, the wholesale price of $10.75 included $0.75 for manufacturing the CD and booklet, $5 for marketing, $2 for overhead and mailing, and $3 for artist payments ("Is Biz Posed," 2000).

Renegade business model and productivity. Most renegade P2P organizations have no sales or profits because they are in the early stages of a business model. As described earlier, some of the renegade organizations have advertising revenue and are implementing strategies to attempt a transformation to a legitimate business with a billing system.

New business model and productivity. Before Apple iTunes introduced its service in May 2003, both the media and consumers had declared the first generation of legitimate music services online to be failures (Mullaney, 2002). Legitimate music sales on the Internet grew from 0.3% in 1997 to 3.4% in 2002 (RIAA.com, 2003). Currently, there are two basic types of new business models that are online music downloading services, with the possibility of having a combination of the first two as a third model. The first successful online business model in the music industry is pay-per-download (priced at $0.99 per song download) introduced by Apple iTunes in May 2003 for Mac users, and in October 2003 for Windows users. Initially, Apple iTunes does not expect its service to be a money-maker; its main goal is to stimulate sales for its iPods (portable MP3 digital music players). Similarly, Dell is planning to introduce an online service for similar reasons, to promote demand for its new DJ player (Burrows, Grover, & Greene, 2003). The second current Internet business model stimulating some interest is the subscription service model (e.g., firms such as Rhapsody, Musicmatch, and Roxio's Napster 2.0). Napster's parent company's chief executive officer asserted that the subscription model provides greater flexibility and value to consumers and delivers higher profits (Legrand, 2004).

In the United States, the cost structure for Apple iTunes is as follows: At the price of $0.99 a song, $0.75 goes to the record label and credit card companies get $0.05 cents, leaving only $0.20 for Apple to cover all of its costs, such as marketing and technology (Burrows et al., 2003). That $0.99 provides consumers with the ability to burn the song to as many CDs as they want for personal use and to play the song on up to three PCs or other mobile devices (e.g., Apple's iPod; Burrows et al., 2003), and consumers get a picture of the CD cover (Mossberg, 2003).

In March 2004 in Europe, artists Peter Gabriel and Brian Eno introduced a new digital music store called SonicSelector through On Demand Distribution (OD2), the leading digital music distributor in Europe. Pricing will range from 99 eurocents to up to 2 euros for each song (www.whatsthedownload.com, 2004). OD2 licenses its service to more than 30 retailers in Europe, including HMV, and Microsoft's MSN. OD2 made a significant investment in establishing its infrastructure to manage 1 million tracks, which was necessary to become a "volume player" and achieve economies of scale. According to an executive vice president from the EMI Group, online music firms need to sell between 50 million and 100 million songs a month to recoup all fixed costs and make a profit. Forrester research predicted that by 2006, there will be a major shakeout in the business, because there will be at least three times as many services than the market will be able to support (Legrand, 2004).

Place

Place includes how the product or service is acquired at physical locations (e.g., bricks-and-mortar stores, or home delivery), on the Internet, or both (e.g., multichannel marketing).

Traditional business model and place. Because traditional music stores are losing CD sales, they need to find other sources of income, or they risk going out of business. In the United States, a consortium of six top retailers, including Best Buy and Tower Records, started investing in their own online download service called Echo Networks. Wal-Mart, the world's largest retailer, acquired Liquid Audio to enter the online music business in 2003.

Established e-tailers such as Amazon.com are also planning to offer online downloading services.

Renegade business model and place. Renegade digital music distribution services are delivered online and provide a high level of convenience—one of the key reasons consumers are online to acquire products and services.

New business model and place. In regards to the six Cs, shopping online at both traditional e-tailers and at online downloading services provides convenience 24 hr a day, 7 days a week, without traffic, parking, crowded stores, and waiting on long checkout lines. As far as convergent marketing goes, some consumers want the convenience of multichannel options—to be able to shop online and offline (e.g., via catalogs, phone, direct mail, etc.). An example of a convergent marketing strategy is the promotional deal between online giant America Online (AOL) and Music Monitor Network, a coalition of nine independent retail chains, to install AOL kiosks into more than 100 stores in the United States. The kiosks will demonstrate AOL's music programming service, and will allow customers to listen to all of the songs of 20 featured artists, which are updated bimonthly (Garrity, 2004).

Price

Price includes financial costs as well as nonfinancial outlays or risks (i.e., waiting time, mental and physical effort, sensory experiences, etc.).

Traditional business model and price. Traditional record labels and retailers have employed a production orientation philosophy, dictating price (as well as product, place, and promotion) to consumers. Such an orientation no longer is effective when consumers have other choices (e.g., P2P, pirated copies of CDs, etc.). For the past few years, especially during economic recession, consumers have complained that CD prices are too high. In response, some record companies have lowered CD prices to stimulate sales. There are also indirect, nonfinancial costs associated with the purchase of a CD. If shopping in stores, there are travel costs, as well as time and effort for in-store search and purchase. If buying a CD online, there are costs associated with time and effort online, as well as shipping costs and time waiting for delivery.

Renegade business model and price. The ability to acquire digital music online for free has been a major impetus for millions to participate in illegal P2P services. However, there are also indirect financial costs such as Internet service provider (ISP) fees and the costs of purchase and operation of the hardware (e.g., the computer, CD burner, portable digital music player, etc.). Nonfinancial costs include temporal risks such as the time involved in search and trade activities, the possibility that the sound quality of the file obtained may be less than ideal, and the fact that now there is a real risk for some file traders to receive computer viruses or be the target of lawsuits.

Kazaa has proposed a billing plan to the major record labels for P2P networks that would initially use credit cards, with future payments automatically charged to monthly ISP bills (Lowe, 2003). This plan is similar to Kazaa's legitimate service in the games industry ("P2P Industry," 2003). In the future, "P2P leaders may lobby for new surcharges on blank CDs, MP3 players, and CD burners to help create a $3 billion annual royalty pool for the music industry. A $5 fee on monthly broadband connections is on their wish list" (Yang, 2003, p. 96).

New business model and price.   In regards to the six Cs, consumers often find costs are lower online than in retail stores. Prices at online downloading services are more cost-effective than purchasing CDs from traditional retail firms. However, actual financial outlays are still higher for online business models than for renegade services that are "free." Apple's $0.99 per download is a good starting price to stimulate trial and purchases from certain older, higher income segments. In the future, to generate acceptable profit levels, the services will have to sell high volumes of songs. To convert P2P file traders, it will be necessary to drastically decrease prices to $0.25 or less per song (Green, 2002). In comparison to the renegade services, the indirect financial costs are similar in terms of the search process. However, two of the nonfinancial costs are different: The files are better quality, and there is no risk of lawsuits, which give legitimate online services two competitive advantages over renegade services.

Product

Product includes both the core benefit (main reason for the consumers' interest in acquiring it) and supplementary services related to acquisition, delivery, and consumption (Lovelock & Wright, 2002).

Traditional business model and product.   In regards to product, major record labels and large retailers in the traditional music industry have pursued a mass production orientation without thoroughly researching consumers' needs. "Companies adopting [a production] orientation run a major risk of focusing too narrowly on their own operations and losing sight of the real objective—satisfying consumers' needs" (Kotler & Armstrong, 2004, p. 12).

Record companies control the amount of product choice by offering for legitimate sale (both in stores and online) only a limited selection of their catalogs. In comparison, a much larger selection of music is available on P2P. In regards to choice in stores, a limited selection of

CDs is available due to shelf space and costs. In regards to control, some music retailers do not offer the ability to listen to or preview all of their songs before purchase. However, in metropolitan areas such as New York City, music stores (e.g., Virgin Records) provide consumers with the ability to hear songs from CDs via headphones connected to a preview service before making a buying decision. This "technological selling tool ... has made music dramatically more shopper-friendly" (Underhill, 2004, p. 139), but the store environment still leaves a great deal to be desired. In comparison, online services provide the advantage of being able to listen to part of a song for free before purchase with at-home convenience. In reference to customizability, buying CDs in a traditional bricks-and-mortar store or from an e-tailer (e.g., Amazon.com) does not give consumers control over the option of customizing a CD with their own selection of songs. Both the renegade and legitimate online services offer customizability as a benefit to using their service.

As far as new product formats are concerned, traditional record labels investigated using copy protection technology to create CDs that limit or curtail P2P file trading. "New copy-protection technology won't save the industry from falling sales and may encounter resistance in the marketplace, music executives recently warned" (Garrity, 2003, p. 71). One record executive noted that the market has not yet welcomed alternative formats for the CD such as DVD-A or Super Audio CD (Garrity, 2003).

There is also the artist and repertoire (A & R) issue of what types of new music to produce and what artists to market. Some investment bankers believe that cost-cutting strategies will decrease the creative output of the major labels (Grover & Lowry, 2003). Industry experts have asserted that the major record labels will pursue a risk-averse strategy by focusing only on marketing clones of artists with mass appeal and large sales potential. Some industry experts predict that more creative talent will be signed and marketed to consumer niches by independent labels, as well as by the artists themselves, especially with the Internet and new media such as satellite radio (e.g., Lefsetz, 2003a, 2003b).

Renegade business model and product.   As previously mentioned, users who trade files via P2P have the largest choice of music in the world (millions of songs), much larger than on any legitimate online service or from traditional retailers. Renegade P2P users can create their own customized compilations by burning their favorite songs onto a blank CD, which is possible with new legitimate services, but not with the purchase of traditional CDs.

New business model and product.   With the Internet empowering smaller independent record labels and musicians (e.g., Hughes & Lang, 2003), consumers will have more types of musical choices in the future (e.g., Freedman, 2003; Lefsetz, 2003a, 2003b). For instance, a new on-line service, www.CDBaby.com, sells CDs of "hundreds of thousands of musicians who've been left behind" by the traditional music industry. For each CD sale made, the Portland, Oregon, firm gets $4 and the artist gets on average $8 per CD on a U.S. $12 disc. Because the majority of major-label musicians receive only about $1 per CD sold, CDbaby.com is a great opportunity for artists and consumers (Langer, 2003).

In regards to product choice for legitimate music downloading, most online services currently offer anywhere up to 800,000 songs. Apple iTunes selection includes songs from every major genre and era (Mossberg, 2003). This is a good start but more choice will be needed to be competitive with renegade P2P services. In reference to convergent strategies, customerization means empowering consumers to customize or create their own product or service using the Internet and other technologies. As mentioned for the renegade business model, consumers can also produce customized compilations. One recommendation for legitimate online music services is to use "choiceboards" and other technologies (e.g., Slywotsky, 2000; Wind & Mahajan, 2002) on the Internet and in stores for music-related products, services, and information to be customized and to generate income.

Another key strategic recommendation is for the major labels to open their catalogs of out-of-print recordings, which would provide the record firms with an opportunity to increase sales via legitimate online services. To accomplish this from a practical viewpoint, industry firms would need to loosen their licensing (Green, 2002; Van Buskirk, 2003). At present this is a complex challenge because licenses to provide tracks for legitimate download have to be negotiated with every copyright holder. Also, there are some artists who refuse to be included in any service, notably the Beatles. Implementing compulsory licensing (along the lines of the radio broadcast remuneration model) could work. It has been suggested that digital rights management (DRM) technology makes possible a business model where ISPs become digital retailers for all types of digital content; this business model may be more effective than the tax and royalty system if certain problems can be resolved (Sobel, 2003).

Process

Process consists of the steps in the service creation and delivery experience that are performed by the service provider or the customer and can be considered an extension of a product or service.

Traditional business model and process. The process of purchasing CDs in a store is perceived by many consumers as slow, inefficient, and inconvenient. The time and effort spent traveling to the store, searching for music, waiting on line to check out, and being in an often unpleasant store atmosphere have contributed to lower sales at bricks-and-mortar retailers. CD stores in particular are inept when it comes to attracting consumers. Windows are poorly designed and point of purchase displays are either to difficult to see or nonexistent (Underhill, 2004). In addition, older baby boomers who dislike rap and hip-hop music would prefer not to shop in today's record stores that often blast this type of music at loud levels. Digital Music Express, a retail music programming firm, has found that "the wrong music can drive (customers) out of the store" (Rubel, 1996, p. 1).

Renegade business model and process. The convenient process of acquiring digital music via P2P file trading on one's computer can be time-consuming, but it is an enjoyable experience to millions of users who are hooked. However,

> on Kazaa, the songs can be hard to find, especially in the version you want. There's a lot of trial and error. Also, the quality can be poor, with pops and hissing and the endings cut off. There's no album art ... lots of people ... have received viruses and spyware ... at the very least [it's] unethical, and ... illegal. (Mossberg, 2003, p. D1)

The processes involved in downloading MP3 files, as well as the interfaces encountered by users, are continuously in a state of evolution. The renegade model is similar to an arms race: As legal and technological actions are taken to defeat illegal downloading, P2P file-sharing software authors respond with steps toward anonymity. For example, there is EarthStation5, which may or may not work as advertised. There is also distributed uploading (e.g., BitTorrent), where pieces of one file are recovered from many different machines at once, which greatly increases the efficiency of the P2P process. Thus, the renegade model subsumes a basket of related and evolving processes, which is critical as to why it is such a threat to traditional and new business models.

New business model and process. One benefit of purchasing digital music from legitimate online services is that consumers are spared being potential lawsuit targets. The acquisition process may also be superior to P2P. Apple Computer's iTunes, the most popular, successful legitimate service online to date, has been described as "the first really useful, and enjoyable, legal music service ... [which] basically work[s] as promised ... well designed, with minimum clutter and maximum usability ... with [quick] search [features]" (Mossberg, 2003, p. D1). As previously discussed, the ability to customize and create one's own music compilations is comparable to the P2P process. The control issue is related to consumers' desire to be able to download and play music on any devices they have including their computers, home entertainment systems, and portable MP3 players (Burrows et al., 2003).

Physical Evidence

Physical evidence includes all tangible and visible aspects of the organization associated with image and perceived quality of the product or service (i.e., related to the product, packaging, or promotion).

Traditional business model and physical evidence. With a CD, the physical evidence consists of the plastic shrinkwrap, the jewel case container, CD, cover art, and liner notes. In addition, the store-bought enhanced CD, when played on a computer, may include cover art, a music video, and lyrics. The enhanced CD is one way in which the music industry is trying to increase product value. However, research suggests that only a small group of fans are interested in these types of products, which may be better for enhancing customer loyalty by building a stronger relationship between fans and artists than for enticing legions of consumers to buy new CDs; also, in their current state, enhanced CDs can be copied and pirated (Clement, Engh, & Thielmann, 2003).

In regard to the in-store shopping experience, physical evidence includes store design, signage, and atmospherics (e.g., lighting, music). The direct mail model includes the actual physical package used to ship the CD. The online shopping experience of purchasing CDs also includes the visual aspects of the Web site design.

Renegade business model and physical evidence. The only evidence associated with P2P file trading would usually be the MP3 file and file name in this pure exchange of information over the Internet (Hughes & Lang, 2003).

New business model and physical evidence. With Apple iTunes, as mentioned earlier, consumers who purchase a song also receive a picture of the CD cover (Mossberg, 2003). It is recommended that legitimate online digital music distribution services do market research to find out what types of physical evidence, information, or services could be offered with the core product of music to provide added value to different consumer market segments and generate higher profits.

Promotion

Promotion refers to the communication of informational messages of persuasion about the product via media (e.g., broadcast, print, the Internet) or salespeople (Lovelock & Wright, 2002).

Traditional business model and promotion. Major record labels and large retailers in the music industry have traditionally employed a sales orientation philosophy toward promotion, which is focused on the firm making transactions, rather than developing and maintaining long-term, profitable customer relationships. This promotional philosophy includes pushing the product using large budgets for promotion in traditional media such as expensive videos (to air on cable television stations such as MTV and VH1), radio promotion, heavy advertising, and publicity. The promotional power of traditional media still can have a huge impact on music sales, such as having artists perform on network television. For instance, 2 days after the 2004 Grammy Awards aired on CBS television, "Merchants reported sales increases of anywhere from 200% to 300% ... for artists who performed or won on the Grammy show" (Christman, 2004, p. 1).

The industry is also promoting an antipiracy campaign via various strategies to discourage P2P illegal usage using political, legal, technological, educational, and fear tactics addressed to individual users and P2P organizations (Freedman, 2003). Recent educational efforts have been made to inform users about the issues of copyright infringement and the benefits of using legitimate online services. During the 2004 Grammy Awards, the President of the National Academy of Recording Arts and Sciences gave a speech that appealed to music fans to visit the new Web site, www.whatsthedownload.com (Portnow, 2004). Also, the International Federation of the Phonographic Industry (IFPI; www.ifpi.org) sponsors another educational Web site (www.music.org) for consumers in Europe (IFPI, 2004). The chairman of the IFPI emphasized the importance of promoting the right message in the media to various stakeholders (IFPI, 2004).

Renegade business model and promotion. Positive word-of-mouth spreads on a global basis to millions of individual users in the digital online community about the benefits of participating in unauthorized, "free" P2P file trading services. In addition, as discussed earlier, all users who download the free version of Kazaa are exposed to advertising via adware and may also receive free digital television programming with sponsors distributed by Kazaa.

From an organizational view, Kazaa established a trade association called the Distributed Computing Industry Association (DCIA) to persuade record companies to help transform them into a legitimate P2P venture (Girard, 2003; "P2P Industry," 2003). In 2003, Kazaa spent $1 million on a promotional campaign. Kazaa ran advertising in newspapers and on Web sites in the United States (e.g., the *Wall Street Journal, Los Angeles Times,* and *Rolling Stone*), the United Kingdom (e.g., *The Guardian* and *The Metro*), and Australia (e.g., the *Sydney Morning Herald*). Kazaa placed banner ads on Yahoo.com, Wired, and RollingStone.com, and distributed posters to more than 30 large U.S. college campuses. Kazaa also established a Web site called Kazaa Revolution (Kazaa.com/revolution) where P2P fans could send letters to congressmen, journalists, and record label executives, and obtain information on legitimate, licensed content available on Kazaa ("Kazaa Launches," 2003).

According to the executive director of Sharman, the company that operates Kazaa, record companies' refusal to work with Sharman "regrettably condemns the music industry to continued piracy and endless litigation against its own customers" (Needham, 2003).

Other renegade organizations including Grokster, Morpheus, Blubster, Limewire, EDonkey2000, and Bearshare have joined forces as P2P United to achieve a similar objective to DCIA ("P2P Industry," 2003). P2P United supports a compulsory licensing solution where the government would require labels and artists to license their music to the P2P organizations; DCIA, which has Kazaa as its only member, supports the use of a different business model of having the major labels use digital rights managment via a universal Internet service provider-based billing system ("P2P Industry Bodies," 2003).

New business model and promotion. There are three main ways communication can occur on the Internet between marketers and consumers: (a) business-to-consumer e-mails and promotions, (b) consumer-to-business purchases and information requests, and (c) consumer-to-consumer communication (e.g., instant messaging, e-mails, and chat rooms).

The first major convergent media promotion (combining traditional media and the Internet) to garner attention and publicity was the Pepsi–Apple iTunes advertising and sales promotion campaign that kicked off during the 2004 Super Bowl on network television. One hundred million bottle caps on a number of Pepsi soft drinks included a code for a free song download on the Apple iTunes Web site (Graham, 2004). The creative premise featured teenagers who settled lawsuits with the RIAA for illegal P2P file trading who switched their allegiance to downloading on Apple's iTunes; the song in the ad was Green Day's version of the song "I Fought the Law (and the Law Won)" (Graham, 2004).

It is recommended that music firms use a number of new convergent strategies such as customerization by personalizing marketing communications, customer relationship management strategies such as loyalty programs, database management (e.g., Winer, 2001), customer lifetime value assessment (e.g., Gupta & Lehmann, 2003), and services marketing to help develop a competitive advantage (e.g., Lovelock & Wright, 2002, Zeithaml, Parasuraman, & Berry, 1990). There is also no doubt that advertising and promotion in traditional media will continue to be important in stimulating awareness and purchase at online firms using a new business model in the music industry.

People

In the services marketing mix, *people* usually refers to the employees or individuals who deliver the service. This article expands the element of people from a producer paradigm to a true marketing orientation by including the consumer. Thus, part of this section focuses on the third business model question: Who is the customer?

Traditional business model and people. Traditional bricks-and-mortar stores have fixed overhead and labor costs. Most store employees are cashiers, and do not help with the search or purchase decision process. In regards to e-tailers, the people include management and employees such as customer service representatives. Traditional members of the music industry have been criticized for treating customers as mainly a mass market (e.g., Hughes & Lang, 2003) and of neglecting the needs of older baby boomers. The music industry does segment consumer markets according to demographics such as age, gender, ethnicity, and musical tastes (e.g., RIAA.com, NARM.com). However, in today's information age, and with customer dissatisfaction at high levels with the traditional music industry, it is necessary to go beyond traditional customer market definitions.

Renegade business model and people. The people involved in the renegade model include the P2P users who trade files and the owners and executives who operate the renegade organizations. In addition, there are people who play a critical role in initially making MP3 versions of new songs available on P2P networks before they are publicly released onto the retailers' CD shelves or are available for legitimate purchase online. This may occur somehow via music industry insiders who have access to master tapes, disks, or promotional copies. For instance,

> New albums by Madonna, Radiohead and others are available online long before their official release; ... Madonna even resorted to flooding file-sharing services with expletive-carrying bogus files in an attempt to confuse pirates and boost sales of her new album, "American Life." Hackers promptly posted a free copy of the album on her website. ("How to Pay the Piper," 2003, p. 1)

New business model and people. With new downloading services, the part of the services marketing mix related to people refers to the organizations' management and employees who may work in customer service operations. In addition, there are the customers of the new services. Apple iTunes segmented the market into consumers under 18 years old and those over 25 years old (Legrand, 2004). The 18- to 25-year-old market was not targeted because Apple's management believe these are illegal P2P file traders, who are "a lost cause" (Legrand, 2004, p. 68). Apple iTunes found success with the over-25 market, who have the income to afford the service and the motivation to use the legitimate, reliable, easy-to-use service to save time. Napster 2.0 is also targeting the over-25 demographic (Legrand, 2004). There is also geographic market segmentation by major online services. Apple iTunes and Napster 2.0 both announced plans to introduce their services in Europe (Legrand, 2004).

The music industry needs to better understand its consumers. Organizations need to conduct in-depth market research on customers using additional bases for market segmentation to determine its impact on music purchasing behavior. These bases can include psychographics (e.g., attitudes, interests, opinions, lifestyle), technographics (e.g., Forrester.com), and consumer values and music-buying behavior (e.g., Bhattacharjee et al., 2003; Cohn & Vaccaro, 2002; Molteni & Ordanini, 2003).

An overview of the aforementioned discussion on the services marketing mix for traditional, renegade, and new business models in the music industry is provided in Table 1. In addition, a summary of key recommendations for new business models in the music industry is provided in Table 2.

Conclusion

The revolution in the distribution of music on the Internet via P2P file trading started by renegade organizations in 1999 is still in the growth stage. The renegade business model, enabled by digital technology and the Internet, has become the impetus for sweeping changes in the music industry for both traditional and new business models. These three business models are competing for consumers' hearts, minds, and wallets.

The outcomes of new business strategies and legal issues will have implications not just for the music industry, but for the entertainment industry on a global scale—for all content that can be digitized, downloaded, and traded on the Internet (e.g., movies, television, video games, etc.). "On-demand services are the future of entertainment delivery. CDs, DVDs, and any other forms of physical media will become obsolete" (Legon, 2004). The firms with winning business model strategies will most likely be "those with sufficient scale to convert meager per-song margins into meaningful profits and those that use music to sell add-ons, be it hardware, subscriptions to online music magazines, or concert tickets" (Burrows et al., 2003, p. 42). Successful firms are predicted to also turn to m-commerce by creating alliances with online music services, phone and cable companies that provide broadband services, and "music to go" equipment manufacturers (Legrand, 2004).

Members of the music industry have been operating with traditional business models and have never completely embraced the customer philosophy of a true marketing orientation (e.g., Keith, 1960; Kotler & Armstrong, 2004). From a services marketing viewpoint, a knowledge gap (e.g., the difference between what a service provider thinks customers want and what the actual needs and wants of customers are; Zeithaml et al., 1990) still exists between the record labels with their traditional business model approach and consumer expectations of the music industry. Traditional firms have been accused of lacking the cultural capital to make a successful transition to a new business model in the information age, and it has

Table 1. The Services Marketing Mix for Traditional, Renegade, and New Business Models in the Music Industry

Services Marketing Mix	Traditional Business Model	Renegade Business Model	New Business Model
Productivity	Declining store sales; high operational costs.	Some interest and actions to become legitimate firms.	Sales growth. Low or no profits. Low distribution costs. High infrastructure costs.
Place	Visit physical store. Home delivery via snail mail for online CD purchases and music clubs.	Online delivery.	Online delivery.
Price	Medium to high prices. Indirect costs.	Free (no price). Indirect costs.	Medium Prices. Indirect costs.
Product (the music)	Low to medium choice. No customizability.	High choice of songs. High customizability.	Medium choice. High customizability.
Process (related to place)	Medium to high steps for waiting and search time. Inconvenient acquisition process.	Low to medium search time. Enjoyable process for millions of users.	Low to medium search time. Process for each service varies and must be learned.
Physical evidence (related to promotion)	High physical evidence re: in-store atmosphere, promotional ads and Web site design.	Low physical evidence. MP3 file and file name.	Medium level of physical evidence: Web site design, product information.
Promotion	Medium to high level of promotion in traditional and some new media.	High word-of-mouth on the Internet throughout the digital Internet community. Adware. Press coverage. Media ads. Web sites.	Medium to high level of promotion in both traditional and new media.
People (related to promotion and customer service)	Management and employees. Salespeople or customer service representatives. Customers.	Organizations' executives. Industry hackers. Consumer-to-consumer information.	Management and employees of firm. Customers of service.

Table 2. Services Marketing Strategy Recommendations for the Music Industry

Place	Increase choice in regards to where and when consumers can acquire music on and off the Internet (using convergent strategies).
Price	Lower prices per song download. Offer better value and rewards for subscription services. Use CRM. Expand the availability of prepaid cards to appeal to consumers without credit cards (e.g., young age groups), as well as to consumers with security concerns about buying online.
Product	Increase choice of music available legitimately (e.g., major label record catalog must be offered in different forms offline and online, which can include audio and video at reasonable prices). Make more new music-related choices available that speak to the hearts and minds of consumers (niches). Create product and service packages of core and supplementary benefits (e.g., access to satellite and Web radio stations; concert tickets, etc.) that are unique or exclusive to each firm.
Process	Use technology to offer customizability of music compilations selected by consumers in stores and online. All services should enhance ease of use and consumer satisfaction with the process of search, acquisition, and consumption of music delivered via technology and people (e.g., employees, musicians, customer service, etc.). Do research on needs of various consumer segments in regards to process and satisfaction.
Physical evidence	Find out what physical evidence consumers want and offer tangible benefits (e.g., liner notes, books, band merchandise) to those target markets that value them at various prices to create added value, brand preference, profitability, and productivity.
Promotion	Increase usage of convergent promotional strategies utilizing the Internet and traditional media, depending on target market preferences. Use CRM, permission marketing, and viral marketing.
People	Harness digital community networks to generate positive word of mouth. Do viral marketing (forward promotional offers from legitimate firms to friends). Train employees to be customer-oriented in delivering services and products.

Note. CRM = customer relationship management.

been suggested that the record labels need to change their orientation from lawsuits to a marketing and promotional orientation (Freedman, 2003).

The marketing orientation recommended in this article includes a services marketing mix framework (Lovelock & Wright, 2002) and includes relationship marketing, and convergent, interactive marketing paradigms (e.g., Wind & Mahajan, 2002; Winer, 2001) that can be utilized to help create a competitive advantage (Webster, 1992, 2002). These strategies can light the path for winning the legitimate music business model revolution.

Valerie L. Vaccaro

(vaccarov@oldwestbury.edu)

is an Assistant Professor of Marketing at SUNY– College at Old Westbury, USA. Before entering academia, Dr. Vaccaro worked in the areas of market research, advertising, sales promotion, and public relations, and in the music industry. Her research interests include services marketing, Internet marketing, promotion, and consumer behavior.

Deborah Y. Cohn

(cohn@yu.edu)

is an Assistant Professor of Marketing in the Sy Syms School of Business at Yeshiva University, USA. Before entering higher education, Dr. Cohn worked in consumer products and in the retail industry. Her research interests include Internet marketing, consumer behavior, and integrated marketing communications.

References

Afuah, A., & Tucci, C. L. (2003). *Internet business models and strategies* (2nd ed.). New York: McGraw-Hill.

American Marketing Association dictionary of marketing terms. (2004). Retrieved March 12, 2004, from http://tinyurl.com/3g671

Bambury, P. (1998). A taxonomy of Internet commerce. *First Monday.* Retrieved February 2, 2004, from http://tinyurl.com/2q9mq

Bhattacharjee, S., Gopal, R. D., & Sanders, G. L. (2003). Digital music and online sharing: Software piracy 2.0? *Communications of the ACM, 46*(7), 107–111.

Borland, J. (2003, January 27). Kazaa strikes back at Hollywood, labels. *CNET News.com.* Retrieved May 17, 2004, from http://tinyurl.com/3fukp

Burrows, P., Grover, R., & Greene, J. (2003, October 13). Tuning up like nobody's business: Making a buck selling music online will be tough, but a raft of sites are at the ready. *Business Week, 3853,* 42.

Christman, E. (2004, February 21). Retail sales sizzle from Grammy heat. *Billboard, 21,* 1.

Clement, M., Engh, M., & Thielmann, B. (2003). Innovative product and customer retention strategies in the music business: An analysis of Santana's enhanced album. *International Journal on Media Management, 5*(3). Retrieved April 24, 2004, from http://tinyurl.com/3hcgl

Cohn, D. Y., & Vaccaro, V. (2002). Diffusion of innovation theory and peer-to-peer music file exchange on the Internet. *Proceedings of the American Society of Business and Behavioral Sciences, 9*(1), 234–244.

Dean, K. (2004, March 16). Honey, I shrunk the URL. *Wired News.* Retrieved March 16, 2004, from http://tinyurl.com/yteyt

Donovan, P. (2003, January 24). Piracy and DVDs share blame for CD sales dive. *Sydney Morning Herald.* Retrieved January 24, 2003, from http://tinyurl.com/2qm5e

Ewing, J., & Green, H. (2003, October). Global downloading, local lawsuits hauling U.S. file-sharers to court won't stop the flow of free tunes from overseas. *Business Week, 3852*, 32, 64.

Fadner, R. (2004, May 1). Riding shotgun with adware. *MediaPost's Online MEDIA*. Retrieved May 17, 2004, from http://tinyurl.com/2z9q6

Freedman, D. (2003). Managing pirate culture: Corporate responses to peer-to-peer networking. *International Journal on Media Management, 5*(3). Retrieved April 23, 2004, from http://tinyurl.com/2t5u3

Garrity, B. (2003, October 11). Execs: Copy-protection could spur consumer wrath. *Billboard, 115*, 71.

Garrity, B. (2004, February 21). AOL in kiosk venture with indie coalition. *Billboard, 116*, 39–40.

Girard, K. (2003, October 11). Kazaa's endgame: A deal. *Billboard, 115*, 12.

Graham, J. (2004, January 28). Pepsi, Apple team to tout music downloads. *USA Today*. Retrieved January 28, 2004, from http://www.usatoday.com/tech/news/2004-01-28-sb-apple_x.htm

Graves, T. (2004, February 12). Music: An aging customer base. *Standard & Poor's Movies and Home Entertainment Industry Survey*. Retrieved February 12, 2004, from http://tinyurl.com/2a8hw

Green, H. (2002, October 14). Digital media: Don't clamp down too hard: Lots of armor on CDs, books, and movies could spook buyers and stifle innovation. *Business Week, 3803*, 140.

Greenfeld, K. T. (2000, October 2). Meet the Napster: Shawn Fanning was 18 when he wrote the code that changed the world. *Time, 156*, 61–66.

Grover, R., & Lowry, T. (2003, December). Will Bronfman have the last laugh? If piracy keeps falling and web sales keep climbing, Warner music has a chance .*Business Week, 3861*, 42.

Gupta, S., & Lehmann, D. R. (2003). Customers as assets. *Journal of Interactive Marketing, 17*, 9–24.

Hachman, M. (2003, March 17). Kazaa users paying for legit content, Altnet says. *ExtremeTech.com*. Retrieved May 17, 2004, from http://tinyurl.com/2pmby

How to pay the piper. (2003, May 1). *Economist*. Retrieved May 1, 2003, from www.economist.com

Hull, G. P. (1997). *The recording industry*. Boston: Allyn & Bacon.

Hughes, J., & Lang, K. R. (2003). If I had a song: The culture of digital community networks and its impact on the music industry. *International Journal on Media Management, 5*(3). Retrieved April 23, 2004, from http://tinyurl.com/yr6e5

IFPI. (2003, June 25). IFPI statement on action announced by U.S. recording industry against illegal music uploaders. Retrieved June 25, 2003, from http://tinyurl.com/2lhtw

IFPI. (2004, January 22). IFPI report says music industry's Internet strategy is turning the corner. Retrieved January 22, 2004, from http://tinyurl.com/3ae28

Is biz poised for renewed price wars? (2000, January 8). *Billboard, 112*(2), 3.

iTunes tops 100m downloads mark. (2004, July 12). *BBC News World Edition*. Retrieved from http://newsvote.bbc.co.uk/mpapps/pagetools/print/news.bbc.co.uk/2/hi/entertainment/3886309.stm

Jesdanun, A. (2003, January 31). Kazaa looks to legitimate arm for salvation. *HoustonChronicle.com*. Retrieved May 17, 2004, from http://tinyurl.com/29np2

Kazaa. (2004). *SearchNetworking.com definitions*. Retrieved May 17, 2004, from http://tinyurl.com/2ucgy

Kazaa launches ad campaign to counter critics. (2003, November 20). *New Media Age*, 1.

Keith, R. J. (1960). The marketing revolution. *Journal of Marketing, 24*(1), 35–38.

Kerin, R., Hartley, S. W., & Rudelius, W. (2003). *Marketing: The core*. New York: McGraw-Hill.

Kotler, P., & Armstrong, G. (2004). *Principles of marketing* (10th ed.). Upper Saddle River, NJ: Pearson/Prentice Hall.

Langer, A. (2003, December 1). Derek Sivers. *Esquire, 140*(6), 173.

Lefsetz, B. (2003a, March 27). Damien Rice at the Wiltern. *The Lefsetz Letters*. Retrieved March 27, 2003, from www.celebrityaccess.com

Lefsetz, B. (2003b, January 23). The week on KLSX. *The Lefsetz Letters*. Retrieved January 23, 2003, from www.celebrityaccess.com

Lechner, U., & Hummel J. (2002). Business models and system architectures of virtual communities: From a sociological phenomenon to peer-to-peer architectures. *International Journal of Electronic Commerce, 6*(3), 41–53.

Legon, J. (2004, January 23). Study: CDs may soon go the way of vinyl. *CNN.com*. Retrieved January 23, 2004, from http://tinyurl.com/3ya5z

Legrand, E. (2004, February 7). At MIDEM, newfound taste for online music, *Billboard, 5*, 68.

Levack, K. (2003, April). Ta da! Kazaa pulls a countersuit out of a hat. *Econtent, 26*(4), 14–16.

Lovelock, C., & Wright, L. (2002). *Principles of services marketing and management* (2nd ed.). Upper Saddle River, NJ: Prentice Hall.

Lowe, S. (2003, October 10). Kazaa backs plan that could spell an end to the days of free music. *Sydney Morning Herald*. Retrieved from http://www.smh.com.au/articles/2003/10/09/1065676097116.html

Lyman, J. (2003, September 2). Google pulls P2P links over Kazaa copyright claims. *TechNewsWorld.com*. Retrieved May 17, 2004, from http://tinyurl.com/m7cv

Magretta, J. (2002, May). Why business models matter. *Harvard Business Review, 80*, 86–92.

Maney, K. (2000, June 7). File-sharing software may transform the net. *USA Today*, pp. B1–B2.

Molteni, L., & Ordanini, A. (2003). Consumption patterns, digital technology and music downloading. *Long Range Planning, 36*, 389–406.

Mossberg, W. S. (2003, April 30). Music that you don't have to steal: We test Apple's new service. *Wall Street Journal* (Eastern ed.), p. D1.

Most downloaded program on the Web? Kazaa: 230 million downloads and counting. (2003, May 23). *CNN.com*. Retrieved February 10, 2004, http://tinyurl.com/2lsg2

Mullaney, T. J. (2002, February 18). Napster they're not. *Business Week Online*. Retrieved February 18, 2002, from http://tinyurl.com/2sol2

Needham, K. (2003, September 12). Last blast for the music moguls. *Sydney Morning Herald*. Retrieved September 12, 2003, from http://tinyurl.com/2zukf

Olsen, S. (2003, March 6). Pseudo spins hip-hop TV show on Kazaa. *CNET News.com*. Retrieved May 17, 2004, from http://tinyurl.com/2p79z

P2P industry bodies fail to agree on copyright strategy. (2003, October 16). *New Media Age*, 7.

Portnow, N. (2004, February 8). Recording Academy President Neil Portnow's 46th GRAMMY telecast remarks. *Grammy Magazine*. Retrieved February 8, 2004, from http://tinyurl.com/2t8vv

RIAA.com. (2003). *2002 consumer purchasing trends.* Retrieved January 4, 2004, from http://tinyurl.com/2wuar

Richtel, M. (2001, November 29). Free music service is expected to surpass Napster. *The New York Times,* p. C4.

Rivkin, J., & Meier, G. (2002). BMG entertainment. In T. R. Eisenmann (Ed.), *Internet business models: Text and cases* (pp. 277–298). New York: McGraw-Hill.

Rubel, C. (1996). Marketing with music. *Marketing News, 30*(17), 1, 21.

Slywotzky, A. J. (2000, January–February). The age of the choiceboard. *Harvard Business Review,* 40–41.

Sobel, L. S. (2003). DRM as an enabler of business models: ISPs as digital retailers. *Berkeley Technology Law Journal, 18*(2), 667.

Strauss, N. (2001, August 20). Foraging for music in the digital jungle. *The New York Times,* p. E1.

Strauss, N. (2003, September 9). Executives can see problems beyond file sharing, *The New York Times,* p. C1.

Taylor, C. (2003, May 19). Online music turns up the volume. *Brandweek, 44*(20), 34.

Timmers, P. (1998). Business models for electronic markets. *EM-Electronic Commerce in Europe, EM-Electronic Markets, 8*(2). Retrieved July 31, 1998, from http://tinyurl.com/ywamk

Top 50 key players: Alan Morris. (2003, December 11). *New Media Age,* 35.

Tower records files for bankruptcy. (2004, February 9). *CBS News.com.* Retrieved February 9, 2004, from http://www.cbsnews.com/stories/2004/02/09/entertainment/main599008.shtml

Twist, J. (2004, May 20). Napster joins UK online music fray. *BBC News Online.* Retrieved from http://news.bbc.co.uk/1/hi/technology/3729217.stm

Underhill, P. (2004). *Call of the mall.* New York: Simon & Schuster.

Van Buskirk, E. (2003, November 19). What the labels still don't comprehend. *CNET.com.* Retrieved November 19, 2003, from http://reviews.cnet.com/4520-6450_7-5107938.html

Webster, F. E., Jr. (1992, October). The changing role of the marketing in the corporation. *Journal of Marketing, 11, 56,* 1–17.

Webster, F. E., Jr. (2002, January–February). Marketing management in changing times. *Marketing Management,* 18–23.

Wind, Y., & Mahajan, V. (2002). Convergence marketing, *Journal of Interactive Marketing, 16*(2), 64–79.

Winer, R. S. (2001). A framework for customer relationship management. *California Management Review, 43*(4), 89–105.

Yang, C. (2003, September 29). A rising chorus of music downloaders? *Business Week, 3851,* 96.

Zeithaml, V. A., Parasuraman, A., & Berry, L. L. (1990). *Delivering quality service: Balancing customer perceptions and expectations.* New York: Free Press.

Strategies for Selling Paid Content on Newspaper and Magazine Web Sites: An Empirical Analysis of Bundling and Splitting of News and Magazine Articles

Florian Stahl, Marc-Frederic Schäfer, and Wolfgang Maass
University of St. Gallen, Switzerland

More and more newspaper and magazine Web sites offer paid content. However, selling information goods at a price higher than the marginal cost means finding a strategy for product or price differentiation. A possible strategy to solve this problem is the bundling of information goods.

In this article, we analyze empirically, with quantitative statistic methods, strategies for selling bundled and unbundled content on newspaper and magazine Web sites. This analysis is based on the theoretical approach of Bakos and Brynjolfsson (1996).

The article shows that a cannibalization takes place if the same bundle of information goods is offered in offline (printed) and online (digital) media at the same time. Traditional bundling models work nonetheless in an online media if the online content is rebundled (e.g., as dossiers about a topic), but thereby do not compete with the printed version.

For studying the economics of paid content, newspaper and magazine markets are of particular importance and interest, because the convergence of media is very strong in these markets, so the submarkets of online and print are often interrelated (Chyi & Sylvie, 2000). Many newspaper and magazine publishers reuse the contents of the printed version online. The printed newspaper is offered for a fee; the online content is mostly for free. On account of this, one must consider online and printed newspapers as substitute goods (Chyi & Sylvie, 1998) involving a potential risk of cannibalization of the printed version. An indicator for such cannibalization is the fact that young people do not subscribe to daily newspapers but substitute information consumption from news or magazine Web sites during work breaks (Glotz & Meyer-Lucht, 2003).

From a business perspective, various revenue models exist for newspaper and magazine Web sites: advertising, vertical partnerships in e-commerce, paid content, and so on. The most common revenue model is advertising, but combinations of several revenue models are also observable (Chyi & Sylvie, 2000). The study of Glotz and Meyer-Lucht (2003) shows that converting the business model of a newspaper Web site from a freely available content, which is financed through advertising revenues, to a subscription model or paid content is not a successful solution to solve the cannibalization problem. This is true because the decrease of advertising revenues is greater than the increase of revenues through paid content. However, the slump in the online advertising market has forced newspaper Web sites to seek new revenue sources.

To offer paid content as premium content in addition to free and advertised content is one possibility to generate new revenues. Since the beginning of the World Wide Web the debate and discussion about paid content has been very ideological. Articles like "The ROI of free" (Eisenberg, 2002) or scientific contributions like "follow the free" (Loebbecke, 1999) or "Selling More by Giving It All Away Approach" (Zerdick et al., 1999) stress the special importance of free content both from the user and business perspective.

However, the ideological debate about paid content also has an economic background, because selling content online differs from selling content outside the Web as well as from the e-commerce of nondigital products.

In this context, newspaper and magazine Web sites tend more and more to offer bundled information for fees. This phenomenon is well described in the economic literature of bundling of information goods where various

Address correspondence to Florian Stahl, mcm *institute*, Blumenbergplatz 9, St. Gallen, Switzerland. E-mail: Florian.Stahl@unisg.ch

models exist, explaining why bundling of information goods leads to higher prices and revenues compared to unbundled single articles (Bakos & Brynjolfsson, 1996; Fay & MacKie-Mason, 2001; Varian, 2001). Bundling of information goods is a form of price discrimination and a reasonable revenue model, because selling information goods based on traditional economic rules such as price should equal marginal cost do not seem to be feasible in this context (Varian, 2001). Siegel (2002) explained that in the electronic paid content market of news and magazines, single articles are offered more often as complete magazines. On the other hand, scientists like Bakos and Brynjolfsson (1997) conclude that bundling is not always maximizing profit and that in certain circumstances disaggregation leads to higher revenues than bundling. However, low marginal cost facilitates bundling strategies of digital services and goods and thus improves revenues by skimming the willingness to pay of consumers (Siegel, 2002).

In the newspaper and magazine market three main types of paid information goods were identified. The first type of information goods can be classified as bundles, which are also offered as printed versions in the traditional newspaper and magazine market. Henceforth this kind of bundle is just called *bundle* or *bundled information.* The second type of information goods is a single digital article, which can be bought at a set price (e.g., archive articles). The third type is rebundled information. Rebundled information mostly consists of bundled digital articles, which are offered by a supplier in a specific way (e.g., on specific topics) and thus are only available in the online world (e.g., dossiers at Spiegel online).

We present findings on which of these strategies for the bundling of paid content attracts the highest demand (measured by the number of purchase transactions) and maximizes the revenues of the publishers.

Research Question

This led to the following research question: Which strategy for bundling and splitting maximizes the demand and the revenues of paid content on newspaper and magazine Web sites? Different strategies for paid content on newspaper and magazine Web sites are analyzed, with a special focus on three different types of information bundling (bundles, single articles, and rebundles). Empirical research has shown that sometimes the revenues and the demand of bundles outperform that of single information goods and sometimes they do not. This phenomenon is examined and explained in this article.

The following section gives an overview about the literature of bundling of information goods. Based on these theories, an approach is derived and tested empirically. In the last section, the impact of the empirical findings on the bundling theories and the implications of these empirical findings are discussed.

Literature Review: Strategies for Bundling

In this section, an overview of the literature of the bundling of information goods is provided as a basis for empirical research of paid content on newspaper and magazine Web sites. At first glance, three periods in this discussion and citations could be identified (see Figure 1). In the first period, until 1995, bundling was only discussed for certain nonelectronic goods, which had nearly the same characteristics as information goods. Then Varian (1995) and Salinger (1995) discussed bundling in the context of electronically available information goods. Between 1995 and 2000, models from Bakos and Brynjolfsson (1996, 1997, 2000) systematically analyzed why information goods can be sold with higher profits as bundles. From 2000 on, the discussion shifted to analyzing how competition influences bundling strategies of firms that sell information goods. With the advent of paid content on the Web it was possible to apply these theoretical bundling concepts in real-life settings and thus to test them empirically.

If we go back, Schmalensee (1984) was one of the first authors who discussed bundling in a context that fits the characteristics of e-commerce. In his article, he described the phenomenon of heterogeneous buyers' taste in a monopolistic market, where the monopolist produces two goods. He assumed the marginal utility for the second (reproduced) good to be zero for all buyers. In this setting, Schmalensee showed that with a pure bundle of these two goods, sellers can capture the consumer surplus and thus achieve a higher price through price discrimination. Therefore this model fits very well the situation in the online world, where consumers of information goods in the electronic media have heterogeneous preferences and marginal costs of reproduction are near zero.

Salinger (1995) enriched the model of Schmalensee (1984) by showing how the correlation of customers' demands influences the incentive to bundle. Given the assumption that bundling does not affect costs, negative correlated reservation values and low component costs create an incentive to bundle, because reservation value of customers will converge. If, in addition to that, marginal costs of the elements of the bundle are below this reservation value, the seller of the bundle can extract a surplus. These characteristics described by Salinger fit to information goods sold in the electronic media almost perfectly.

Varian (1995) discussed various forms of price discrimination by market segmentation in low-demand and

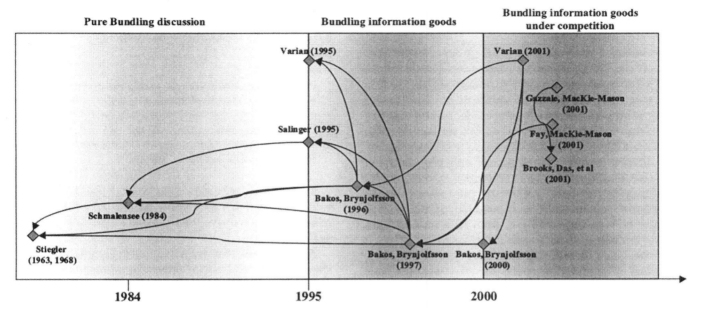

Figure 1. The models from Schmalensee (1984) to Gazzale and MacKie-Mason (2001).

high-demand sectors through product differentiation. In this article he also mentions that bundling can be profitable through the reduction of the heterogeneity of the customers' willingness to pay. Besides this effect, he identifies various other effects like reduction of searching costs if the bundled articles are on similar topics.

Bakos and Brynjolfsson (1996) analyzed optimal strategies for a monopolist offering multiple products and showed that the profit and consumer valuation of large bundles dominates small bundles of information goods. They found that bundling a large number of unrelated information goods could be surprisingly profitable. In their approach, they considered

> a setting with a single seller providing *n* information goods to a set of consumers Ω. Each consumer can consume either 0 or 1 unit of each information good, and resale is not permitted (or is unprofitable for consumers). For each consumer ω ∈ W, let $v_{ni}(\omega)$ denote the valuation of good *i*, when a total of n goods are purchased. (Bakos & Brynjolfsson, 1996, p. 3f)

The valuation of good *i* further depends on the number of goods purchased *n*, so that distribution of valuations for individual goods changes with *n*. The per-good valuation of the bundle can be described with

$$x_n = \frac{1}{n}\sum_{k=1}^{n} v_{nk}$$

Bakos and Brynjolfsson (1996) assumed that the following conditions hold:

A1: The marginal cost of copies of all information goods is zero to the seller.

A2: For all *n*, consumer valuations v_{ni} are independent and uniformly bound, with continuous density functions, nonnegative support, mean μ_{ni} and variance σ^2_{ni}.

A3: Consumers have free disposal. In particular, for all *n* > 1,

$$\sum_{k=1}^{n} v_{nk} \geq \sum_{k=1}^{n-1} v(n-1)k$$

If A1, A2, and A3 hold, selling a bundle of all information goods *n* can be remarkably superior to selling goods separately; the profit of bundling grows, and the bigger the bundle is because "as *n* increases, the seller captures an increasing fraction of the total area under the demand curve, correspondingly reducing both the deadweight loss and the consumer surplus related to selling the goods separately."

By introducing marginal, transaction, and distribution costs, Bakos and Brynjolfsson (1997) showed that constellations exist where bundling dominates unbundled sales and vice versa, as well as where both forms of sales can be unprofitable. However, in contrast to their model, in practice, firms like the FIRSTGATE Internet AG offer technologies for micropayment, which are widely used to sell single information goods at negligible transaction costs.

By another extension of their model, Bakos and Brynjolfsson (2000) showed a nonmonopolistic environment of competition for information goods. In the first case, they analyzed upstream competition: That means sellers of information goods compete for inputs they can sell. In this context, rivals try to bid in a strategic race for the largest bundle, which is similar to traditional economies of scale markets. In the second case they analyzed downstream competition: That means sellers compete for customers in the same market of information goods. Bakos and Brynjolfsson (2000) showed that in competition benefits of bundling are lower than in a monopolistic market but higher than marginal cost.

Varian (2001) mentioned another effect of bundling. Suppliers of information goods can effectively use bundling to hinder new competitors from entering the market, because most attractive buyers are already taken.

A new aspect of information bundling was introduced by Brooks et al. (2001). In their model they took a closer look at the development of bundles and their price over time. They showed that bundling strategies cannot be considered as a steady state but have to change over time to maximize profit. Constant learning and readjustment of bundles allow suppliers to gain the highest profit. This simple model is tested by some experiments.

Fay and MacKie-Mason (2001) showed in their approach that competition between two firms selling information goods lowers prices significantly, whereas the reduction of profits is only moderate. They mainly analyzed four combinations. On the one hand they compared monopolistic and duopolistic sellers and on the other hand they compared homogenous and heterogeneous consumers. They showed that under certain conditions results gained from a monopolistic model also hold in a duopoly, and competitive bundling leads to more potential readers due to lower fees through this competition between firms.

Gazzale and MacKie-Mason (2001) also analyzed how competition in a market of information goods leads to a firm's choice to either stay in a competitive mass market or enter a less competitive niche market with fewer customers.

Bakos and Brynjolfsson (1996) showed in their paper that the profit of bundling grows the bigger a bundle is because

> the law of large numbers assures that the distribution for the valuation of the bundle has an increasing fraction of consumers with "moderate" valuations near the mean of the underlying distribution ... the demand curve becomes more elastic near the mean and less elastic away from the mean. (Bakos & Brynjolfsson, 1996, p. 5)

The reasons for a deadweight loss per good and the consumer surplus per good for a bundle of n information goods converge to zero, and the seller's profit per good is maximized.

Empirical evidence for Bakos and Brynjolfsson (1996) is shown for Web sites that offer a bundle of information goods for a single price (printed newspapers or magazines; e.g., a bundle of different articles on different topics or software products like the Microsoft operating system, a bundle of different software programs developed by other firms and previously sold separately). However, there also exists empirical evidence that challenges the model of Bakos and Brynjolfsson. Web sites of printed newspapers and magazines offer digital content in the form of single articles (often in the archive)— they do not offer bundles of information goods (like a digital version of the newspaper or the magazine). Examples are the *New York Times* (http://www.nytimes.com/) or *The Economist* (http://www.economist.com). This implies that the model of Bakos and Brynjolfsson, especially Assumption A3, does not work for all kinds of information goods.

Based on these observations the demand and the revenues of paid content is analyzed by different strategies of bundling and splitting. The goal of this empirical analysis is on the one hand to review the theories of Bakos and Brynjolfsson (1996, 1997) and on the other hand to show which strategy optimizes the demand and the revenues of paid content on newspaper and magazine Web sites. In the empirical analysis, three types of bundles are included: the same information bundle offered online (digital) and offline (printed), single articles, and rebundled information goods (e.g., as dossiers on a distinct topic). In the following section we show the empirical relation between offline (printed) bundles sold online, single articles, and rebundled article collections.

Empirical Analysis of Strategies for Selling Paid Content

The empirical analysis of strategies for selling paid content on newspaper or magazine Web sites is based on theories and approaches for bundling and splitting of information goods presented in the last section.

Data

The strategies for bundling paid content of newspaper or magazine Web sites were tested on a set of data from the German micropayment provider FIRSTGATE Internet AG. FIRSTGATE Internet AG is the leading micropayment provider in Germany with 2,500 suppliers of paid content

Table 1. List of Analyzed Newspaper and Magazine Web Sites

Supplier	Same Bundle of Information as the Printed Bundle	Unbundled Single Articles	Rebundled, New Combinations of Articles
capital.de		X	X
FAZ.net			X
Financial Times Deutschland	X	X	X
Focus online	X	X	X
heise online		X	
manager magazine		X	X
Harvard Businessmanager Deutschland		X	X
PC-WELT		X	X
SPIEGEL ONLINE	X	X	X
WELT.de	X		

and paid services and 2.5 million registered users. The data set of the seller contains ID, seller name, the Web sites with uniform resource locator, and the different prices of the offered goods stored.

For the empirical analysis a subsample of 10 newspaper and magazine suppliers was drawn. The criterion of extraction was the following: Each supplier offering bundled information offline (in the form of a printed newspaper or magazine) and aggregated or disaggregated paid content online was extracted. The sample of these 10 newspaper and magazine suppliers and the type of bundling and splitting of information goods is listed in Table 1. This sample includes 91,456 purchase transaction from 48,264 customers in the period from October 2003 to December 2003 (all purchase transactions of the suppliers in this period). In addition, the number of page visits to the Web sites of these suppliers was added to the data set. Page visits were used for standardization and scaling, allowing the comparison of sellers with different market share and media coverage.

First, the revenues of suppliers were assigned to the three types of information bundles (bundle, single article, rebundle). In a second step, the number of purchase transactions and the sum of revenues were assigned to each type of information bundle by month and supplier. To gain comparable data the results were scaled by the number of purchase transactions and the revenues were scaled per million visits for each supplier, type of information bundle, and month.

Methodology and Results

The analysis of the data was performed in three steps. First, average transaction volume and revenues per type of information bundling were computed (bundling, single document, and rebundling). Second, the correlation between the type of bundling and revenues, in the form of the number of purchase transactions per million visits, was analyzed. Third, the significance of results from Step 1 and 2 was analyzed by computing an analysis of variance (ANOVA). To show the relation among the three types of information bundles empirically, Table 1 presents the means of transaction volume and the revenues per million visits.

The results in Table 2 show that suppliers offering the same bundle of information goods online and offline achieve only 46% of the revenues per million visits compared to suppliers who offer their information goods in unbundled or disaggregated form, compared with rebundled information goods, for which the revenues per million visits account only for 8%.

If we compare the difference in transaction volume per million visits between same bundle of information goods and unbundled single articles with the difference between same bundle of information goods and rebundled information goods, we can identify nearly the same ratio.

These statistics provide a first indication that bundles that are offered offline (printed) and online (digital) at the same time are outperformed by single (digital) articles, which are in turn outperformed by rebundled (digital) articles.

The statistics in Table 2 do not show if this conclusion holds if sellers provide more than one type of bundle of information goods. Therefore correlation between revenues and purchase transaction for sellers offering several types of bundles at the same time is analyzed. The correlation coefficient between the revenues per million visits of suppliers selling their content both as a bundle of information goods and as single information goods is .5763; the covariance is 27.1009. The positive correlation shows that the difference in purchase transactions and revenues is due to the type of information goods provided. This means that there is a strong positive correlation between revenues and the kind of bundling type if sellers offer their content unbundled.

Table 2. Revenue and Number of Purchase Transactions per Million Visits for Each Kind of Selling Paid Content Online

Kind of Selling Paid Content	Revenue per Million Visits (in €)	Number of Purchase Transactions per Million Visits
Same bundle of information as the printed bundle	69.94	35.32952
Unbundled single articles	149.92	173.9007
Rebundled, new combinations of articles	839.51	173.3987

Table 3. Correlation Coefficient and Covariance

Kind of Selling Paid Content	Revenue per Million Visits		Number of Purchase Transactions per Million Visits	
	Correlation Coefficient	Covariance	Correlation Coefficient	Covariance
Same bundle of information as the printed bundle and unbundled single articles	.5763	27.1009	.6295	33.5252
Unbundled single articles and rebundled, new combination of articles	.3998	171.115	−.2177	−10.9613

Table 4. Transaction Volume in Relation to the Type of Bundling

Source	Partial SS	df	MS	F	p > F
Model	1074183.19	2	537091.595	44.72	.0002
Bundling type	1074183.19	2	537091.595	44.72	.0002
Residual	72056.056	76	12009.3427		
Total	1146239.25	80	143279.906		

Note. N = 81. Root MSE = 109.587. R^2 = .9371. Adjusted R^2 = .9162.

Table 5. Revenues in Relation With Type of Bundling

Source	Partial SS	df	MS	F	p > F
Model	38265.3156	2	19132.6578	479.59	.0000
Bundling type	38265.3156	2	19132.6578	479.59	.0000
Residual	239.362651	76	39.8937751		
Total	38504.6783	80	4813.08479		

Note. N = 81. Root MSE = 6.31615. R^2 = .9938. Adjusted R^2 = 0.9917.

The correlation coefficient between the revenues per million visits of suppliers selling their content both as unbundled single articles and as rebundled, new combinations of articles is .3998 and has a covariance of 171.115.

As displayed in Table 3, correlation between the bundle of information goods and single articles measured in transaction volume per million visits is strongly positive (.6295), but in the second case, where suppliers offer both unbundled single articles and rebundled information goods, we find a negative correlation (−.2177). This means rebundling of articles helps to raise the revenues but lowers the number of purchase transactions.

The means of revenues and purchase transactions per million visits and the correlation coefficient indicate a strong relation to the kind of bundling and splitting. To analyze the significance of this relation, an ANOVA was computed. The ANOVA is a method that analyzes the effect of one or several independent variables (e.g., the kind of bundling or splitting) in relation to one dependent variable (e.g., revenues or transaction volume per million visits; Backhaus, Erichson, & Plinke, 2003). To analyze the impact of aggregation and disaggregation on each of the dependent variables (revenues and transaction volume per million visits) a one-way ANOVA was computed.

As shown in Table 4, a highly significant influence of the type of bundling on the transaction volume can be identified. With a 99% confidence interval a Prob > F value of .0002 is found, which is an indicator for very high significance.

In Table 5 an even more significant influence of the type of bundling on the revenues can be identified. With 99% confidence interval a Prob > F value of .0000 and an F value of 479.59 were computed. This shows that the results in Steps 1 and 2 are significant.

These statistics fully support the conclusion that single articles in terms of purchase transactions and revenues outperform offline (printed) bundles sold online and that single articles are outperformed by revenues, but not by transaction volume of rebundled article bundles.

Discussion and Implications

The previous section showed that the same information bundle offered online (digital) and offline (printed) generates nearly no demand in the online world and therefore the valuations (measured revenues and purchase transactions) are higher for single articles. If these single information goods are rebundled, the valuation of this bundle is much higher.

To explain the phenomenon that in the online newspaper and magazine market some bundles are outperformed in revenues and transaction volume by single articles and single articles are outperformed by other bundles, we make a proposition in addition to the three assumptions of Bakos and Brynjolfsson (1997).

Under the proposition of Bakos and Brynjolfson (1996), if the same bundle of information goods is provided offline (printed) and online (digital), customers prefer the offline bundle, so we can conclude that the valuation of a printed bundle v_p sold in the offline world is outperformed by the valuation v_i of any single digital article i in the online world. On the other hand, the valuation of any bundle v_d, where $d \neq p$ outperforms a single article i sold online (Bakos & Brynjolfsson, 1997). Therefore we can conclude in the competition of information goods that the relation between valuation v is the following:

$$v_p < v_i < v_d$$

where p = digital version of a printed information bundle, i = single digital article, d = digital bundle of articles, and $d \neq p$.

The empirical analysis shows that existing theoretical approaches and models in the bundling literature do not explain all aspects of bundling information goods because they take into consideration only one medium as the distribution channel. The implication of these findings is that a printed bundle of newspaper and magazine content must be split or rebundled on the Web so that a demand for this content exists.

These findings indicate that there is competition between offline and online newspapers, but not in the way Chyi and Sylvie (2000) identified it. Online newspapers may compete with their offline versions and influence their sales volume. However, if we look at it another way, offline newspapers are a strong competitor for online newspapers and magazines as well. In addition to Chyi and Sylvie (1998) showing the cannibalization of printed versions of information bundles, it has been shown in this article that the cannibalization problem also exists for digital information goods through the printed information bundles. Therefore online newspapers have to differentiate information goods against the offline versions by selling single articles or using the potential of rebundling in electronic media. Under this aspect the convergence of online and offline newspapers has to be further analyzed from the online perspective, which suffers strong competition from the offline world. As several newspaper and magazine Web sites show by offering dossiers on specific topics, such a convergence of media

can be used to produce complementary goods, raising the benefits of both sectors (the online and the offline sectors).

Practical implications of the empirical findings presented in this article are that the same information bundle cannot be sold in two or more different media at the same time if there exists a well-established habit to consume this content. These habits can change through digital media (Palmer & Eriksen, 1999). Therefore the business models of traditional newspaper and magazine markets cannot be transferred one-to-one to the online world without product differentiation. Possible alternatives of product differentiation are splitting of the information bundle supplied in the printed version of the newspaper or magazine on the Web or rebundling it into new digital information goods.

Conclusions

In this article it is shown that bundling theories, especially the approach of Bakos and Brynjolfsson (1996), seem to work within a single medium and that the revenues of rebundled information goods outperform the online revenues of split newspaper or magazine articles. However, in addition to their approach, we show that their approach has to be extended if information bundles are offered in various media at the same time. A conclusion that can be derived from the findings in this article is that the revenues of paid content on newspaper or magazine Web sites are higher if information is rebundled (e.g., as dossiers) and not sold as single articles (e.g., in the archive of the Web site) or as bundles that are identical to the printed version.

Of course further research has to be done in this area to analyze the competition and complementary effects of the convergence of the offline and the online world. Only a look at newspapers and magazines with a broad range of topics has been given. Therefore it is possible that the identified correlations are not observable for magazines with a very specific focus (e.g., magazines for handymen or magazines about cars).

Whether these findings can be extended to other media sectors and markets has to be analyzed. It is not clear yet if these strategies for bundling and splitting are also applicable to, for example, the music market and if thus music CDs would achieve higher revenues when sold disaggregated or rebundled on online media. However, the existence of rebundled compilations with different artists in addition to albums of a single artist and the high demand for single music files on online music stores as MyCokeMusic.com or the Apple iTunes music store (http://www.apple.com/itunes/) give a first idea that the findings presented in this article might also be relevant in other media sectors.

Florian Stahl

(florian.stahl@unisg.ch)

is a Research Assistant at the mcm institute, University of St. Gallen, Switzerland. His research focuses on the economics of paid content and the interrelation of product and price differentiation of digital goods.

Marc-Frédéric Schäfer

(marc-frederic.schaefer@gmx.de)

is a Research Assistant and PhD student at the mcm institute, University of St. Gallen, Switzerland. He studied economics with a major in finance at University of St. Gallen, Switzerland, and at HEC Paris, France, and holds a degree from University of St. Gallen, where he finished his master's studies in October 2002. Prior to joining the mcm institute, Marc-Frédéric worked for the mcm institute as a programmer, IBM Consulting Group in Zürich, Switzerland, and the Landesbank Baden-Württemburg in Stuttgart, Germany.

Wolfgang Maass

(wmaass@acm.org)

is a senior researcher at the mcm institute, University of St. Gallen, Switzerland. He studied computer science at the University of Aachen (RWTH) and at the University of Saarbrücken. His doctoral studies have been in the domain of cognitive science. He worked at the German Research Center for Artificial Intelligence (DFKI) and the National Center for Geographic Information and Analysis (NCGIA), UCSB.

References

Backhaus, K., Erichson, B., & Plinke, W. (2003). *Multivariate Analysemethoden* [Multivariate methods of data analysis]. Berlin: Springer Verlag.

Bakos, Y., & Brynjolfsson, E. (1996). *Bundling information goods: Pricing, profits and efficiency.* Retrieved January 1, 2004, from http://papers.ssrn.com/sol3/Delivery.cfm/98111102.pdf?abstractid=11488

Bakos, Y., & Brynjolfsson, E. (1997). Aggregation and disaggregation of information goods: Implications for bundling, site licensing and micropayment. In B. K. D. Hurley & H. Varian (Eds.), *Internet publishing and beyond: The economics of digital information* (pp. 114-137). Cambridge, MA: MIT Press.

Bakos, Y., & Brynjolfsson, E. (2000). Bundling and competition on the Internet. *Marketing Science, 19*(1), 63-82.

Brooks, C. H., Das, R., Kephart, J. O., MacKie-Mason, J. K., Gazzale, R. S., & Durfee, E. H. (2001, October). *Information bundling in a dynamic environment.* Paper presented at the Third ACM Conference on Electronic Commerce, Tampa, FL, USA.

Chyi, H. I., & Sylvie, G. (1998). Competing with whom? Where? And how? A structural analysis of the electronic newspaper market. *The Journal of Media Economics, 11*(2), 1-18.

Chyi, H. I., & Sylvie, G. (2000). Online newspapers in the U.S. *International Journal on Media Management, 2*(2), 69-77.

Eisenberg, B. (2002). *The ROI of free.* Retrieved January 10, 2004, from http://www.clickz.com/experts/design/traffic/article.php/1368441

Fay, S. A., & MacKie-Mason, J. K. (2001). *Competition between firms that bundle information goods.* Retrieved January 18, 2004, from www-personal.umich.edu/~jmm/courses/econ731/bundle-13nov98.pdf

Gazzale, R. S., & MacKie-Mason, J. K. (2001, October). *Endogenous differentiation of information goods under uncertainty.* Paper presented at the EC'01, Tampa, FL.

Glotz, P., & Meyer-Lucht, R. (2003). *Zeitung und Zeitschrift in der digitalen Ökonomie - Delphi-Studie* [Newspapers and magazines in the digital economy]. Retrieved from http://www.unisg.ch/org/mcm/web.nsf/forum?openpage

Loebbecke, C. (1999, June). *Electronic publishing: Investigating a new reference frontier, global networked organzations.* Paper presented at the Twelfth Bled Electronic Commerce Conference, Bled, Slovenia.

Palmer, J. W., & Eriksen, L. (1999). Digital news: Paper, broadcast and more converge on the Internet. *International Journal on Media Management, 1*(1), 31-34.

Salinger, M. A. (1995). A graphical analysis of bundling. *The Journal of Business, 68*(1), 85-98.

Schmalensee, R. (1984). Gaussian demand and commodity bundling. *The Journal of Business, 57*(1), 211-230.

Siegel, F. (2002). Preisfindung für den Vertrieb digitaler Dienstleistungen und Güter [Pricing for sales of digital services and goods]. In *Proceedings of LIT 2002.* Leipzig, Germany.

Varian, H. R. (1995, May). *Pricing information goods.* Paper presented at the Proceedings of Scholarship in the New Information Environment Symposium, Harvard Law School, Cambridge, MA.

Varian, H. R. (2001). *Economics of information technology.* Retrieved April 23, 2003, from www.sims.berkeley.edu/~hal/Papers/mattioli/mattioli.pdf

Zerdick, A., Picot, A., Scharpe, K., Artope, A., Goldhammer, K., Lange, U. T., et al. (1999). *Die Internet-Ökonomie. Strategien für die digitale Wirtschaft* [The Internet economy: Strategies for the digital economy] (3rd ed.). Heidelberg, Germany: Springer.

Dayparting Online: Living Up to Its Potential?

Hans Beyers
University of Antwerp, Belgium

Dayparting is (mainly) an old concept used by television stations that show different programs at different times of the day. These distinctions are based on the usage patterns of the television audience. Dayparting exists in many broadcast media and is profoundly changing the makeup of programming and advertising campaigns. Two 2003 studies found that these dayparts are also applicable to the online media.

On the Internet, the breakdown looks like this: In the morning users want to read their e-mail and consult the news, during the afternoon at work use slows down and entertainment becomes more important (e.g., checking movie times, downloads, online games). In the evening, users switch to goal-driven mode and start looking for cars, jobs, and other products (e-commerce and online shopping). This article examines dayparting as a new online concept and its potential for news sites and online newspapers, and discusses some examples and possibilities.

For some years now, dayparts have been a familiar and frequently used (marketing) concept in broadcast media (Comstock & Scharrer, 1999; Dominick, Sherman, & Copeland, 1996). A *daypart* consists of a consecutive block of time in which a certain program (or a series of related programs) is broadcast and of which receivers can be characterized by a demographic homogeneity and similar features. This is done by measuring the audience flow throughout the day and matching similar programs (Sherman, 1995).

Within these dayparts, networks compete for audiences. By means of block programming, they try to capture and keep their audiences. Television stations broadcast different kinds of content at different times of the day, based on the usage patterns of audiences: soaps and talk shows during the day, news when people get home from work, and sitcoms after dinner (Sherman, 1995; Smith, Wright, & Ostroff, 1998). These dayparts are used to schedule programs by trying to appeal to the audience group most dominant during a given time slot.

In other words, each of these time sections has its own audience and features, and by consequence, provides interesting data for advertising. Advertisers can use these time spans to address specific audiences. Prime time is the most well-known daypart because the period between about 7 p.m. and 10 p.m. attracts the highest amount of television spectators and thus is highly interesting for media companies as well as advertisers (Newspaper Association of America [NAA], 2003; Sherman, 1995; Smith et al., 1998). Prime time "represents the most important revenue source for television managers" (Sherman, 1995). Research found those time slots do not only apply to television and radio, but also to the Internet (NAA, 2003; Online Publishers Association [OPA], 2003b).

The fact that Web site traffic to news sites slips in the late afternoon and drops dramatically during the evening was the immediate cause for establishing these dayparts. On most news sites, the end of the workday coincides with a troubling drop in visitor numbers. Also, evidence was provided that these sites still were consulted during the evening and on the weekend, only not in the same way. Via the United States, dayparting is now making its way into online media (NAA, 2002, 2003; Trombly, 2003).

On the basis of U.S. studies, examples, figures, and remarks, this article tries to work out the potential created by dayparts and to what extent they can influence traffic and Web site revenues. Before we focus, we take a look at the current situation concerning Internet population and media use. Subsequently, we go deeply into dayparting. Its importance for both online journalism and advertising is treated separately. We also try to formulate some considerations and suggestions for the implementation of this new approach.

Address correspondence to Hans Beyers, University of Antwerp, Universiteitsplein 1, B-2610 Wilrijk (Antwerp), Belgium. E-mail: hans.beyers@ua.ac.be

The Internet Population and Its Media Use

The Online Population in the United States

According to research at the University of California (UCLA), 71.1% of all North Americans went online in 2002, and 47% of nonusers said they probably would in 2003 (UCLA Internet Report, 2003). Data by eMarketer found a total of 566 million online users for 2002. Berthelsen (2003) expects this figure to rise to about 725 million by 2004. However, the image of the United States as a wired and connected society must be put into perspective: As in any country, there are a lot of digital have-nots in the United States. These nonusers can roughly be divided into three categories. A first group, the net evaders, consists of people who avoid the Internet by relying on others (family, partner, or friends) to search the Internet and send e-mail (20% of nonusers). Second, there are the so-called dropouts[1] (17% of nonusers, possibly somewhat overlapping with the evaders), who used to surf the Internet. Finally there are those who are truly offline and by consequence do not have any online experience at all (69% of all nonusers and some 24% of the U.S. population). We also mention the intermittent users (27%–44% of the current Internet population), who are back online after being offline for some time. We should conclude that Internet use is very fluid and that the Internet population is ever shifting (see Figure 1; Pew Internet & American Life Project, 2003a).

Online Media Use

Research for the NAA by Minnesota Opinion Research, Inc. (MORI), has shown a shifting media use depending on time of day (see Figure 2; NAA, 2002, 2003). Next to radio (53%) and Web sites (30%), online newspapers (27%) are the most used media before 8 a.m. (NAA, 2003). Between 8 a.m. and 11 a.m., Web sites and online newspapers own the audience with, respectively, 59% and 49%. Until about 6 p.m. both media stay in first place; later on television takes over. As already said, 49% of users access

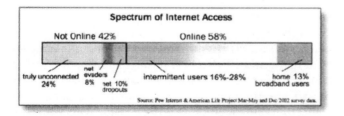

Figure 1. *Spectrum of Internet access in the United States, N = 3,553 (Pew Internet & American Life Project, 2003a, p. 26).*

online newspapers between 8 a.m. and 11 a.m., but this percentage falls to 28% from 6 p.m. to 10 p.m., and plummets to 13% at night. Newspaper Web sites are left largely depopulated because most users (58%) access them at work. At the same time, there still is considerable traffic to (general) Web sites at night (25%), signifying that Web sites are the only media to compete with television (35%) during that time slot (see Figure 2). During the weekend, online traffic is highest between 1 p.m. and 10 p.m. Television is still in a strong position, especially at night (see Figure 3).

Without a doubt, the priorities of online newspaper users are not constant across a 24-hr period. Information and entertainment seem to be very important factors in the changes that occur throughout distinct dayparts. Almost half of U.S. broadband users surveyed (N = 999) go online for news on a daily basis. The main reasons are that they like to consult up-to-the-minute (63%) news from various sources (66%; Pew Internet & American Life Project, 2003b).

Dayparting

Term Description

Two recent American studies, one by MORI[2] for the NAA and another by the OPA, prove that temporal influences affect Internet audiences. Dayparts differ significantly by the demographics of their audiences, frequency of use, and type of content that is accessed. Every time slot corresponds to a specific audience that can be targeted because its profile is known and available to advertisers (NAA, 2003; OPA, 2003a). By modifying content and layout throughout the day, online news sites can meet the appetites of their visitors by offering different information at different times: In the morning surfers want to check the news, by the afternoon they long for entertainment, and in the evening and at night they prefer online shopping and personals or classifieds. The basic idea is to emphasize hard content in the morning and to gradually add more entertainment stories as the day goes by (Coats, 2003; Deuze, 2003; Morrissey, 2003a).

Online dayparting can thus be defined as "promoting different editorial and advertising content online during different segments of the day to better serve readers' interests" (CyberJournalist, 2003; NAA, 2003; OPA, 2003b). In the following, we look at both aspects (journalism and advertising) separately. Clearly, two assumptions are at the very heart of dayparting: First, Web traffic has to be large and continuous so it can be split up in segments, and, second, that information on distinct online behavior can be used for the benefit of both user and advertiser. Finally,

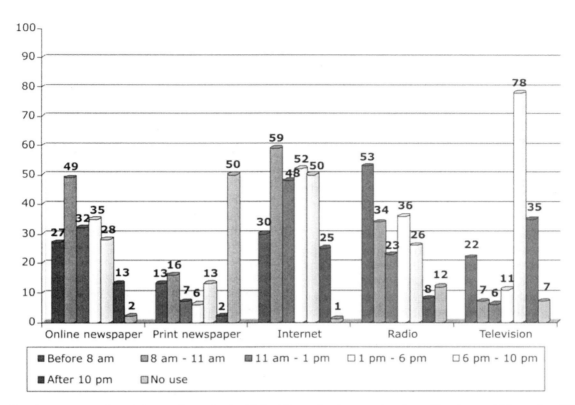

Figure 2. Percentages of workday media use in the United States by daypart, data from October and November 2002, N = 11,133 (NAA, 2003, p. 9).

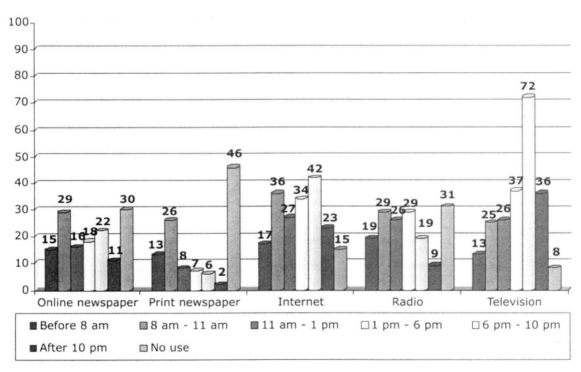

Figure 3. Percentages of weekend media use in the United States by daypart, data from October and November 2002, N = 11,133 (NAA, 2003, p. 9).

we discuss some examples of sites using dayparting strategies and their results.

Different Sets of Dayparts

The OPA study used average minute audience[3] as an estimate to indicate the number of people using the Internet at a certain point in time. Also on the basis of these data, the OPA derives five distinct internet dayparts: early morning, daytime, evening, late night, and weekends (see Table 1).

The NAA defines a working day as the period from 6 a.m. to 6 p.m. to create some flexibility concerning the traditional nine-to-five-job. This results in a timetable that is less refined: In the morning (6 a.m.–2 p.m.) surfers are almost as interested in news as they are in e-mail (UCLA Internet Report, 2003). This goes for breaking news, as well as for local, international, business, and sports news. In the course of the afternoon (2 p.m.–6 p.m.) the attention to news begins slipping and entertainment sites and related databases (e.g., movies, music, restaurants) become more important. The share of this kind of information has to be extended, but updates and breaking news are still advised. When the evening comes (6 p.m.–6 a.m.) surfers become more attracted to e-commerce and online shopping, and especially to personals and classifieds (NAA, 2003).

Dayparting on News Sites

The ideal news site. Based on the outcomes of these studies we conclude that a news site ideally consists of four components: a part with breaking news and headlines, a component focusing on entertainment and hobby content (e.g., movie programming, online games, downloads, etc.), personals and classifieds (jobs, real estate, cars, etc.), and an online shopping component.

Of course daypart productivity relies on more than just audience because prime time is changing by type of product or service. In fact, some products or services perform best outside the daytime time slot. Combined with the Internet as a real-time medium able to provide immediate satisfaction, targeting by product type—next to type of consumer and daypart—is of high importance for advertisers and news sites. Peter Daboll, president of ComScore Media Metrix, concluded, "Dayparting is becoming more important if you want to reach different audiences better, by understanding when they are likely to be online and on certain sites" (Olsen, 2003). However, several news sites are afraid of downgrading their brand names by shifting to a more trendy approach at night and thus most of them have been fairly slow to adopt dayparting strategies (Kaye, 2004).

Suggestions and notes. A nice example of news site traffic is provided by azcentral.com (*The Arizona Republic*). On a typical day, first users come on at 6 a.m., with peaks at 8 a.m., 9 a.m., and again at noon. Until 4 p.m. an average of 120,000 page views an hour is counted, then traffic takes a plunge to some 50,000 page views (6 p.m.), and ultimately drops to only 25,000 page views around 9 p.m. To offset this traffic dip, azcentral.com came up with the idea of a trendier version, starting in May 2003. Azcentral now rebrands and transforms into azcentral@night, focusing on entertainment, shopping guides and personals, and news is relegated to a secondary status. A similar decision has been made at the *Lawrence Journal-World* (LJWorld.com) in the beginning of March 2003. "We decided to make this change because our traffic was really great between 8 and noon, and between noon and 3 it starts to die. After 5 or so it's a virtual ghost town," said general manager Rob Curley. Editors rewrite headlines

Table 1. Distinct Internet Dayparts According to OPA

Daypart	Time Slot	AMA (of U.S. Surfers)	Remarks
Early morning	6 a.m.–8 a.m., weekdays	1.38 million	Online newspapers are the second most powerful media with 27%.
Daytime	8 a.m.–5 p.m., weekdays	3.84 million	Largest audience Online prime time News sites are very popular (high % of working people between the ages of 25 –54).
Evening	5 p.m.–11 p.m., weekdays	2.79 million	Entertainment, search engines, and portals take over.
Late night	11 p.m.–6 a.m., weekdays	676.000	
Weekends	Saturday and Sunday	1.6 million	Kids are three times more likely to go online during the evening and weekend than persons between 25 and 54 (shift toward more interest in entertainment and sports).

Note. Online Publishers Association, 2003b, pp. 5–6.

and try to add some fun, now prominently inserting items like calender listings, sports, and a focus on students. Video, screen savers, local weblogs, and MP3 downloads of local bands are also featured in the sundown edition, which is published around 4 or 5 p.m. (Saul, 2003; Trombly, 2003).

We therefore suggest that news sites interested in using dayparting strategies hire young, trendy editors to take care of their editions at night. It also seems rather clear that such adjustments mean a high workload for the editorial staff, although success is not always guaranteed.

Dayparting in Online Advertising

The concept of dayparting is not only applicable to news, but also to online advertising: Daytime is prime time online. Working days also provide the highest levels of Web site traffic, but not all days are the same. A study from OneStat.com found that Monday is the busiest day online (15.31% of worldwide traffic). By moving online advertising expenses to the right daypart, costs can be cut down, and efficiency and return on investment increase (OneStat.com, 2003).

A handful of major American Web sites (e.g., America Online, The New York Times Digital, CBS Marketwatch, Yahoo!) started selling advertising space during certain times of the day (Saunders, 2002). For example, Budweiser bought all available advertising space at CBS Marketwatch toward the end of the workday, because that is the time when a lot of CBS's audience (chiefly men working in financial business) go to a pub. On February 10, 2003 (from 9 a.m.–1 p.m.) Sun Microsystems did the same at Forbes.com: Banners promoted a Web event taking place at 9:30 a.m. (Hall, 2003; Van Camp, 2003). Because the Internet is a global medium, this approach causes some problems. For example, how can you make sure you reach people at lunchtime? The campaign on Sun Microsystems announced that the event was going on "right now," so different time zones were not taken into account. Yet another possible application of dayparting includes travel advertising focusing on the weather, but the same critique (region) is valid here. Dayparting can also come in useful when using online coupons. Advertisers could offer coupons for donuts in the morning or a lunch coupon at noon.

According to Tacoda Systems, the next big thing in targeted online advertising is *roadblocking*. Roadblocking buys advertising space in different media and channels and is a technique to program advertising in such a way that consumers cannot avoid the messages of advertisers. Data on online behavior are matched with consumer databases of print versions (e.g., survey data), meaning not only a very narrow public can be reached, but this can also

be broadened to the offline market by using (direct) mail or adding advertising appendices to the print version (Outing, 2003; Wani, 2003).

The fact remains that during daytime the at-work audience has the highest potential for advertisers. This group is more likely to consult online media, shops more frequently, and as a consequence, spends more money online (Elkin, 2002; OPA, 2003b). This "desk-public" accounts for over 80% of all consumed online advertisements (Avenue A, 2003). Bearing all of this in mind, dayparting might be worth considering if one is trying to reach people in a certain state of mind, or in the middle of the purchase decision process.

Results at Some American News Sites

Research by the OPA showed a 40.2% increase in advertising revenues at 24 online publications during the first quarter of 2003. Revenues at New York Times Digital rose from $16.2 dollars during the first quarter of 2002 to $19.6 million for the first quarter of 2003 (+21%). By the end of the first quarter of 2004, this figure grew another 31.1% to $25.7 million. With $8.4 million, the digital unit of The New York Times Co. also achieved its highest operating profit ever, primarily due to higher advertising revenues. The Washington Post.com reported a 78% increase in local and national advertisements for the first quarter of 2003, equaling a surplus of 26.7% in revenues ($7.5 to $9.5 million) between the first quarters of 2002 and 2003 (Morrissey, 2003b; Runett, 2003). During 2003, revenues generated by the online activities of The Washington Post Company increased 30% to $46.9 million (The Washington Post Company, 2004). The Arizona Republic's AZCentral.com reported a roughly 70% increase in online advertising sales from 2001 to 2003.

The increase in revenues is partly due to a higher level of online advertisements to capture the at-work audience. Nowadays, online advertising is looked at as a complementary element in a larger campaign that uses all kinds of available media (a lot of traditional advertisers are more familiar with using larger advertising formats often including video and animation). Of course, other aspects are in play here and the revival of the online advertising market in the United States is not fully attributable to dayparting as such. This conclusion would surely be premature. The staff of LJWorld.com noticed increased traffic numbers in the evening. However, "We're not seeing the type of traffic we see in the morning or when there is bad weather," said Robert Curley of LJWorld.com (Rabasca, 2004). However, it is self-evident that selling online dayparts leads to a more transparent and measurable online advertising market, thus making it easier for advertisers to understand how online advertising fits in their general strategy.

Conclusion

Dayparts promise better targeting for advertisers, more profits for publishers, and a maturation of the industry as a whole. Dayparting also opens new perspectives for the study of online advertising effectivity. On the other hand, dayparting will not be profitable for all Web sites, depending on target group and purpose. As a consequence, news sites should test the concept of dayparting on a smaller scale before investing in additional editors or content management systems. Another point is the risk of ignoring Internet users without Internet access at work: When they come home, they can no longer consult the "daytime" edition of news sites using dayparts. Therefore, Rusty Coats of MORI suggested adding a "recap module" containing the daytime stories (Kaye, 2004).

A lot of U.S. news sites are starting to rotate their headlines throughout the day, but depending on the time of day general approaches may vary as well. However, we could ask ourselves if users want information to be forced on them. Users will eventually find the movie or shopping information they are looking for without a prominent display on a home page. Selectivity and interactivity are essential features of the World Wide Web, meaning that users can access any site no matter when or where. In fact, the element of free choice is somehow affected here. For most American news sites, dayparting will be technically easy to implement, as their core audiences tend to be local (and hence within the same time zone). The availability of editors to rotate sites is yet another matter.

As a consequence of a large volume of Web site traffic at work, news sites are particularly suitable for advertising. Moreover, the Internet is the only medium to rival television in the evening and at night. Finally, the growing amount of online newspapers offering digital replicas in some sort of portable document format might influence advertising strategies because this allows companies to simply transfer ads from the print version to an online environment, avoiding annoying pop-ups or other (sometimes rather aggresive) online ad forms (Berthelsen, 2003).

Hans Beyers

(hans.beyers@ua.ac.be)

is been an Assistant in Communication Sciences at the University of Antwerp, Belgium, since 1999. His research focuses on the impact of the Internet on traditional mass media and more specifically on online newspapers and their repercussions for print newspapers and traditional journalistic values.

Endnotes

1. The main reasons for this dropout are: "no longer have or use of a computer" (19%), "didn't like it/want it/not interesting or useful" (13%), and "didn't have time to use it/wasn't a good use of my time" (12%; Pew Internet & American Life Project, 2003b, p. 22).

2. The study questioned 11,133 respondents during October and November 2002.

3. Average minute audience was proposed in 2001 Coffey and Stipp. The formula calculates the total number of Internet users within a given period × the average number of minutes online divided by 60 min per hour (OPA, 2003b).

References

Avenue A. (2003). *The influence of broadband on Internet advertising.* Retrieved January 21, 2004, from http://www.avenuea.com/insights/expert_Broadband.asp

Berthelsen, J. (2003). Internet hacks: Web news cashes in. *Asia Times Online.* Retrieved April 12, 2003, from http://www.atimes.com/atimes/Global_Economy/ED12Dj01.html

Coats, R. (2003). Programming for dayparts. Online users' content, commerce habits change throughout the day. *The Digital Edge.* Retrieved March 27, 2003, from: http://www.digitaledge.org/DigArtPage.cfm?AID=4712

Comstock, G., & Scharrer, E. (1999). *Television: What's on, who's watching, and what it means.* San Diego, CA: Academic.

CyberJournalist. (2003). News sites move toward 'dayparting'. *CyberJournalist.net.* Retrieved April 28, 2003, from http://www.cyberjournalist.net/news/000338.php

Deuze, M. (2003). Dayparting. *De Internetjournalist.* Retrieved April 11, 2003 from http://www.xs4all.nl/~ijour/columns/deuze/column9.htm

Dominick, J. R., Sherman, B. L., & Copeland, G. A. (1996). *Broadcasting/cable and beyond: An introduction to modern electronic media.* New York: McGraw-Hill.

Elkin, T. (2002). At-work Internet users biggest online spenders: Consume more online media than TV, study finds. *AdAge.com.* Retrieved September 24, 2002, from http://www.adage.com/news.cms?newsId=36121

Hall, S. (2003). Online dayparting roadblock on Forbes.com. *Marketing Vox.* Retrieved February 5, 2003, from http://www.marketingwonk.com/archives/2003/02/05/online_daypartingroadblock_on_forbescom/

Kaye, K. (2004). Newspaper sites' dayparted content lures readers throughout the day. *Mediapost.com.* Retrieved February 26, 2004, from http://www.mediapost.com/dtls_dsp_news.cfm?newsID=239662

Morrissey, B. (2003a). Defining dayparts. *Internetnews.com.* Retrieved February 6, 2003, from http://www.atnewyork.com/news/article.php/1580701

Morrissey, B. (2003b). The promise of dayparts. *Internetnews.com.* Retrieved January 24, 2003, from http://www.internetnews.com/IAR/article.php/1574281

Newspaper Association of America. (2002, May). *Digital edge report: Power use. A profile of online newspaper consumers.* Retrieved April 7,

2003, from www.digitaledge.org/pdf/2002_Online_Consumer_Study.pdf

Newspaper Association of America. (2003, January). *Online dayparting: Claiming the day, seizing the night.* Retrieved January 28, 2003, from http://www.online-publishers.org/naa_daypart_report.pdf

Olsen, S. (2003). Advertisers to be offered 'daypart' data on website traffic: It's not just TV that has peak time viewing. *Silicon.com.* Retrieved March 11, 2003, from http://www.silicon.com/news/500019/1/3247.html?et=search

OneStat.com. (2003). *Monday is the most popular day of the week to surf the Web according to OneStat.com.* Retrieved April 9, 2003, from http://www.onestat.com/html/aboutus_pressbox19.html

Online Publishers Association. (2003a, May). *At work Internet audience media consumption study.* Retrieved June 11, 2003, from http://www.online-publishers.org/opa_media_consumption_050203.pdf

Online Publishers Association. (2003b, January). *The OPA white papers: The existence and characteristics of dayparts on the Internet.* Retrieved January 28, 2003, from http://www.online-publishers.org/internet_dayparts%20_020603.pdf

Outing, S. (2003). Stop the presses! *Editor & Publisher Online.* Retrieved June 11, 2003, from http://www.editorandpublisher.com/editorandpublisher/features_columns/article_display.jsp?vnu_content_id=1910312

Pew Internet & American Life Project. (2003a, April). *The ever-shifting Internet population: A new look at Internet access and the digital divide.* Retrieved April 16, 2003, from http://www.pewinternet.org/reports/pdfs/PIP_Shifting_Net_Pop_Report.pdf

Pew Internet & American Life Project. (2003b, April). *The Internet and the Iraq War: How online Americans have used the Internet to learn war news, understand events, and promote their views.* Retrieved April 7, 2003, from http://www.pewinternet.org/reports/pdfs/PIP_Iraq_War_Report.pdf

Rabasca, L. (2004). Plugged in. *Presstime.* Retrieved April 18, 2004, from http://www.naa.org/Presstime/PTArtPage.cfm? AID=6024

Runett, R. (2003). Web units show solid growth during first quarter 2003. *The Digital Edge.* Retrieved May 5, 2003, from http://www.digitaledge.org/DigArtPage.cfm?AID=4956

Saul, A. (2003). Connections 2003 highlights: 'Dayparts' and web-site registration. *Gannett News Watch.* Retrieved February 14, 2003, from http://www.gannett.com/go/newswatch/2003/february/nw0214-1.htm

Saunders, C. (2002). NYTimes.com debuts dayparts. *Internetnews.com.* Retrieved June 3, 2002, from http://www.atnewyork.com/news/article.php/1181811

Sherman, B. L. (1995). *Telecommunications management: Broadcasting/cable and the new technologies.* New York: McGraw-Hill.

Smith, F. L., Wright, J. W., & Ostroff, D. H. (1998). *Perspectives on radio and television: Telecommunication in the United States.* Mahwah, NJ: Lawrence Erlbaum Associates, Inc.

The Washington Post Company. (2004). *The Washington Post Company reports 2003 fourth quarter and year-end earnings.* Retrieved January 29, 2004, from http://phx.corporate-ir.net/phoenix.zhtml?c=62487&p=irol-pressArticle&t=Regular&id=489637&

Trombly, M. (2003). News sites experiment with "dayparting" by tailoring content. *Online Journalism Review.* Retrieved June 18, 2003, from http://www.ojr.org/ojr/aboutjr/1055792590.php

UCLA Internet Report. (2003, January). *Surveying the digital future: Year three.* Retrieved January 31, 2003, from http://ccp.ucla.edu/pdf/UCLA-Internet-Report-Year-Three.pdf

Van Camp, S. (2003). Sun to rise on Forbes.com. *Technology Marketing.* Retrieved February 5, 2003, from http://www.technologymarketing.com/mc/news/article_display.jsp?vnu_content_id=1809491

Wani, A. (2003). Targeting lessons for online publications. *Online Journalism Review.* Retrieved June 12, 2003, from http://www.onlinejournalism.com/topics/brief.php?briefID=54705

Webcasting Business Models of Clicks-and-Bricks and Pure-Play Media: A Comparative Study of Leading Webcasters in South Korea and the United States

■

Louisa Ha
Bowling Green State University

Richard Ganahl
Bloomsburg University, USA

This article identifies the business models of leading Webcasters in the United States and South Korea and proposes a cross-cultural framework to analyze the determinants of business models. The file transmission methods, content strategies, and revenue sources of clicks-and-bricks and pure-play Webcasters were compared in the study. After analyzing the business practices of 48 leading Webcasters—using a content analysis of their sites—we found that the content aggregator model and the branded content model are the 2 most commonly used business models of leading Webcasters in the United States and South Korea. Although clicks-and-bricks and pure-play Webcasters in both countries have a similar reliance on advertising as their major source of revenue, they employ different content strategies to their own media's advantages. Korean Webcasters are more likely to use pay-per-view as a revenue source than U.S. Webcasters.

Traditional broadcasters have extended their presence to the Internet through their Web sites. With the advancement of streaming technology, their Web sites can be used for Webcasting audio and video content. By compressing the digital signal and enabling the user's computer to decode and play the signal almost immediately in the correct order, consumers can enjoy video and audio content in quality similar to television and radio. Such Webcasting technology also enables dot-com Webcasters such as RealNetworks and Yahoo! to offer Webcasting services to Internet users. Webcasting has become a battlefield between traditional electronic media (clicks-and-bricks) and the dot-com media (pure plays). Although the extent of their Webcasts varies, almost all television networks and stations have a presence on the Web to compete with the pure-play Webcasters such as America Online, Yahoo! and RealNetworks (Accustream, 2003).

Webcasting can be broadly defined as the delivery of media content on the Web. More specifically it is the broadcasting of video and audio content on the Web. The multimedia capacity of the Web facilitates both traditional media and online-only media to provide information and

entertainment services to Internet users (Miles & Sakai, 2001). Although Webcasting can be used both by businesses and consumers, this study focuses on the Webcasting services that supply either prepared audio or video content to consumers because they can present a threat or an opportunity to traditional electronic media such as television and radio. How existing electronic media make use of Webcasting to consolidate their audience base or enlarge their audience reach, and the dynamics of online-only Webcasters can illuminate the future of the media industry.

This study compares the business models used by leading Webcasters in South Korea and the United States. Because of the global nature in audience reach for Webcasting, we seek to create a cross-national theoretical framework that will be useful for studying business models for emerging media such as Webcasting. Broadband penetration is an important factor in studying Webcasting because of the bandwidth requirement for transmitting video and audio files over the Internet. The increasing broadband penetration in South Korea and the United States makes these markets ideal for exploring the business viability of Webcasting.

The United States is the world's biggest user of the Internet, with 165.7 million Internet users (The World Factbook, 2002). According to an International Telecom-

Address correspondence to Louisa Ha, Department of Telecommunications, Bowling Green State University, Room 108 West Hall, Bowling Green, OH 43403, USA. E-mail: louisah@bgnet.bgsu.edu

munications Union (2003) report, 18% of all U.S. Internet subscribers are broadband subscribers. The average monthly broadband subscription price is about $40 (Fischer, Tom, & Ming, 2003). The cost of 100 kilobits per second is 0.13% of an average individual's monthly income (Reynolds, 2003). Also, the United States has the world's most successful entertainment industry with eight broadcast TV networks, more than 305 national cable networks, 12,300 radio stations, and Hollywood's famous movie studios. It is also the largest advertising market in the world.

The well-developed media industry in the United States has cultivated an American audience that is accustomed to abundant popular culture choices in electronic media and on the Web. The overwhelmingly large number of Web sites originating from the United States easily positions it as a "global trader" that can export large amounts of American media content to other countries over the Web (Zook, 2001). Essentially, the United States is an immigrant country with citizens from many ethnic origins using the same common language of English.

South Korea is the third biggest user of the Internet in Asia with 25.6 million Internet users (The World Factbook, 2002) and the second largest advertising market in Asia. South Korea has the world's highest Internet broadband connection penetration rate. Ninety-four percent of all Internet subscribers are broadband subscribers (International Telecommunications Union, 2003). The high broadband adoption rate in South Korea can be attributed to the strong government support of broadband as a technology infrastructure and the cultural characteristics of South Korean consumers (Han, 2003; Lee, O'Keefe, & Yun, 2003). The government supported several programs to promote broadband and the Internet including the Ten Million People Internet Education Project, Internet education programs targeting housewives, the cyberbuilding certification system, and deregulation of the Internet access service industry to encourage market competition. The broadband subscription price is highly affordable at about U.S. $25 a month (Fischer et al., 2003). Cost for 100 kilobits per second is only 0.03% of an individual's monthly income, four times less than the price charged in the United States (Reynolds, 2003).

In addition to government support, the homogeneous and gregarious culture of South Korea is also a big factor in the rapid adoption of broadband. Less than 1% of the Korean population is immigrants (The World Factbook, 2002). Korean is the only common language used in the country. High-density urban dwellings such as high-rise apartments facilitate the installation of broadband connections. Because technology ownership is viewed as a social status symbol and the Internet is viewed as the gateway to education and success, Korean consumers enthusiastically use their broadband connections (Han, 2003).

The South Korean government formerly controlled the media through the government-owned monopoly of television. Nevertheless, with the market liberalization reforms under Kim Dae-Jung beginning in the mid-1990s, South Korea's media industry has been transformed to a very competitive commercial industry with many newcomers, including cable television providers (Chang, Palasthira, & Kim, 1995). South Koreans are famous for their long working hours, 500 hr more than Americans annually (Anderson, 2001). The Webcasting business was valued at approximately $600 million by the end of 2002 according to the Korea Network Information Center's estimates (Park, 2003).

Literature Review

Online Media Business Model Controversies

Business models are conceptions of how a firm operates, including potential benefits for the various actors and the sources of revenues for the business (Picard, 2000). Two aspects of Webcasting must be addressed to understand its business model: One is the content and revenue source of the Webcast; the other is the technical requirement of Webcasting. Both can be barriers to consumption.

One major controversy in the online media business model is whether consumers will pay for online content. U.S. market researchers such as Cyberatlas (2003) and critics such as Rojas (2001) have documented consumers' resistance to paying for online content. According to a worldwide study by eMarketer, only 8% of all revenues for online content are from general consumers (Crosbie, 2002). The explanations for such resistance are that consumers are accustomed to free content on the Web, and they see parity between online and offline media content. To these skeptics, Webcasting to consumers as a business is doomed to failure. Following the dot-com bust, the press repeatedly reported the failures of various Webcasting ventures such as NBCi.com, Netradio.com, Digital Entertainment Network, and Pseudo Networks (e.g., Lee, 2000; Lefton, 2001; Rich, 2000). Nevertheless, with recent increases in broadband penetration, several notable major American Webcasters such as America Online, RealNetworks, and Yahoo! are committed to the business future of Webcasting, and offer consumers a wide range of Webcasting services (Gough, 2003; Sloan, 2003).

Baird (2003) and Bartussek (2003) argued that it is a misconception that consumers will never pay for online content. Although consumers will not pay for content that is perceived to be low in value or that competes with a free online substitute, they will pay for content online perceived as highly valuable such as *Consumer Reports* and the *Wall Street Journal*. Baird (2003) suggested that online media content can be highly profitable if online publishers use a tiered business model for content. This model provides visitors some free content and then uses a subscription model for access to exclusive content and features such as archives and database search.

Thus, the essence of the controversy is whether online media content creates value so compelling to consumers that they will pay for it. Among the handful of successful Webcasters such as sports leader ESPN and RealNetworks that offer cooperative deals with leading TV networks, most profitable consumer Webcast businesses are pornographic sites (Lubove, 2002). Consumers are accustomed to paying for pornographic content because it is not free in offline media.

Some established media see the online media as a repurposing platform or exhibiting window for their offline media content. The value of such repurposed content depends on the desire of offline viewers for repeated viewing, or on the interest of nonviewers to see the original show. Stand-alone online media that do not have their own production facilities may adopt the aired content in a syndication mode, and use the show's past audience ratings as an indicator of the content's potential attractiveness.

Picard (2000) viewed business models as evolutionary and proposed that the emergence of one business model is an improvement over previous business models. We, however, contend that business models can coexist and one model is not necessarily better than the other. Certain business models are better suited for certain Webcasters. The business model itself cannot guarantee business success, but it can serve as the framework for business operation and provide the means to achieve the business goals of a company.

For the purpose of this study, we first examine five revenue sources for Webcasters: (a) advertising and sponsorship, (b) e-commerce, (c) content syndication, (d) subscription, and (e) pay-per use, view, or /download. The first three modes all assume that the audience will not pay for the content, or the payment will be so minimal that it cannot provide sufficient revenue. The advertising and sponsorship mode assumes that audiences will not mind viewing or reading advertising as long as they do not need to pay for the content. Even if they pay, the amount they are willing to spend may be too little to support the online media. The audience for the content is large enough to attract advertisers at a cost-efficient level. The e-commerce revenue mode also assumes that audiences will not pay for the content. Instead of relying on advertisers for revenue, the e-commerce mode uses the revenue generated from selling merchandise on the site to make a profit. The free content is the bait; the business transactions are the ends. The content syndication mode uses the Web site as the showcase of content that can be readily transferable or adapted to other sites.

The assumption of the syndication mode is that consumers will not pay for the content. There are many sites that need the content but do not have the facilities or expertise to produce it. The profit comes from syndicating the content to other sites.

The subscription mode and the pay-per-use mode, on the other hand, assume audiences are willing to pay for the Webcast content. The subscription mode is the most commonly used business model for payment because it avoids the trouble of charging consumers every time they use the content, and it encourages consumers to use the content without worrying about additional payments. The content is bundled as a package so that all is available to the subscribers. The pay-per-use mode is particularly viable if individual content items are so attractive to the audience members that they will pay to own a copy (download) or view it on demand. A few attractive items may be able to generate sufficient revenue for the Webcaster. However, there must be a substantial number of people willing to pay for each item if the price is to remain competitive and affordable.

These revenue sources are not mutually exclusive. Webcasters can choose one source or a combination of sources that are appropriate. Webcasters that appeal to a broad audience can choose revenue sources that do not need an audience to pay directly for the content to survive. Webcasters that appeal to a niche audience may have fewer choices because the audience size may not be large enough to attract advertisers or sponsors. Despite the hype about online advertising customized by Web site content, the harsh reality of online advertising still follows the golden rule of cost efficiency. Online advertising dollars are concentrated on those sites with the highest traffic. Indeed, the top 20 most visited sites receive 80% of the online advertising revenue (Pastore, 2001). Specialized sites with small audiences have little advertising.

This study sheds light on the debate about online media business models by examining the business models of leading Webcasters in South Korea and the United States, the two largest Webcasting markets in America and Asia, respectively. It identifies the factors shaping Webcasting business models and shows how leading Webcasters overcome the problem of the consumers' unwillingness to pay for online media content.

Cannibalization of Media Consumption

Another controversy regarding Webcasting as a business is its potential to cannibalize offline media consumption. Those who view Webcasting as competition to the broadcast media see it as a cannibalizing force. They argue that Webcasting will steal audiences from the broadcast media. It is viewed as a better medium than broadcast media and popular music record labels because Webcasting has the advantages of interactivity, 24-hr on-demand access, and easy storage and retrieval (e.g., Cho, Byun, & Sung, 2003; Fox & Wrenn, 2001; Waterman, 2001).

Yet many view Webcasting as a complement or a companion to broadcast media (Stacy, 2001). Some think it is an opportunity or a new window for traditional media such as record labels to expand additional revenue sources (Bhatia, Krishan, & Honey, 2003). For those at work, Webcasting is an important substitute for TV viewing and radio listening. eMarketer (2003) reported that more than one third of Americans go online at work, 84% of workers have broadband access, and 60% of consumer online dollars are spent targeting the workplace. At-home audiences prefer the lean-back experience of watching TV from their couch or listening to radio in their cars. The geographical distance from the broadcast source is also an important factor in watching or listening to Webcasts. In fact, Arbitron/Edison's study concludes 55% of U.S. Web radio listeners listen to stations outside their local market (Rose & Lenski, 2003).

Technical Requirements and Barriers to Webcast Consumption

Another important aspect related to Webcasting is its technical requirements. They can create barriers to Webcast consumption and raise questions about the Webcast content's value. Pagani's (1999) analysis of the economics of interactive television stresses the importance of understanding the technical factors in shaping the economic models of the new technology. Currently, the access to and applications of the Web are not standardized. First, Webcasting of video and audio files requires high bandwidth from the provider and a broadband Internet connection from the user. The speed of the Internet connection can determine the quality of the user's Webcast experience. If the Internet connection is slow—such as a dial-up connection—the transmission of video and audio files becomes garbled and incomprehensible. Hence the full enjoyment of a Webcast is highly dependent on whether the user has a broadband connection. Many studies of Internet use show that broadband Internet users are much more likely to consume Webcasts than narrowband users (Cho, Byun, & Sung, 2003; Rao, 2001).

Second, there are three types of multimedia file transmission methods available to Webcasters at this time: (a) live streaming, (b) on-demand, and (c) push (Ha, 2004). Recent advancement of live streaming technology allows instant transmission of video files in streams by compression and decompression techniques. Web users can enjoy video and audio content in real time through the live streaming method. In live streaming, users must follow the Webcast schedule. On-demand is a transmission method that offers content based on a specific request from consumers at a time convenient to them. Users can retrieve the video or audio files any time. When the video displays instantly at retrieval but disallows storage, it is using the streaming technology. However, when it plays back after being fully downloaded on the user's computer, the Webcast is transmitted on-demand by downloading files. The files are stored on the user's computer system. The last transmission method is push, which is the automatic transmission of files displayed on the user's computer without his or her explicit request: The Webcast comes to the user. Microsoft's Windows Update and many other software companies use the push technology to remind users to upgrade or download patches of their products. Because of the high bandwidth required for video and audio files, push is seldom used for Webcasting of video and audio.

In addition to transmission method differences, there are other usability issues in Webcasting. Usability refers to the ease for users to navigate a Web site. First, Web site designs vary in usability. Some Webcasts with complex and confusing designs are very difficult to navigate. Because of the self-paced navigation design of the Web, the user must know where to locate the materials he or she wants to open. If one is confused and gets frustrated, one may leave the Webcast. Second, the compatibility of media players is another issue. Whether the user can view or listen to the Webcast depends on the compatibility of media players used by the Webcaster and the user. For example, if the Webcaster uses the Windows Media Player file format and the user only has a Quicktime player, the user cannot open the Webcast. To be a regular user of Webcasting, consumers need to own several media players to play the Webcasts in different formats. In addition, some Webcasts require additional software such as Macromedia Flash to view the page and the Webcast. A U.S. study by Ha and Chan-Olmsted (2002) reveals over half of the Internet users did not download additional software to view specific features of a Web site. For Webcasting to be successful in capturing the largest audience possible, it must be highly usable. To be highly usable, a Webcast should accommodate different Internet connection speeds and provide both live streaming and on-demand services to consumers. Also, it must be organized with an easy-to-navigate design and a search engine for fast location of materials, it should display a description of the content with file size and length, and accommodate multiple player platforms with little or minimal additional software to display the majority of the materials. Figure 1 illustrates the framework we employ in this study to analyze business models for Webcasters.

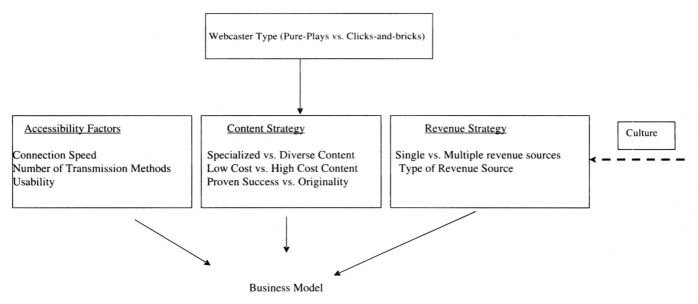

Figure 1. A framework for analyzing Webcasting business models.

Research Questions

To understand the business practices of Webcasters, this study examines the leading Webcasters in South Korea and the United States. Both countries have high broadband penetration rates that facilitate the Webcast industry, the support of the government, and a vibrant commercial interest in the Internet industry. In general, the study identifies the general business models of Webcasters. Specifically, this study attempts to answer the following five research questions:

1. What are the revenue sources used by the leading Webcasters in South Korea and the United States?
2. What are the content sources and program genres provided by the leading Webcasters in South Korea and the United States?
3. What are the file transmission methods used by the leading Webcasters in South Korea and the United States and are they related to the business model?
4. Are there differences in revenue sources, content sources, program genres, and file transmission methods between those with offline counterparts such as radio stations (clicks-and-bricks) and those that only Webcast on the Internet (pure plays)?
5. If there are differences in revenue sources and content, can those differences be attributed to cultural differences?

Method

The content analysis method was employed to examine the practices of leading Webcasters in both South Korea

and the United States. Because the Webcasting industry is still in its infancy, many Webcasters are just hobbyists or amateurs who are not serious about making their Webcasting a successful business. Studying a random sample will not help illuminate the direction of Webcasting business models. Only a handful of commercial Webcasters with larger audiences are important in this regard. Also, these leading Webcasters may set the trend for other Webcasters who are learning how to make Webcasting a profitable business. We selected 12 leading video Webcasting services and 12 leading radio Webcasting services for analysis in each country. After consultation with the International Association of Webcasters and the Webcasting-Digest listserv, we found there is no authoritative list of Webcasting services with audience information in both countries. We consulted various sources to design a list of the leading Webcasters in both countries.

As in all cross-national comparative studies, it is difficult to achieve complete equivalence. For example, the United States is more advanced in media audience research and more quantitative data are available. In addition, the top Webcasters in Korea have a much smaller audience because of language limitations and fewer total Internet users. As long as the purpose of the research is to test abstract dimensions across countries, it can be a justified approach (Livingstone, 2003). In this study, we attempt to apply a standard theoretical framework to apply to both countries with the expectation that there may be a difference in the business models based on the countries' different market environments.

In the United States, only Web radio sites are regularly monitored by commercial audience research services such as Measurecast (now part of Arbitron). Audience traffic for sites dedicated to videos, except popular TV network sites, is not regularly reported (one reason may be their small audience). To identify leading video Webcasting services, we first reviewed trade magazines such as *Streaming Magazine* and the *PC Magazine* for the sites recommended to readers. The top 12 video sites came from the "Video Prime-Time Players" article in the January 2002 issue of *PC Magazine*. Leading Web radio sites were identified from the top 10 list in the March 2003 list of Measurecast and the top three Web radio services reported in Arbitron/Edison Media Research's Internet 8 Report (Rose & Robin, 2002). Because MusicMatch was listed twice for its two different services, only one was selected. It must be noted that some video sites also provide audio services such as Windows Media and ESPN.com.

Internet use in South Korea is primarily concentrated among younger Koreans (Ko, 2001). The Korea Network Information Center estimates more than 90% of those between 6 and 19 years old use the Internet, 86% of those between 20 and 29 and more than 66% of those between 30 and 31 years old do so. Only 9.6% of those over 50 use the Internet. This concentration of Internet use among younger South Koreans is reflected in the 2002 election of President Roh and his 2% margin of victory. The campaign Web site received more than 500,000 daily visits to its chat rooms, video clips, and audio broadcasts. It received 7,000 e-mails daily offering policy ideas and campaign suggestions. On Election Day, the campaign sent 800,000 midday text messages reminding younger voters to cast their ballots.

Selection of South Korea's leading Webcasting sites reflects this emphasis on younger users. We consulted primary sources including government statistics and industry rankings, and also informally surveyed college students at leading universities in Seoul, the capital of South Korea, regarding the popularity of various Webcasting sites. Consequently we came up with 12 video and 12 audio Webcasting services that are most popular among the college student population (Please refer to the Appendix for the list of leading Webcasters chosen for this study).

The coding scheme was designed to identify the revenue sources and content characteristics of the Webcast. The coders recorded information about the content of the Webcast and the amount of money it charged to users if any. They also recorded the various revenue sources found on the site. The coding scheme was originally in English. The Korean version was a translation of the English coding scheme. To assure accuracy of the translation, the back translation technique was used: A Korean translated the Korean version back to English and the discrepancies were identified and resolved. In the United States, coders were senior undergraduate students at a midwestern state university who were taking a new media course with a focus on Webcasting. In South Korea, coders were native Korean graduate students in a communication program at a

university located in Seoul. Coders in both countries were trained on how to use the coding sheet and coded sites with a demonstration session. The coding was conducted from late March to early April 2003.

The coding sheet was a list of categories of Webcaster type, program genres, revenue sources, content sources, and transmission methods used by the Webcaster. Coders checked the presence of each category on the Webcaster's site. Coder reliability was calculated through double-coding 20% of the services by the researchers. To ensure that the double-coding was coding the same site, the second coders used the same printout of the site coded by the first coder in entering the information. Perreault and Leigh's (1989) Reliability Index was used to compute the intercoder reliability because it is an estimate of the true population level of agreement (Neuendorf, 2002). Taking into account the multiple coders involved in this study, the average reliability of items across all pairs of coders ranged from .81 (e.g., type of program genres) to 1.0 (e.g., Webcaster type) with an overall average reliability of .88.

Results

We had no intention to have an equal number of pure-play Webcasting services and clicks-and-bricks Webcasting services for both South Korea and the United States. In the resultant sample, both countries have slightly more pure-play Webcasters (54.2%) than clicks-and-bricks Webcasters. Among the 14 Webcasters that charge a monthly subscription fee, the subscription fee ranged from U.S. $3 to U.S. $21 a month with an average of U.S. $9. The monthly subscription fees for U.S. webcasters (average = U.S. $13) are significantly higher than their Korean counterparts, which on average charge $6, $t(12) = 2.53$, $p = .02$. For pay-per-view charges, they range from $1 to $2 per view.

Revenue Sources Used by the Leading Webcasters in South Korea and the United States

Among all modes of revenue sources, advertising and sponsorship is the most commonly used by leading webcasters in both South Korea and the United States, with e-commerce a distant second (Table 1). Nevertheless, there are quite a number of significant differences between the revenue sources used by South Korean Webcasters and American Webcasters. In South Korea, there are many more Webcasters using the advertising and sponsorship mode than in the United States. Almost all of the sites (except one) have some forms of advertisements or sponsor logos. Moreover, Korea's Webcasters are much more likely to employ several revenue sources than their American counterparts, $t(46) = -3.01$, $p < .01$.

Table 1. Revenue Sources of Leading Webcasters

Revenue Source	U.S.[a] n	%	South Korea[a] n	%	Total[b]
Advertising/sponsorship	19	79.2	23	95.8	42
E-commerce	8	33.3	12	50.0	20
Subscription	7	29.2	6	25.0	13
Pay-per-view**	1	4.2	9	37.5	10
Content syndication*	2	8.3	7	29.2	9
Other (tip jar, donation)	4	16.7	5	20.8	9

[a]$n = 24.$ [b]$N = 48.$
*Significantly different at $p < .05.$ **Significantly different at $p < .01.$

For example, on average, Korea's Webcasters have 2.85 revenue sources, whereas American Webcasters only have 1.7 revenue sources. In the United States, about 80% of the leading Webcasters employ the advertising and sponsorship mode, but this might be their only source of income. In Korea, both advertising and e-commerce can be easily found on the same site. Another significant difference is the use of pay-per-view and content syndication. Although pay-per-view and content syndication are not as popular as the other revenue sources, the South Korean Webcasters' use of pay-per-view is much more than the American sites. Nine South Korean Webcasters use pay-per-view, whereas only one U.S. Webcaster uses pay-per-view. Seven leading South Korean Webcasters syndicate their content to other sites, but only two leading American Webcasters syndicate their content.

To better understand the issues related to the business models' differences, we examine the content sources and program genres offered by the Webcasters.

Content Sources and Program Genres of Leading Webcasters

South Korean and U.S. Webcasters have similar proportions of original content, repurposed content, and simulcast of their offline counterparts' content in their Webcasts (Table 2). Hence the difference in revenue sources is not related to content originality or sources.

When we further examine the program genres offered in the Webcasts, there are also very few significant differences between the two countries. As shown in Table 3, there are a wide variety of program genres offered by the leading video Webcasters with very few dominating program genres. Among video content, music videos are just slightly more popular than news. Leading South Korean Webcasters are significantly more likely to carry TV entertainment programs, general news, and educational content than their American counterparts.

Music is undisputedly the most commonly available genre among Webcasters' audio content. Talk shows, speeches, or interviews are the second most common Webcast program genre. The only significant difference between leading American and South Korean Webcasters is the presence of news. American Webcasters are much more likely to carry news audio than their South Korean counterparts.

File Transmission Methods Used by the Leading Webcasters

As Korean and American Webcasters generally offer similar content sources and program genres, we explored if the file transmission method employed by the Webcasters can be associated with differences in revenue sources. First, it is interesting to find that South Korean Webcasters are much more likely to use on-demand transmission than American Webcasters. All except two lead-

Table 2. Media Content Sources of Leading Webcasters in the United States and South Korea

Content Source	U.S.[a] n	%	South Korea[a] n	%	Total[b] n	%
Original	11	45.8	13	54.2	24	50
Repurposed	13	54.2	11	45.8	24	50
Simulcast	13	54.2	11	45.8	24	50

Note. Each webcaster can have more than one content source.
[a]$n = 24.$ [b]$N = 48.$

Table 3. Program Genres of Leading Webcasters in the United States and South Korea

Genre	U.S.[a]		South Korea[a]		Total[b]	
	n	%	n	%	n	%
Video						
Blockbuster movies	2	8.3	4	16.7	6	12.5
TV commercials	2	8.3	4	16.7	6	12.5
TV programs (entertainment)	1	4.2	5	20.8	6	12.5
Education/instruction*	2	8.3	9	37.5	11	22.9
Trailers/highlights	5	20.8	6	25.0	11	22.9
Business (business news/speech/conference)	4	16.7	8	33.3	12	25.0
News clips/interviews (nonbusiness)*	6	25.0	13	54.2	19	39.6
Talk shows	2	8.3	6	25.0	8	16.7
Music videos	7	29.2	14	58.3	21	43.8
Documentaries	3	12.5	6	25	9	18.8
Cartoons/animation	5	20.8	7	29.2	12	25.0
Sports	6	25.0	7	29.2	13	27.1
Other	4	16.7	4	16.7	8	16.7
Audio						
Music	15	65.2	17	70.8	32	66.7
News	10	43.5	5	20.8	15	31.3
Talk/speech/interview	7	30.4	10	41.7	17	35.4
Sports	4	13.0	4	16.7	8	16.7
Other	3	13.0	1	4.2	4	8.3

[a] $n = 24$. [b] $N = 48$.
*Significantly different at $p < .05$.

ing South Korean Webcasters offer on-demand Webcasts to consumers so that consumers can access the service at any time. In contrast, slightly less than half of the American Webcasters offer on-demand Webcasts. Yet, South Korean Webcasters are almost as likely as U.S. Webcasters to provide live streaming to their consumers. As only two Webcasters offer push technology in Webcasting their content, we focus our comparison on live streaming and on-demand streaming.

In analyzing the transmission method, it is important to remember that Webcasters can use several transmission methods at the same time. Table 4 compares the file transmission method and the corresponding revenue sources. Among the leading Webcasters, only 14 exclusively provide on-demand transmission and 14 exclusively provide live streaming transmission. There are slightly more leading Webcasters ($n = 18$) that offer both live

streaming and on-demand transmission. Because South Korean Webcasters are more likely to use on-demand transmission than American Webcasters, we examine the relation between business model and on-demand transmission. Among the five most common revenue sources, pay-per-view is the only revenue source that can be attributed directly to the on-demand transmission method. Other revenue sources have no significant differences among transmission methods.

Remarkably, the transmission method seems to have an impact on the variety of revenue sources being used. Webcasters using live-streaming transmission have a much more limited choice of revenue sources than those using on-demand or both live and on-demand. They use a significantly lower number of revenue sources ($M = 1.5$) than Webcasters using on-demand only ($M = 2.14$) and both live and on-demand ($M = 2.7$).

Table 4. File Transmission Method and Revenue Sources

Revenue Source	OD Only[a]	Live Only[a]	Both Live and OD[b]
Advertising/sponsorship	92.9%	71.4%	94.4%
E-commerce	42.9%	29.6%	55.6%
Subscription	28.6%	28.6%	27.8%
Pay-per-view	21.4%	0.0%	38.9%
Content syndication	7.1%	7.1%	30.3%
Other (tip jar, donation)	21.4%	14.3%	22.2%

Note. OD = on demand.
[a] $n = 14$. [b] $n = 18$.

Comparison Between Pure-Play and Clicks-and-Bricks Webcasters

A recent study of a random sample of global Webcasters (Ren & Chan-Olmsted, 2003) reported no difference in revenue sources of pure-play Webcasters versus clicks-and-bricks Webcasters. However, among leading Webcasters who are serious in making Webcasting a profitable business, would the same pattern hold? After examining the leading Webcasters, we find that clicks-and-bricks Webcasters are not significantly different from pure-play Webcasters in their choice of revenue sources. As shown in Table 5, both clicks-and-bricks and pure-play Webcasters rely primarily on advertising and sponsorship as their revenue source supplemented with e-commerce. Although clicks-and-bricks Webcasters are more likely than pure-play Webcasters to use subscription as the revenue source, the difference is not statistically significant.

Although the type of Webcasters do not differ much in their revenue sources, it is associated with their content sources. As shown in Table 6, clicks-and-bricks Webcasters, with their advantage of possessing readily available content from their offline counterparts, are much more likely than pure-play Webcasters to use repurposed content or simulcast. To compete with clicks-and-bricks Webcasters, pure-play Webcasters are much more likely to offer original content. The cost of repurposed content to them can be much higher because pure-play Webcasters do not own any of the traditional media content. RealNetworks, for example, shares revenue sources with its program content suppliers to pay for the cost of nonoriginal content featured in its RealOne SuperPass.

To examine if the type of Webcaster may be related to the difference in program genres, we also compare the Webcast program genres offered by clicks-and-bricks and pure-play Webcasters. Indeed, as shown in Table 7, clicks-and-bricks Webcasters are more likely than pure-play Webcasters to offer education, business, talk shows, and sports, which are costly to produce and obtain the broadcast rights. Pure-play Webcasters commonly feature music videos, which are available at low cost and supplied to the station for free.

Discussion

This analysis of leading Webcasters in South Korea and the United States indicates that most Webcasters acknowledge the "free-rider" online consumption culture, and users' reluctance to pay for online Webcasts. Advertising and e-commerce are the most commonly used revenue sources that do not require users to directly pay for the content. Subscription is used by only seven Webcasters in Korea and six Webcasters in the United States. Yet in Korea, where broadband connections are much more prevalent, it seems pay-per-view is considered a viable revenue source for more than one third of the leading Korean Webcasters. With broadband connections that are readily available and affordable, Korean consumers seem more willing to pay for private consumption of quality Webcasts than American consumers.

Table 5. Revenue Source by Webcaster Type

Revenue Source	Clicks-and-Bricks[a]		Pure Play[b]		Significance
	n	%	n	%	
Advertising/sponsorship	20	90.9	22	84.6	ns
E-commerce	9	40.9	11	42.3	ns
Subscription	4	18.2	9	34.6	ns
Pay-per-view	6	27.3	4	15.4	ns
Content syndication	6	27.3	3	11.5	ns
Other (tip jar, donation)	4	18.2	5	19.2	ns

[a]n = 22. [b]n = 26.

Table 6. Content Sources by Webcaster Type

Content Source	Clicks-and-Bricks[a]		Pure Play[b]		Total[c]	
	n	%	n	%	n	%
Original*	3	13.6	21	80.8	24	50.0
Repurposed*	17	77.3	7	26.9	24	50.0
Simulcast*	18	81.8	6	23.1	24	50.0

Note. Each webcaster can have more than one content source.
[a]n = 22. [b]n = 26. [c]n = 48.
*Significantly different at $p < .01$.

Table 7. Program Genre Comparison by Webcaster Types

Program Genre	Clicks-and-Bricks[a]		Pure Play[b]		Total[c]	
	n	%	n	%	n	%
Video						
Blockbuster movies	1	4.5	5	19.2	6	12.5
TV commercials	4	18.2	2	7.7	6	12.5
TV programs (entertainment)	5	22.7	1	3.8	6	12.5
Education/instruction*	8	36.4	3	11.5	11	22.9
Trailers/highlights	5	22.7	6	23.6	11	22.9
Business (business news/speech/conference)*	9	40.9	3	11.5	12	25.0
News clips/interviews (nonbusiness)	11	50.0	8	30.8	19	39.6
Talk shows	6	27.3	2	7.7	8	16.7
Music videos**	4	18.2	17	65.4	21	43.8
Documentaries	6	27.3	3	11.5	9	18.8
Cartoons/animation	4	18.2	8	30.8	12	25.0
Sports**	10	45.5	3	11.5	13	27.1
Other*	1	4.5	7	26.9	8	16.7
Audio						
Music	12	57.1	20	76.9	32	66.7
News**	11	52.4	4	15.4	15	31.3
Talk/speech/interview*	11	52.4	6	23.1	17	35.4
Sports	6	27.3	2	7.7	8	16.7
Other	2	9.1	2	7.7	4	8.3

[a]$n = 22$. [b]$n = 26$. [c]$N = 48$.
*Significantly different at $p < .05$. **Significantly different at $p < .01$.

Culture may also play a role in the relatively higher presence of paying directly for media content as a viable revenue source in South Korea. As stated before, because Koreans have longer working hours, the need for quick entertainment and relaxation after work may be higher. Indeed, entertainment is the dominant program genre that the nine leading Korean Webcasters charge for in a pay-per-view format. Also, consumers of Webcasts are offered a wider variety of programs than those regularly broadcast on TV. Because these pay-per-view Webcasts are available on demand, it is more convenient for the busy Korean consumers to access the content when they want. When we further examine those leading Korean Webcasters that offer pay-per-view, the program genres are indeed highly diversified, with no particular type of program genre dominating the service. In addition, the high penetration of broadband connection among Koreans also makes Webcasting consumption an enjoyable experience so that Korean Webcasters can expect users to pay for a quality experience on individual items. The relatively higher presence of educational content in South Korean Webcasts is also in line with the Korean consumers' enthusiasm for education.

Concurring with the findings of Ren and Chan-Olmsted (2003), this study finds no significant difference between types of the Webcasters (pure-play or clicks-and-bricks) and their revenue sources. The file transmission method chosen by the Webcaster is most associated with the revenue source. A wider variety of trans-mission methods must be provided if the Webcaster wants to charge consumers for the content. All leading Webcasters that use dual transmission methods can command more revenue sources than those that only use one single transmission method.

Two Commonly Used Webcasting Business Models

Based on the findings of this study, we can deduce two commonly used Webcasting business models: (a) the content aggregator model, and (b) the branded content model (please refer to the Appendix for the designation of model for each Webcaster). The content aggregator model refers to the operation of the Webcaster as an entertainment or information portal. The Webcaster serves as a one-stop entertainment or information source to provide consumers with convenient service. Like a cable system operator, the Webcaster collects and packages content from a number of different sources. Consumers use the Webcasting service for a wide selection of content. In addition, the Webcasting service offers multiple transmission methods and maximizes usability with an easy-to-use interface and navigation design. Webcasters operating under the content aggregator model are likely to employ multiple revenue sources. They will also provide either repurposed programs with proven success such as high-rating reality shows or low-cost programs such as music videos as their content strategy.

In contrast, Webcasters employing the branded content model build their business success on specialized content. The specialized content can be original content if they have no offline media partners, or the Webcaster can arrange exclusive deals on repurposed or simulcast content from partners or offline media counterparts. As with cable networks, many branded content Webcasters cannot afford high-quality original content to fill their lineup. Much of their content offering will be a mix of original content and repurposed or simulcast content. However, their reputation and popularity depends on the original content they offer. Because of their special focus, they should expect a smaller audience size. They are likely to focus on a single revenue source and a single transmission method. If their transmission method is live streaming, they have to rely on indirect consumer payment such as advertising and e-commerce. If they can provide the content on-demand and the content is of high value to consumers, then they can charge users by subscription or pay-per-view.

Inevitably, all clicks-and-bricks Webcasters work on the branded content model because they will not carry the media content of offline and online competitors. They can choose transmission methods and revenue sources for their Webcast. In contrast, pure-play Webcasters have the choice between the branded content model and the content aggregator model. If they want to build a strong media brand with unique content, and they have the supply of content, then a branded content model is viable. However, if they do not have a reliable supply of content, they have to count on the convenience and comprehensiveness of the content to consumers and assemble a portfolio of content suppliers from various sources as content aggregators and operate like cable system operators.

Limitations and Suggestions for Future Research

Achieving both conceptual and methodological equivalence is an ideal for all cross-national comparative research. Yet it is hard in reality when different markets have different levels of sophistication and data availability. For example, in this study, the United States is much more advanced in commercial audience research with much more available data about audience size than South Korea. Compiling a list of leading Webcasters using the same source of audience research data is impossible. Ultimately, we used popularity as the definition for leading Webcasters. In the United States where audience research

data are available, the Measurecast ratings can be used to select leading Webcasters by largest audience size. However, in Korea, where no such ratings data are available, the collective opinion of college students who are the most frequent users of Webcasting was used to determine popularity. Future comparative research on Webcasting may need to establish an informant panel composed of industry experts in each country to create a list of leading Webcasters.

Because of the global nature of Webcasting and the fact that there is an unequal media content production capacity across countries, future research should examine the content's country of origin to assess the possible domination of foreign media content in countries with weaker media production facilities. For example, South Korea is similar to an isolated island because of the limited use of the Korean language. U.S. Webcasters, however, benefit from English as a universal second language. It becomes a global trader and may tend to dominate the Webcast medium. Such imbalance may perpetuate other countries' dependency on American media content on the Web. An expanded study with more countries can further address such concerns.

A further test of the study's proposed framework will be an assessment of the business performance of Webcasters using different business models. However, until the Webcasting industry has matured with more and more of the companies available for public trading with financial data available, it is difficult to systematically assess the profit potential of the Webcasters. In the meantime, the high volatility of many Webcasting services (many U.S. small Webcasters closed their Webcasts as a result of the copyright payment arbitration) indicates that it will take some time for consumer Webcasts to be profitable businesses.

Conclusion

Can Webcasters really make money from their Webcasts? Among the 48 leading Webcasters we examined in this study, there is no single formula. However, one thing the Webcasters have in common is that they either charge consumers directly (pay-per-view or subscription or donations of some sort) or indirectly (advertising and e-commerce). Advertising is the primary revenue source for most leading Webcasters examined in this study because they seem successful in drawing audience traffic that advertisers value. However, only a few Webcasters command enough traffic to be attractive to advertisers. For example, even among the top 10 radio Webcasts in the United States, none of them have a monthly cumulative measured audience of more than 400,000 listeners (Arbitron, Inc., 2004). For those Webcasters that are not leading Webcasters, relying on advertising as the only revenue source is not a viable business model. Such a harsh reality applies to both Korean and American Webcasters. For Webcasters who do not plan to assume leadership roles in audience traffic or in a particular audience segment, the other revenue sources should be pursued, particularly pay-per-view and subscription models that offer consumers much more flexibility in consuming the content.

Apart from revenue sources, the cost of Webcast media content will be critical to the development of Webcasting in all markets. The royalty payment to record labels in the United States as outlined in the Small Webcaster Settlement Act, and the statutory licensing system issued by the Digital Millennium Copyright Act written by the United Nations World Intellectual Property Organization are going to increase the content cost for Webcasters (Ha, 2004; Lam & Tan, 2001). A successful Webcaster must be able to keep the Webcast content's cost reasonable to run the Webcast on a regular basis.

What are the implications of Webcasting to the business of traditional offline electronic media? This study shows no apparent advantage of clicks-and-bricks over pure plays in being ranked as leading Webcasters in audience traffic in either South Korea or the United States. In addition, the study finds few signs of cannibalization of offline media by Webcasters. Rather, we see much offline media content emerging in a new form online, similar to how Hollywood movies become part of the staple of television. This is especially true of Webcasters that have offline counterparts. Webcasts have become another window for traditional media (Bhatia et al., 2003). When Webcasters simulcast offline content, they are actually reaching an audience that otherwise would not be able to use the content. The audience that is able to use the content in traditional media will not take the extra effort to use the Webcast. When Webcasters repurpose the content previously shown in offline media, they are entertaining fans that cannot have enough of the content or servicing those who missed the aired show. Indeed the fact that almost half of the leading Webcasters in this study are established television networks or radio stations demonstrates that some offline media succeed in extending their media brand online.

It may take many years for Webcasting to be as common as the television and radio broadcasts of today. However, the versatility of Webcasting in content diversity, transmission method, and display devices will eventually give it prominent roles in the media diet of consumers. At this nascent stage, Webcasters must promote to the consumers their content offering, the exclusivity of the content, and the benefits of the Webcasts, such as convenience and customization to create a compelling demand for their Webcasting service.

Louisa Ha

(louisah@bgnet.bgsu.edu)

is an Associate Professor in Telecommunications at Bowling Green State University, Bowling Green, Ohio. Her research areas are media convergence and media management, international advertising, media technology, and media entrepreneurship.

Richard Ganahl

(rganahl@bloomu.edu)

is a Professor at Bloomsburg University, Bloomsburg, Pennsylvania. His research interests are media management and media technologies with an international focus.

Acknowledgments

We would like to acknowledge the assistance of Bo Ra Hyun, Chae Eun Park, and Song Young Sun of Yonsei University, and the 12 undergraduate students at Bowling Green State University, in the collection of data and coding.

References

Accustream. (2003). *Accustream research report shows declining market share for broadcast and cable TV networks as stand alone brands in streaming media.* Retrieved April 10, 2004, from http://www.webcasters.org/news/20040219.htm

Anderson, P. (2001). Study: U.S. employees put in most hours. *Cable News Network.* Retrieved April 10, 2004, from http://www.cnn.com/2001/CAREER/trends/08/30/ilo.study/

Arbitron Inc. (2004). Top Internet broadcasters show significant audience gains according to Arbitron Internet broadcast ratings. Retrieved August 25, 2004, from http://www.arbitron.com/internetbroadcast/home.htm

Baird, B. (2003, April). Keys to developing paid online content. *Circulation Management,* pp. 30–33.

Bartussek, J. (2003). From newspaper to news filter. In A. Vizjak & M. Ringlstetter (Eds.), *Media management: Leveraging content for profitable growth* (pp. 43–52). New York: Springer-Verlag.

Bhatia, G. R., Krishan, C. G., & Honey, W. R. (2003). Windows into the future: How lessons from Hollywood will shape the music industry. *Journal of Interactive Marketing, 17*(2), 70–80.

Chan-Olmsted, S., & Ha, L. (2003). Internet business models for broadcasters: How television stations perceive and integrate the Internet. *Journal of Broadcasting and Electronic Media, 47,* 597–617.

Chang, W. H., Palasthira, T. S., & Kim, H. K. (1995). *The rise of Asian advertising.* Seoul, Korea: Nanam Publishing.

Cho, S., Byun, J., & Sung, M. (2003). Impact of the high-speed Internet on user behaviors: Case study in Korea. *Internet Research: Electronic Networking Applications and Policy, 13,* 49–60.

Crosbie, V. (2002). *Online content: The 2002 report. Publishing: Free or fee?* Retrieved February 20, 2003, from http://www.clickz.com/design/freefee/article.php/1557571

Cyberatlas. (2003). Users still resistant to paid content. *Cyberatlas.* Retrieved April 11, 2003, from http://cyberatlas.internet.com/markets/retailing/print/0,,6061_2189551,00.html

eMarketer. (2003, February). *More than one-third of working Americans go online at office, new online journal/eMarketer report finds.* Retrieved February 20, 2003, from http://www.emarketer.com/news/article.php?1002068

Fischer, J. S., Tom, R. L., & Ming, L. (2003, January). *Broadband in the United States and Europe: What went wrong and what are the lessons for Asia.* Paper presented at the 2003 Pacific Telecommunications Conference, Honolulu, HI. Retrieved April 10, 2004, from: http://www.dynastycap.com/about/PTC/PTC2003_paper.pdf

Fox, M., & Wrenn, B. (2001). A broadcasting model for the music industry. *International Journal on Media Management, 3*(2), 112–119.

Gough, P. (2003). AOL Broadband head sees good future. *MediaPost's Media Daily News.* Retrieved February 20, 2003, from http://www.media post.com/PrintFriend.cfm?articleId-204831

Ha, L. (2004). Webcasting. In H. Bidgoli (Ed.), *The Internet encyclopedia* (Vol. 3, pp. 674–686). New York: Wiley.

Ha, L., & Chan-Olmsted, S. (2002). *Enhanced TV as brand extension: The economics and pragmatics of enhanced TV to cable TV network viewership* (A Magness Institute Research Report). Retrieved April 10, 2004, from http://www.bgsu.edu/departments/faculty/ha/magness.pdf

Han, G. (2003). Broadband adoption in the United States and Korea: Business driven rational model versus culture sensitive policy model. *Trends in Communication, 11,* 3–25.

International Telecommunications Union. (2003). *Top 15 economies by 2002 broadband penetration.* Retrieved April 10, 2004, from http://www.itu.int/ITU-D/ict/statistics/at_glance/top15_broad.html

Ko, H. (2001). Internet uses and gratifications: Similarities and differences in motivations for using the Internet between the United States and Korea. In M. S. Roberts & R. L. King (Eds.), *International conference proceedings of the American Academy of Advertising* (pp. 44–50). Gainsville, FL: American Academy of Advertising.

Lam, C. K., & Tan, B. C. Y. (2001). The Internet is changing the music industry. *Communications of the ACM, 44*(8), 62–68.

Lee, H. C. (2000, November 27). Online radio hears static. *The Industry Standard,* 90–92.

Lee, H., O'Keefe, R. M., & Yun, K. (2003). The growth of broadband and electronic commerce in South Korea: Contributing factors. *The Information Society, 19,* 81–93.

Lefton, T. (2001, July 23). Still on their feet. *The Industry Standard,* 48–49.

Livingstone, S. (2003). On the challenges of cross-national comparative media research. *European Journal of Communication, 18,* 477–500.

Lubove, S. (2002, May 13). Streaming media. *Forbes,* pp. 50–52.

Miles, P., & Sakai, D. (2001). *Internet age broadcaster* (2nd ed.). Washington, DC: National Association of Broadcasters.

Neuendorf, K. A. (2002). *The content analysis guidebook.* Thousand Oaks, CA: Sage.

Pagani, M. (1999). Interactive television: A model of analysis of business economics dynamics. In S. Klein & B. Schneider (Eds.), *Proceedings of the Sixth Research Symposium on Emerging Electronic Markets* (pp. 5–30). Muenster, Germany: Arbetisberichte des Institute für Wirtschaftsinformatik.

Park, J. (2003). *The Internet content business in Korea* (Working paper). Seoul, Korea: Korea Culture and Tourism Policy Institute.

Pastore, M. (2001, December 19). It's diversify or die for online media firms. *Cyberatlas.* Retrieved August 7, 2002, from http://cyberatlas.internet.com/markets/advertising/article/0,,5941_943041,00.html

Perreault, W. D., Jr., & Leigh, L. E. (1989). Reliability of nominal data based on qualitative judgments. *Journal of Marketing Research, 26,* 135–148.

Picard, R. G. (2000). Changing business models of online content services: Their implications for multimedia and other content producers. *International Journal on Media Management, 2*(2), 60–68.

Rao, B. (2001). Broadband innovation and the customer experience imperative. *International Journal on Media Management, 3*(2), 56–65.

Ren, W., & Chan-Olmsted, S. (2003, July). *Radio business on the World Wide Web: An examination of the streaming clicks and bricks and Internet-based radio stations in the United States.* Paper presented at the Association for Education in Journalism and Mass Communication Annual Convention, Kansas City, MO.

Reynolds, T. (2003). *Broadband competition, penetration, speed and prices* (International Telecommunications Union Strategy and Policy Unit Presentation). Retrieved April 10, 2004, from: http://www.itu.int/osg/spu/presentations/2003/BoB-Brussels-NZ%20change.pdf

Rich, L. (2000, December 11). Entertainment sites squeezed by narrowband. *The Industry Standard,* 150–154.

Rojas, P. (2001, August 15). New habits die hard: College students have grown accustomed to getting online entertainment for free. What's Hollywood to do? *Red Herring,* pp. 49–53.

Rose, B., & Lenski, J. (2003). *Arbitron/Edison Media Research Internet and multimedia 10: The emerging digital consumer.* Retrieved September 2, 2003, from http://www.arbitron.com/downloads/Internet10_Summary.pdf

Rose, B., & Robin, L. (2002). *Internet 8: Advertising vs. subscription—Which streaming model will win?* Arbitron, Edison Media Research. Retrieved August 7, 2002, from http://www.arbitron.com/home.content.stm

Sloan, P. (2003, July). Sultan of stream. *Business 2.0,* 72–75.

Stacy, P. (2001, August–September). Multichannel cross-platform synergy is mega, yo. *Business 2.0,* 164–165.

Video prime-time players. (2002, January 28). *PC Magazine,* pp. 98–107.

Waterman, D. (2001). The economics of Internet TV: New niches vs. mass audiences. *Info, 3,* 215–229.

The World Factbook. (2002). *Central Intelligence Agency (CIA) of the United States.* Retrieved August 10, 2003, from http://www.cia.gov/ia/publications/factbook

Zook, M. A. (2001). Old hierarchies or new networks of centrality? The global geography of the Internet content market. *American Behavioral Scientist, 44,* 1679–1696.

Appendix. List of Leading United States and South Korean Webcasters in the Study

United States	Model	South Korea	Model
Video/Television			
1. FMiTV	CA	www.gembc.com (gaming)	BC
2. Bloomberg TV	BC	www.sdn.com (fashion)	CA
3. CNN	BC	www.ytn.co.kr (news)	CA
4. iFILM	CA	www.sportal.sbs.co.kr (sports)	BC
5. LikeTelevision	CA	www.clubwow.com (film)	CA
6. ESPN Video Highlights	BC	www.sbs.co.kr (TV network)BC	
7. Adventure TV	CA	www.kbs.co.kr (TV network)	BC
8. Windows Media	CA	www.imbc.com (TV network)	BC
9. Yahoo Music Videos	BC	www.naver.com (portal)	CA
10. Live Music Channels	CA	www.daum.net (portal)	CA
11. CBS SportsLine.com	BC	www.freechal.com (portal)	CA
12. Real Guide (RealOne Super Pass)	CA	www.cbs.co.kr (Christian)	BC
Audio/Radio			
1. WXPN.org	BC	www.zihasil.com	BC
2. Yahoo!Broadcast	CA	www.letscast.com	BC
3. MSN Music	CA	www.click2dj.com	BC
4. AOL Radio	CA	www.tubemusic.com	BC
5. Radio IO Eclectic	BC	www.nine4u.asiamusic.com	BC
6. Musicmatch	CA	www.sbs.co.kr (radio network)	BC
7. WQXR-FM 96.3	BC	www.imbc.com (radio network)	BC
8. KLOVE Radio	BC	www.stoneradio.com	BC
9. KPLU-FM 88.5	BC	www.letsmusic.com	BC
10. KING-FM 98.1	BC	www.24cast.net	CA
11. KFI640.com	BC	www.doobob.com	CA
12. KNAC.com	BC	www.kbs.co.kr (radio network)	BC

Note. CA = content aggregator model; BC = branded content model. In South Korea, if the video Webcaster and the radio Webcaster use the same domain name such as KBS (www.kbs.co.kr), the user chooses the TV network Web cast service or radio network Web caster service and the content is separate.

Online Business Models in Greece and the United Kingdom: A Case of Specialist Versus Generic and Public Versus Privately Owned Online News Media

Alexandros Arampatzis
Edge Hill University College, United Kingdom

This article selects 2 European Union countries (Greece and the United Kingdom) with significant differences in terms of the development of their Internet markets to survey and assess the business models some of the most established online news publishers in these 2 countries utilize. The study analyzes the current developments in the field of online subscriptions by differentiating between generic and specialist news publishers and between public news providers and privately controlled companies. Finally this article examines the impact of the new economy boom and bust on the operations of the online enterprises studied.

The diffusion of the Internet during the recent past has created a substantial industry of content creators in an online environment. However, and despite the dramatic growth in the number of online newspapers, it is still rather unclear whether this medium will become an economically viable business, and if ever so, how.

Although online news media are economic institutions engaged in the production and dissemination of content and operated by private parties for the purpose of generating profit, online newspaper economics appears to be complex. The convergence of the print newspaper and the Internet creates a new medium that must deal with two sets of market factors simultaneously. As Chyi and Sylvie (2000) said,

> Confusion still exists as to how online newspapers define a market between the local and the global, how they position themselves in the market, how they define the relationship between online and print products, and how they define competition and develop market strategies. How, in all, they can create profitable enterprises, which, at the end, mean viable and sustainable businesses. (p. 75)

This study attempts to describe the business models utilized by some of the most established Greek and U.K. online news organizations and explore the criteria and the reasons for choice of these particular models. Moreover, the study examines both public and state-controlled and privately owned online media companies to find the set of challenges they had to confront on the online business environment as well as how they see and position themselves in the marketplace.

The key questions to be addressed are the following:

1. Is there any uniformity in the business models utilized by the Greek and U.K. online media organizations?
2. Are public service new media providers in an advantageous position compared to privately owned ones? If so how do they take advantage of that and how do they assess their role?
3. Do news Web sites that target a niche audience find it easier to charge their customers? How do generic news publishers try to overcome the abundance of free content on the Web before introducing charging policies?
4. How far did the euphoria around the new economy in the years before 2000 influence the developments in online news publishers and how far did the demise of the new economy impact on their business operations?

The structure of this article is as follows: The literature that examines new economy and online business models issues is reviewed and followed by a brief methodology section. The part after that involves the description and

Address correspondence to Alexandros Arampatzis, Edge Hill University College, ST Helens Road, L39 4QP, Ormskirk, United Kingdom. E-mail: arampata@edgehill.ac.uk

assessment of the business models used by the online publications studied, with a particular emphasis on the significance of the introduction of subscription services. As the study separates between state-owned and privately controlled new media firms, the analysis of the position and the role of each follows. The penultimate part of this study looks at the impact of the new economy debate on the Web companies examined. Finally, the study outlines the research conclusions by summarizing the main points made.

Literature Review

New Economy

Because the discussion of business models for media firms falls within the broader theme of media economics, the exploration of business models for online news media is tightly connected with the so-called new economy. In fact, it seems that the new economy debate, underpinned and facilitated by a couple of technological developments (mainly digitization and convergence), alongside all the myths, hyperboles, and inflated and realistic projections that surrounded the economic environment between 1997 and 2000, was one of the main driving forces that, to a certain extent, determined the current shape of the online news media industry.

The digital new economy issue split scholars into opposing camps. Some argued that this, although an important development, is merely a next step within a series of technological innovations. Others claimed that a radically new and very promising epoch in the media landscape in general and media economics in particular, had dawned.

In the early days of euphoria, the new economy enthusiasts were eager to produce bold assertions. Kelly (1998) wrote that "it is possible that the gauges are all broken, but it is much more likely that the world is turning upside down" (p. 4). He went on to explain, focusing on the field of media, "Communication—which in the end is what the digital economy and media are all about—is not just a sector of the economy. Communication is the economy" (p. 4).

Along the same lines, Goldhaber (1997) argued that the Web and the Net can be viewed as spaces in which we increasingly live our lives and therefore the economic laws we live under have to be natural to this new space.

Commentators went so far as to suggest that in a pure attention economy money has no essential function, no real role to play, while companies of all kinds will have less definite and fixed structures because they will be structured not by physical walls and buildings, but through the Net itself and more and more of their pro-

ceedings will be done in the full glare of Web attention, as temporary and rapidly reforming projects.

Nevertheless, and especially after the initial enthusiasm about the new economic environment had withered, largely as a result of the deflation of the value of new-economy-related stocks, theory shifted its focus and employed a more modest approach toward digitization and its impact on the economy and new media economics in particular. Picard (2000), among others, argued that the latest advances in technology have brought significant changes in areas such as content distribution, presentation, and consumption, but traditional economics concepts such as supply and demand for a product are as salient today as ever.

According to Picard (1989), the challenge for new media businesses lies in finding a means of obtaining and maintaining sufficient usage and turnover so that it is not rejected by users, entrepreneurs, or financiers. Consequently, the focus of the attention of the new media economics theory was centred on the notion of value creation, because "technologies and their associated applications will succeed only if the market believes that they create value that is currently absent today" (Picard, 2000, p. 61).

Business Models

Once the notion of value generation (for the consumer) prevailed in industry and theory alike, the exploration and analysis of the various business models available became one of the favorite topics of both researchers and business executives. This is reasonable as the business models are the essential mechanisms employed by businesses to identify the added value of a given product and outline the ways of exploring this value.

In terms of modern communications, "business models need to account for the vital resources of production and distribution technologies, content creation or acquisition, and recovery of costs for creating, assembling and presenting the content" (Picard, 2000, p. 76). Consequently, according to the same scholar, a business model as such embraces the fundamental concept of the value chain, that is, the value that is added to a product or service in each step of its acquisition, transformation, management, marketing, sales, and distribution.

The value chain concept for products and services is now well established in business literature, where it was widely embraced after its initial exploration by Porter (1985). This value chain concept is particularly important in understanding market behavior exactly because it places the emphasis on the value created for the customer who ultimately makes consumption decisions. It seems widely accepted that if one cannot articulate that value, one cannot properly manage and market any product or service.

What needs to be emphasized, though, is the importance of distinguishing between business strategies and business models, as the latter refer directly to fundamental elements, the cornerstone of a business, whereas strategy refers to a set of plans and decisions that help a firm realize its goals and objectives (Karlof, 1989; Smith, 1990).

> Business models are understood and created by stepping back from the business activity itself to look at its bases and the underlying characteristics that make commerce in the product or service possible. A business model involves the conception of how the business operates, its underlying foundations, and the exchange activities and financial flows upon which it can be successful. (Picard, 2000, p. 62)

One of the key studies in the field of business models for online content providers was conducted by Mings and White (2000). Drawing primarily on reports and analyses in the U.S. print and online industry press, the authors identified four basic business models to which online newspapers had turned to achieve profitability: subscriptions, advertisements, transactions, and partnerships with other content providers (what the authors called the *bundled model*).

This study acknowledges the inherent difficulties involved in charging for online news (due to the "information for free" culture within which the Web developed) and suggests that online news publishers need either to first attract online readers with free information and then charge for access once the paper has a sufficient mass of readers or provide most of the content for free and charge only for premium news and information.

Therefore, although a traditional revenue model for print publications has been roughly a split of 20% versus 80% between subscription and advertising income, respectively, this analogy, in the majority of online publications is impossible to be transferred on the Web due to users' reluctance to pay a fee to access specific content because they already pay fees for connection (Mings & White, 2000). In addition, it is commonplace among online news publishers (see also research findings analysis later) that measuring users' willingness to pay and devising accurate and attractive pricing schemes is almost impossible because users, when asked how much they would be willing to pay for accessing content on the Web, would invariably choose the lowest possible price or nothing at all.

However, the same study cites the example of the *Wall Street Journal* to illustrate how specialist news publishers find it easier to identify the value of the product they offer on the Web and therefore can charge for it. However, the authors concluded by arguing that "it is not yet possible to make definitive pronouncements about the success of a subscription model or different implementations of it, or of models that include subscriptions in a mix of revenue strategies" (Mings & White, 2000, p. 54).

Exploring the growing use of subscriptions by online news providers, a study conducted by the Poynter Institute (2002) surveys the variations that have sprung out of the subscription model. According to this study, the subscription model variations are the following:

- Free content; advertisement supported; paid subscription content verticals and paid premium content.

This subscription type is gaining favor among Web news publishers that wish to charge for content, but fear that charging for all or most of that content would be risky. The majority of content on such sites is available free (with or without required user registration) so that it can attract large audiences and therefore become appealing to advertisers, but a minority of high-value or premium content has a price tag that can hopefully bring in cash revenues.

- Free content; advertisement supported; ad-free access paid subscriptions.

This variation entails offering two versions of a site. One version is free access, and includes advertising (often intrusive Web ads such as pop-ups and pop-unders, interstitials, and large animated or flash banners). The other version of the site is for those willing to pay a subscription fee; this version is free from advertisements. A variation of this model is represented by the Web site of *Le Monde*, the French publication, since April 2002.

- Paid subscriptions; no or very limited free content; no advertising.

Although few Web sites can live on subscription fees alone, some can afford to do so. Without exception, news-oriented Web sites that employ this approach are those that enjoy a strong brand and publish content that is valuable to many people and cannot be found elsewhere.

ConsumerReports.org, the Web site of the venerable consumer products review publication, offers a limited amount of free content, as most of its articles and reviews are behind a subscription wall, yet it boasts 800,000 registered subscribers (ConsumerReports.org Web site). "Few mainstream media sites offer anything narrow enough or deep enough to support a subscription-only model,' Coats (2002) explained.

- Paid subscriptions; no or very limited free content; advertising accepted.

Sites adopting this variation of the subscription model typically offer a very limited amount of content for free, putting most of their wares behind a subscription wall. Although they accept advertising, only Web sites with a substantial subscription database (e.g., the *Wall Street Journal*) can hope to attract sufficient numbers of advertisers. These firms tend to view their Web sites as a new line of business and their primary concern is to avoid cannibalization of the print product.

- Free content to in-market Internet users; paid subscriptions for out-of-market.

This is an interesting variation instituted in the United Kingdom by only the Times.co.uk so far, the online edition of the *Times* of London. According to this online revenue-generation strategy, Internet users in the circulation or broadcast area of a media entity are given free access to its Web site. Those outside of the area are required to pay a fee for access.

Thus, in the case of thetimes.co.uk, a subscription fee will be charged to users coming to the site from outside the United Kingdom, whereas British users can visit the site for free. The rationale behind this variation is that, in the case of the *Times* of London again, it helps define the audience primarily to U.K. users, making the site more attractive to advertisers who seek to reach only U.K. customers. It also helps reduce bandwidth costs due to the loss of overseas users and also brings in some subscription revenue from overseas (Poynter Institute Web site, 2002). Nevertheless, and despite the apparent advantages of this variation, some publications will always be reluctant to follow this route because the danger of losing their international leverage looms.

- Regional content providers cooperate in charging scheme; everyone charges.

This rather uncommon variation of the subscription model is based on an agreement (cartel-like) between Web publishers in a confined geographic region, or within a topic niche, to charge for specified content areas or services of their sites. Payment can be a subscription fee that gains access to all Web sites, or microtransaction payments to individual sites. Bringing together Web publishers is a fairly new phenomenon, largely born out of frustration over free content models not being profitable and the drying up of online advertising in 2001 and 2002.

As far as another prominent online business model is concerned, advertising, Mings and White (2000) illustrated the difficulties online news publishers face in making advertisements a steady and profitable stream of revenue. This is mainly because, as opposed to other mass media, online news services "face the challenge of 'narrowcasting,' with exceedingly high costs per thousands reached" (p. 74). Moreover, online advertisements "can be easily ignored and there is currently no consensus on rates for online advertising displays" (p. 74). Although the authors acknowledged the growth potential of classified advertisements (a traditional domain of print media) on the Web, they argued that "currently online news publishers seeking to generate revenues from classified advertising are being challenged on two fronts; notably by specialist online classified operations and by mass market online auction sites such as eBay" (p. 74).

Along the same lines, e-commerce carried out through news Web sites (whereby the news Web site operates as an intermediate between a buyer and a seller) is also problematic when issues around pricing, security, and ease of use are considered, and therefore Mings and White (2000) concluded that "given the complex challenges for online newspaper publishers trying to turn a profit, no single economic model or particular mix of models can be entirely suitable. A successful model for online newspapers will be a mix of revenue models" (p. 87).

Picard (2000) arrived at a similar conclusion, after conducting a historical review of what he called failed or abandoned business models for online content services (notably videotext, paid Internet, free Web, Internet/Web ad push). He stressed the fact that the current dominant business models for online news providers are based on advertising displayed on portals, which in turn is "based on newspaper- and magazine-style advertising in which readers are brought into contact with advertisers' messages while they make other use of the pages" (p. 69). Picard moved on to outline his view of future profit-generating trends and prospects for online content publishers, by introducing the digital portal model, which is a system that will allow users to access a variety of multimedia content and services from a variety of sources, alongside advertisements, and pay for it either via subscription or a micropayment mechanism. Yet, partly due to technological and resource limitations, this is a concept that has not materialized to a reasonably large degree yet.

Overall, what is rather striking in the literature review about online media economics and business models is that the overwhelming emphasis of scholars has been placed on the industry-level analysis and the exploration of generic concepts. What is missing is the application of these concepts and theoretical observations on the firm level to investigate how media firms respond to changes in technology and how they face challenges (and perhaps shape the future itself) in their revenue-generation operations.

Questions about individual companies are important because they provide a clear picture of market dynamics and the process that lead company executives to make economic choices and choices about the way their businesses will be structured, the activities they will undertake and the performance that is subsequently produced. Analyses at the market or industry levels provide collective pictures of media but through their focus on the overall situation miss the pressures, constraints and choices faced by individual firms. (Picard, 2002, p. 114)

This article attempts to do exactly this: Draw on the business practices and strategic decisions of some of the most prominent Greek and U.K. online news media to determine the business models they opted to utilize to respond to the new economy challenges.

Other studies that focus on the firm level in particular include the one conducted by Saksena and Hollifield (2002), who found that newspapers' innovation management processes were generally haphazard and that industry executives should be better prepared in the future to manage innovation. Also Kung (2001) examined the way BBC News Online responded to the Internet, against the framework of Christensen's work on incumbent failure in the face of disruptive technological change (Christensen, 1997). The study found that although there were ample grounds for BBC News Online to conform with Christensen's failure framework, BBC News Online has in fact flourished into a market leader primarily because of the autonomy, clarity of brief, and freedom of implementation the organization enjoyed fairly early on. Along the same lines, BBCi benefits from strong executive support, generous resources, a supportive underlying cultural and cognitive paradigm, and a good intrinsic match between public service status and an Internet news service.

Finally, the latest literature has started decomposing business models into their atomic elements (Afuah & Tucci, 2001; Hamel, 2000; Peterovic, Kittl, & Teksten, 2001; Rayport & Jaworski, 2001; Weill, 2001). By and large, the existing literature adopts a distinction of business models to revenue- and product-specific, business actor and revenue-specific, and marketing-specific.

In terms of the revenue and product aspects, Rappa (2001) and Tapscott (1996) provided a taxonomy of e-business models rather than an explanation of what elements such models contain. Both authors concentrated on revenue- or product-specific aspects, whereas examining the business actor and network aspects, Timmers (1998) provided a taxonomy in which he classified business models according to their degree of innovation and their functional integration. Gordijin and Akkermans (2001) drew a richer and more rigorous business model framework, "which is based on a generic value oriented ontology specifying what is an e-business model" (p. 24). This framework even allows the graphical representation and understanding of value flows among the several actors of a model.

Finally, in his analysis of marketing-specific aspects, Hamel (2000) identified four main business model compo-

nents that are related to each other and are decomposed into different subelements. The main contribution of this methodology, as well as the one of Rayport and Jaworski (2001) is that it takes a view of the overall picture of a firm. Peterovic et al. (2001) divided a business model into submodels, which describe the logic of a business system for creating value that lies behind the actual processes.

Research Methodology

The basic research questions are framed in such a way that call for a descriptive and exploratory approach (as opposed to an explanatory one). Consequently, descriptive and exploratory case studies were chosen as the best suited research methods to address the aforementioned questions.

As Yin (1984) explained, research questions formed with a "how" or "why" and focusing on contemporary events (and what is more contemporary than the analysis of the selection of business models by new media companies?) are ideally approached by conducting case studies.

The case studies were selected in such a way that: (a) they include businesses that constitute the online channel of an established and outstanding analog medium, (b) include media outlets only with an online presence, and (c) represent a wide range of the observable online content providers (newspapers, TV and radio, portal), which has the potential to assist in drawing conclusions referring to the online content provider industry as a whole.

In addition, the selection of case studies from both Greece and the United Kingdom serves a twofold end: First, it allows for a rigorous research of the business models and the consequent survey of the relevant developments in these two countries. Interesting comparisons will be drawn, attempting to place and analyze issues into the wider context of the north versus south European online publishing realities.[1]

For instance, how does the relatively high Internet usage in the United Kingdom compared with the poor corresponding statistics for Greece influence an online publisher's overall strategy?[2] Given that the Internet is still in a premature state in Greece, to what extent do Greek online news providers mimic the developments in the more advanced—as far as online publishing is concerned—Britain?

Moreover, the study opted to explore the state-owned online media enterprises in Greece and the United Kingdom. This is because examining ERT.gr against the BBCi will offer a set of opportunities to explore the similarities and the differences of the Web outlets of the state broadcasters in these two countries, which are, by and large, occupying the two ends of the Internet market on a pan-European level. The British market is a mature northern European Internet market, with a significant diffusion of the medium in the wider population, as opposed to the Greek Internet market, which is still at an infant level, with the majority of the population demonstrating a limited familiarity with this new medium.

Finally, the units of analysis in each case study involve key individuals in each organization (notable managing directors and editors, with whom in-depth interviews were conducted) and organization structures. Miles Palmer, the managing director of the BBC.co.uk; and Myra Hunt, the acting editor of BBCi, World Service were interviewed, as well as the managing director of the Independent Digital, Richard Withey; and the publisher of the Economist.com, Paul Rossi. As far as Greek publications are concerned, interviews were carried out with George Zafolias, the managing director of Naftemporiki.gr; Despina Gabriel, assistant managing director of In.gr; and Christos Stathakopoulos, the director of ERT.gr.

Given the qualitative nature of most of the data sought, triangulation was one of the most important means of increasing the validity of the research by substantiating the findings. Toward this aim, articles from the business press, company press releases, and investor presentations as well as reports from several investment banks were also examined.

What follows is a brief presentation of the Web sites selected for the purposes of this study.

1. The Independent Online: www.independent.co.uk.

One of the first British newspapers to go online (1996) and one of the online pioneers on a worldwide scale, the Web presence of the Independent constitutes the ideal case study for the purposes of this research, primarily because the publication introduced a subscription policy and business model for its Web users in April 2003. This was by and large seen as one of the most pioneering development in the generic news publishers industry (see later). The Web site currently attracts 1 million unique users and 23 million page impressions a month.

2. The Economist Online: www.economist.com.

The specialized nature of the content of Economist.com is the prime factor that made it extremely interesting and relevant to this research. By targeting a niche area, the Economist Online appears to have a significant competitive advantage compared to its generic news rivals, as specialist news publishers find it easier to identify the added value of their products and as a result charge for it.

The Economist.com site introduced content charging schemes before the generic news publishers even started contemplating such an undertaking. As a result it claims to operate a sustainable business (it broke even last year).

3. BBC Online: www.bbc.co.uk.

Much advertised as "the UK's number one digital destination," and one of the most popular in Europe (it boasts 6.5 million unique users monthly), the BBC news Web site is a unique case study. Its uniqueness lies in the fact that BBCi (BBC interactive) is a state- and public-funded organization that nevertheless operates within a fully competitive environment. The main challenge is to explore how this impacts on the performance of the site.

4. Naftemporiki: www.naftemporiki.gr.

Among the 10 most popular Greek news Web sites, Naftemporiki.gr is the Web outlet of one of the most established financial newspapers in Athens, Greece. One of the reasons I chose this online publication as a case study is because it constitutes the Greek counterpart of the Economist.com and as such it will allow me to draw valuable conclusions with regard to how online news publishers of a specialist nature fare on the Web in these two countries.

5. IN.GR: www.in.gr.

In.gr is the first Internet portal of general interest to go online in Greece and currently the most visited Greek news Web site (with more than 1 million page impressions monthly). Reportedly, when the Web site was launched (in 1999, at the height of the dot-com boom) it opted to invest heavily in both the development and the promotion of the site. As a result, In.gr was strongly affected by the bust of the new economy. This is the only online news organization studied that is not supported by an established parent organization.

6. ERT: www.ert.gr.

This case study involves the assessment of the official Web site of the Greek state broadcaster, ERT. Ert.gr has indeed a similar function (and remit) to that of the BBC; both being public service broadcasters, they do not operate within a strictly commercial context and as a result they can afford to concentrate their energy and resources on the quality of their provision. The source of funding for both is the taxpayers' money. But what are the differences in the operation of ERT compared to that of BBCi?

Research Findings

Commercial News Web Sites

Among the most significant findings of this study is that both the Greek and the U.K. news providers examined demonstrate a common pattern as far as their business models are concerned: Irrespective of whether they targeted a niche market or provided generic news content, they employed a similar set of business models: a mixture of subscription services, advertising, and syndication. What differed was the degree of the importance each organization placed on each stream of revenue.

Although the introduction of subscription services appears to constitute the single, relatively recent most important development on all the sites studied, still, all managing directors interviewed (with the exception of Ert.gr and BBCi, the public service Web sites that do not carry any advertising at all) cited advertising as the main source of their Web sites' revenue.

It is indicative that currently about 65% of the Economist Web site income, 55% of the Independent Digital and Naftemporiki.gr revenue, and about 90% of In.gr comes from advertising. However, all the media executives interviewed said that subscriptions are growing fast and they estimate that this will become their main stream of revenue in the near future (yet, they were reluctant to provide any evidence or figures to back up their statement).

Subscriptions

The commercial news Web sites examined present their users with a variety of subscription packages to better meet their needs. The main subscription schemes involve individual article sales, monthly, semester, and annual subscriptions. Only In.gr, the Greek Web site that operates as a news portal, is service-based as far as its subscription services are concerned. The site charges its users for the creation of a professional e-mail account, the building of a Web site using the site's Web authoring tools, and for access to a sophisticated archive of financial news information (see Table 1).

When describing the subscribers' profiles, the managing directors of Independent Digital, Economist.com, and Naftemporiki.gr argue that monthly subscriptions target primarily students and academics, whereas the annual subscriptions are popular with people who use the Web site as a business and professional tool. Individual article purchases are carried out by people on a random basis and tend to be based in regions outside the circulation area of the print product.

Having made the crucial decision to introduce subscriptions, the Web sites examined were confronted with the challenge of appropriately pricing their product. Online publishers had to ensure that the introduction of subscription-based services would not result in the loss of readers to other Web sites that offered similar content for free. In light of that, the choice of the right pricing policy is perceived to be of the utmost importance (P. Rossi, personal communication, June 22, 2003; R. Withey, personal communication, April 12, 2003). This did prove to be an arduous task for many, with rather unclear results.

The managing directors interviewed said that they employed the usual market research tools to gauge how much their readers would pay before attaching a price tag to their news services. They did surveys, reader panels, and focus groups, but none appeared to provide useful and constructive feedback.

Of course, what everybody tells you if you ask them whether they would pay for an online news product is "No" So we had to ask them if they had to pay something for our product and service, what would that be? We presented them with some indicative prices and they always took the lowest. So with these kind of surveys you usually end up with a very odd piece of feedback, because people are always reluctant to pay money for something they believe they can receive for free. (P. Rossi, personal communication, June 22, 2003)

Table 1. Online Business Models

	Currently	*Future*
The Independent	Subscriptions (premium content) Advertising (emphasis on promotion) Content syndication	Charge overseas users
The Economist	Subscriptions Advertising (emphasis on promotions) Content syndication	
The BBC	Content syndication	Subscriptions for overseas users
IN.gr	Subscriptions (financial services) Advertising Content syndication Site development services	Subscriptions for content
Naftemporiki.gr	Subscriptions Advertising Content syndication	
ERT.gr	Content syndication	Advertising Subscriptions but not for content, only for services

To overcome this problem, the online publishers studied had to devise a pricing strategy based primarily on speculation rather than a pragmatic evidence of what their readers were prepared to pay. Drawing on their experiences on how the print subscription packages work and what their online competitors were charging assisted this speculation.

Rossi admitted in his interview that the starting point for the Economist.com charging policy was the print publication:

> The magazine is 135 dollars a year to subscribe to. We thought this is expensive for the Web so we launched the Internet edition at 49 dollars a year. I suspect that at the time it was 49 dollars because the *Wall Street Journal* was 49 dollars also. There was a strong element of comparison and personal guess involved. (P. Rossi, personal communication, June 22, 2003)

At present, the Independent Digital charges £1 pay-as-you-go access to one item for 24 hr, £5 monthly subscription per package, £30 annual subscription per package, and £60 annual subscription for access to all its premium content. The Economist.com charges its users $59 for an annual subscription, $19 for a monthly subscription, and $2.95 for individual article purchases (see Table 2).

The attempt to attract as many subscribers as possible (in the already small Greek market) is reflected in the charging policies adopted by In.gr, where prices have been kept to a minimum. The news portal currently charges its customers 35 euros for a professional e-mail account (20 MB storage space) and 25 euros monthly for access to its sophisticated financial news portfolio. Web site construction services are priced on a bespoke basis.

Nevertheless, the prices charged rise significantly in the case of Naftemporiki.gr. Being a news Web site with a strong business and finance news focus, it draws the majority of its users from businesses and large corporations. Naftemporiki.gr currently charges 75 euros for a 3-month subscription to the print edition (this guarantees access to the Web site content also), 150 euros for 6 months, and 300 euros annually (see Table 2).

The Content Challenge

The views of the media managers interviewed appear to be in line with the growing theory trend, according to which the key to charging for content on the Web lies in identifying its value. In light of this, new media scholars (Rappa, 2001) and industry professionals (M. Palmer, personal communication, April 27, 2003) argue that it is far more challenging for generic news publishers to charge for their online content. This is on the grounds that the constant proliferation of free online news offerings makes it difficult—if not impossible—for them to identify the value of their product and therefore charge for it.

On the other hand, news publishers that target a niche market (e.g., the Economist.com and Naftemporiki.gr in this article's case studies) find themselves in an advantageous situation as their online content has some intrinsic value for a very distinct segment of the market (notably those interested in business and financial news in the examined publications).

Paul Rossi, the publisher of Economist.com, elaborated:

> What differentiates us from the competition and adds value to our online product is the level of clever analysis we provide on news and events around the world. One very big part of the Economist is the perceived value of the brand. Therefore to take something and make it free at one space, but with 100 pounds subscription at another space would be an oddity. (personal communication, June 22, 2003)

Along the same lines, the managing director of Naftemporiki.gr, George Zafolias (personal communication, June 22, 2003), explained, "As our print product is primarily subscription-based, we decided to charge our online users for access to our archives and PDF formats of the print edition right from the start."

However, the fact that specialist news publishers find it easier to charge for their content did not prove to be a factor strong enough to allow them to charge for the totality of their online provision. Currently, Naftemporiki.gr has placed only its archive, PDF formats of the print edition and access to a specialized portfolio of stock exchange

Table 2. Online Charging Schemes

	Annual Subscription	Monthly	Pay as You Go
Independent Digital	£30 per package/£60 for access to all premium content	None	£1 per article
The Economist Online	$69	$29	$2.95 per article
Naftemporiki.gr	300€	150€	75€
In.gr	25€ for a professional e-mail account	25€ for access to stock-exchange portfolio	none
BBCi	none	none	none
ERT.gr	none	none	none

news and services behind a subscription wall. The rest of the site is available free and supported by advertising. In the case of Economist.com, 15% of the site remains free, asking its users to pay for the remaining 85% of the Web site materials. "We say to our readers: if you want to have a read, here is a sample of our site," said Paul Rossi (personal communication, June 22, 2003).

In the case of the generic news publishers studied, all interviewees agreed that a piece of content on its own has no value whatsoever. Value is attached to it according to the ways you deliver it and what it does when you deliver it.

Independent Digital Managing Director Richard Withey explained:

> This is why we have carefully chosen the content that is unique to us to charge for: the crossword, the opinion people, the archive. All of that is unique to us. Nobody else has the Independent archive, nobody else has the Independent crossword, and nobody else has Robert Fisk or some other of our commentators. (personal communication, April 12, 2003)

The news organizations examined appeared to follow the suggestion of Coats (2002) that online generic publications should not overlook areas such as their columnists and other personality-driven pieces. They have tapped into the strengths of their opinion pieces and their columnists. Most important, they avoided launching full subscription models as they felt that charging a fairly heavy up-front subscription before one can even visit the site is a mistake (D. Gabriel, personal communication, June 22, 2003; R. Withey, personal communication, April 12, 2003).

It is probably due to the painstaking selection of the content they put behind a subscription wall that the charging schemes of the generic news publishers studied show a growing degree of success. The Independent Digital, for instance, reported that in the first 6 weeks after it launched the subscription site, 4,000 people bought content from it,[3] of whom about 400 people used the pay-as-you go option to buy individual articles. These figures were far above the expectations of the site's executives (R. Withey, personal interview, April 12, 2003).

Why Now? The Timing Question

According to the responses of the media executives that were interviewed as part of this study, there are various reasons why the introduction of charging policies took place, almost as a whole, in spring 2003.

First, they all felt that there is an increasing trend now developing for charging for content. They argue that from a cultural point of view the market was ready to accommodate these developments, but, nevertheless, none cited any pragmatic evidence of that. Richard Withey from the Independent Digital and Despina Gabriel from In.gr did say, though, that they felt they were increasingly operating under the intense pressure of the board of directors.

Second, the factor that appears to have influenced them significantly is that one of the competitive players did make a start after all, and that was the online section of the Independent:

> The Independent has done it before some others because we are small enough to risk it. If I was publishing the Guardian with the 100 million page impressions, I would be nervous about charging for anything. We have a very small cost base, we are not very far from breaking even, we could even break even this year, certainly next year, and this is because our cost base is so small. (R. Withey, personal communication, April 12, 2003)

Although exact figures with regard to the firm's cost base were not disclosed (as they fell under the firm's confidentiality agreement), the Independent Digital running costs appear to be relatively small indeed. The online department is run with six full-time employees (editorial and technical staff included).

Finally, one of the main reasons online news sites decided to embrace subscriptions as an additional revenue source is based on a significant technical development: Key improvements in the technical infrastructure for processing online transactions emerged, greatly facilitating the whole process.

In the not so distant past, the up-front cost of an investment on an online transaction platform (essentially an e-commerce platform) was almost prohibitive. The result was that online publishers had to undertake an up-front billing investment, which then they had to set against the ultimate success of the service. Yet, some of the online publishers studied managed to address this problem by teaming up with telecommunications companies and therefore achieving economies of scale.

The Independent Digital even had the setup of the installation mechanism delivered at very little cost.

> BT recently launched the Click-and-buy software and agreed to provide this to us almost for free. They do have a nominal charge for the technical development on each side, and we asked them to waive that because we thought we are big enough a site for this initiative. (R. Withey, personal communication, April 12, 2003)

Moreover, one of the distinct advantages of this payment system (and a breakthrough the industry long expected) is that as well as using credit or debit cards, users can also put the micropayment on their phone bills.

Future Plans for Charging

A consistent trend emerged among the online news organizations studied, which points toward two sets of developments in the future in the field of online business models: (a) delivery of paid-for content on various media platforms (primarily mobile phones), and (b) the charging of foreign-based visitors.

The exponential growth of the use of mobile phones in Greece[4] points to a significant revenue stream for the Greek commercial online news providers examined. The Independent Digital also plans to strengthen its provision on the mobile market, whereas Paul Rossi (personal communication, June 22, 2003) believes that the content of the Economist.com is not very well suited for small mobile phone screens, as it is very "wordy."

The second potential area of development involves foreign-based visitors and is based on the principle of offering free content to in-market Internet users and paid subscriptions for those out of market (see earlier).

Online news publishers argue that there is a straightforward commercial reason for that and it is based on the premise that advertisers are not interested in reaching that sector of their visitors that come to the site from outside the site's geographical base (associated with country boundaries). "In other words you are providing a site for people who never pay you at the cost of people who do support you by buying the paper," says Withey (personal communication, April 12, 2003).

Similar plans were outlined by Naftemporiki.gr and In.gr also, for Greeks that visit the sites from abroad. All executives interviewed estimate that about 50% of their traffic comes from visitors based abroad.

Public Service Broadcaster Business Models

The different structure and operation of the public service online news services, as opposed to the commercial news sites, dictated the separate treatment of BBCi and ERT.gr for the purposes of this article.

The fundamental difference lies in the funding of public service online news organizations. The BBC Web site has two streams of funding. One comes from the Foreign and Commonwealth Office, which funds the World Service, whereas the other is taxpayers' money through the license fee.

The public funding of the BBC is reflected in the business model the organization has opted for. Miles Palmer (personal communication, April 27, 2003), the managing director of the organization's online operations, emphasizes that its public nature allows the BBC to afford to overlook the money-making operations. "There is no business model as such [for us]. Our 'business model' is to spend money. We get a grant of money that we decide what we're going to spend it on. So there is no external income to support the content or the Directorate," he said.

However, the absence of institutional pressures in generating revenue does not actually mean that BBCi operates within a context of liberty as far as its business operations are concerned. A set of criteria applies to determine the ways the public money should be spent.

According to Myra Hunt, the BBCi editor-in-chief:

> We don't have a bottom line where we have to make money, however we do have to deliver value for money, we do have to have impact, we do have KPIs (key performance indicators) that we have to achieve, and we also, wherever possible, should be exploiting our content and possibly the technical infrastructure that we have through one of the BBC's commercial infrastructures which is BBC world-wide. (personal communication, April 12, 2003)

During the in-depth interviews, BBCi executives revealed that an ongoing debate takes place within the organization that involves charging online users who access the BBC content from overseas. The rationale behind this lies in the fact that the provision of content (be it broadcasting or online) for people outside the United Kingdom is beyond the responsibilities of the BBC, as defined by the charter that sets out the organization's remits.

> The reason we anticipate charging users who access our site and view our programs from abroad is because providing streaming audio is very expensive. We want to prevent people from getting something for free that the UK user is paying for, said Hunt. (personal communication, April 12, 2003)

The other pillar of the BBC's revenue-making operation involves syndication of content to other news providers, a model similar to the one used by the established BBC radio stations, which syndicate content (particularly World Service radio content) to radio stations around the world (M. Palmer, personal interview, April 27, 2003).

Along the same lines falls the function of the Web site of the Greek state-owned broadcaster, ERT. ERT.gr receives its funding directly through taxation and these state subsidies allow the organization to list profitability further down its priorities. However, and contrary to BBC's function, ERT's TV and radio channels do compete with commercial broadcast players on an equal basis and as a result they do broadcast advertising messages and opt for profit at the end of each financial year.

Similar rules apply for the organization's online operations. ERT.gr, unlike BBCi, is free to carry advertising on its Web pages. Therefore, according to the organization's initial planning, the Web site had to become viable financially after 3 years of operation. Yet, at present, this goal has not been achieved because bureaucratic constraints and the complex and sometimes irrational division of the various departments into separate directories with overlapping responsibilities held back the efficient rollout of the service (C. Stathakopoulos, personal communication, July 2, 2003).

At present, ERT.gr uses only syndication to make money, as technical deficiencies have made it impossible to launch advertising on the site. The organization plans to insert banner advertisements on its pages but rules out the possibility of subscription services, especially news related, considering them to be beyond its remit as a public service broadcaster.

Result: How the BBCi and ERT.gr View Themselves

The luxury of conducting business outside of commercial imperatives is indeed demonstrated in the objectives of both BBCi and ERT.gr.

In the case of BBCi the commercial activities are on the margins:

> As we currently stand as an organization our reason d'etre is not to make lots of money, it is to deliver news and information and have an impact. The commercial activity is at the margins. Primarily what we are looking for is cost recovery: flowing into the business and offsetting costs. (M. Palmer, personal communication, April 27, 2003)

In addition to that, BBCi executives stated that they are very much interested in providing services for the online user. The most notable example of that is the recent launch of the BBC research service, which was initiated partly because according to the BBC's remit, the organization "needs to be a trusted guide to the Internet." In terms of the impact of this initiative, the latest figures show that 50% of news users in the United Kingdom use Google, whereas only 5% use BBC's search facility. This, however, was considered to be quite a satisfactory and promising figure for the future by BBC executives.

Finally, BBCi endeavors to assist as much as possible the digital take up of services in the United Kingdom. "If there is anything the BBC can try to do to help drive the digital take up, we would do it," Hunt (personal communication, April 12, 2003) said.

In the same line lie the objectives of ERT.gr as these are outlined both by official organization documentation and its executives. ERT.gr sees itself as a driver of the Greek Internet and strives to become a trusted source of news for the Greek online user. In addition to that, ERT.gr positions itself as keen to explore new and innovative ways of interactive storytelling right from the start (C. Stathakopoulos, personal communication, July 2, 2003).

The New Economy Debate

This article aims, among other things, to examine both sides of the impact of the new economy on the online news organizations studied: the impact of the new economy rhetoric in the years before 1999 on the creation and development of the sites, as well as the impact of the demise of the new economy on the operations of these organizations.

A factor that clearly emerged during the in-depth interviews with online media executives is that the rules of the economy have not changed. Companies still need to make a profit to reinvest in a profitable business. Those that followed the old business model, the old approach, and were not prepared to invest too heavily up front were those who benefitted most.

In terms of the impact of the euphoric Internet years on the creation and development of online news enterprises, this came primarily from consultants and media analysts who were keen to present an inflated picture of the Internet news market.

The Economist's Paul Rossi said:

> We had a lot of consultants, we had a lot of internal discussions about what other people were doing and an internal recognition that there was a space that we had to fill. We are 50% owned by Pearson so we looked at what the FT.com does and we were also looking at what Time, Business Week, Fortune, Forbes were doing. (personal communication, June 22, 2203)

Independent's Richard Withey and Despina Gabriel from In.gr also cited the influence of consultants as a major drive for entering the online news industry in the first place:

> The analysts and the consultants should take a lot of blame for what happened really. Independent News and Media enjoyed, for a while, a great flowering in its share price on the basis of the so-called new economy. When I first came here, I gave my first talk to analysts for the half-year results and the share price went up. That's how ludicrous it was. (R. Withey, personal communication, April 12, 2003)

Rossi (personal communication, June 22, 2003) recalled the time when consultants hired by Economist.com suggested that the organization should create a brand new payment mechanism online that would charge users in "Economist dollars," an idea that was finally dismissed by the board of directors on the grounds that "real dollars exist already."

All the cases studied for this article revealed that when the bubble burst they were forced to scale down their operations, reduce the cost base by laying off staff, and reorganize the maintenance of the site. However, surprisingly enough, only one of the online enterprises studied (In.gr) admitted that the scaling down of operations took place on a huge scale, impacting considerably on the financial viability of the organization. In.gr employed 120 people in 1999. This number is 14 employees on a full-time basis. The Economist.com, BBCi, and the Independent Digital were also forced to reduce their staffing (although they would not reveal precise figures) and only Naftemporiki.gr and ERT.gr managed to increase their number of employees.

Overall, the online media executives interviewed strongly downplayed the impact of the new economy demise on their operations. Collectively, they cited various factors that allowed them to sustain the industry downfall.

The first was the limited up-front investment required, due to the existence of an established brand with a conservative approach and traditional business logic. These were the companies that never believed in the new economy rhetoric (Economist.com, BBCi, Independent Digital, Naftemporiki.gr). Second, the small size of some organizations made decision making a relatively fast and easy procedure. Third, firms that realized the limitations of the market because of their early presence in the Internet business (Naftemporiki.gr) were also able to fend off the new economy crisis. Moreover, in one particular firm (Independent Digital), managers had made their mistakes in the past, when working for other online organizations. Along the same lines, those that did not invest in third-party dot-com businesses during the boom years found themselves in an advantageous position and, finally, organizations that only entered the online news business scenery at the end of 1999 when the new economy euphoria was withering off (ERT.gr), were also in a position to sustain the crisis.

Reflecting on the issue of how much the euphoria around the new economy impacted on business decisions, Paul Rossi elaborated:

I don't think we were ever euphoric. The board did not allow us to do excessive things. Effectively we are the Economist. The management team told us that there were certain things we could do (you can be casual and you can have a surfboard in the office) but at the end of the day we make our money by being the Economist. Bear in mind that this is a 160-year-old business. That's why we did not do as much as we could have done maybe, but we did not crash as much either. (personal communication, June 22, 2003)

In the case of the Independent Digital, the key to fending off the burst of the bubble was the small size of the organization. Richard Withey elaborated:

We have never in fact had more than 22 staff on the net services here in London. We never invested in third parties dot-com companies, we did not do it big scale, we always set up the Internet side of things with the view to support-

ing print and providing another channel to market for our content, rather than believing this was a new business. (personal interview, April 12, 2003)

Withey also revealed that although the Independent Digital operations in London were left relatively intact by the new economy bust, some parts of the group (notably in South Africa and Ireland) suffered significantly as they opted for big up-front investments. Currently around 60 people work for the group's new media operations around the world.

In any case, though, all online publishers interviewed expressed their disappointment with regard to the actual growth of the online publishing market as a whole. They all fell prey to a vision of the scale of the Web businesses that never materialized. In particular it was the graphs presented to them by media analysts regarding advertising projections back in 1998 and 1999, as they were all forecasting 20%, 30%, and 40% percent growth of some sectors of online advertising, which never materialized. This was reflected in the flattening of their share prices as a result of the withdrawal of funds in the markets.

As far as BBCi is concerned, the demise of the dot-com era came at a very convenient time for the organization. Back in 1999, the English news site was divided into a world edition and a U.K. edition. The world edition covers international news and the U.K. domestic news. An intense debate was taking place within the organization regarding whether advertising should be introduced into the world edition Web site:

Many people in the organization despised the idea of the BBC Web site carrying advertising messages for various reasons, not least because there was lots of worry that U.K. users might end up in the wrong place and see advertising messages. Conveniently the Internet ad market fell apart and removed the impetus. (M. Hunt, personal communication, April 12, 2003)

In tune with his colleague at the BBC, Miles Palmer cited another positive aspect of the burst of the new economy bubble: the fact that competitors had to scale back considerably, which proved to be fortuitous in terms of the BBCi position.

Conclusions

Perhaps the one finding that stands out in this article is the very fact that business models do not differ substantially in the cases studied, irrespective of whether the news organization publishes generic or specialist news content, is commercially driven or not, and irrespective also of whether it is based in Greece or the United Kingdom. The main reason for this is that the online companies studied were keen to copy their competitors' initiatives and developments, and also the rather limited options of business models from which online companies can choose. As expected, all the commercial online news media studied tend to employ a mix of business models to increase their streams of revenue and achieve the best possible financial results.

At the same time, generic news providers both in Greece and the United Kingdom were deemed to be in a far more disadvantaged position compared to their specialist news counterparts. The reason for this is because they find it more challenging to charge their customers a subscription fee on the Web, as there is abundance of generic free content elsewhere. To overcome this problem, they have identified, with varying degrees of success, as areas of potential value on their content the following: online archives, crosswords, columnists and opinion pieces, added-value services (e.g., access to stock and share portfolios). On the other hand, news Web sites both in Greece and the United Kingdom with a niche target audience face fewer difficulties and less user resistance in introducing pricing policies, only because it is easier for them to identify (and then exploit commercially) the value of their product for consumers.

Although subscriptions are forecast to constitute the future of online news publishing by the media executives interviewed, advertising still accounts for the majority of their online revenue. At the time when the interviews were conducted, the online advertising market was just recovering from a prolonged decline, and all future projections appeared to be very positive, a development that was very much welcomed by the media executives interviewed. Yet, their insistence on developing their subscription base as much as possible is, partly at least, due to the steady stream of revenue this business model guarantees, as opposed to the very volatile nature of advertising. Nevertheless, subscription pricing models are based on speculation, as empirical research does not provide valid feedback for the online news industry.

As far as public service online news businesses are concerned, they appear to be very much envied by their commercial competitors, as they can afford to overlook commercial considerations in their operation. As a result they tend to view themselves as "guardians" of the Internet and drivers of the development of online news organizations in the countries in which they operate. In light of this, they develop schemes such as reliable search engines (BBCi) or avoid charging their users for any of the content they produce (ERT.gr).

In terms of the fundamental online media economics, the participants in this study dismissed the new economy concept as a fallacy and argued that the so-called new economy economic rules are very much in tune with the old, basic economic rules that involve the creation of a product that offers added value to consumers.

They all put the blame for the bust of the new economy in 1999 and 2000 on media consultants' and analysts' irresponsible, careless approach and inflated predictions. Meanwhile, the online news providers that (both in Greece and the United Kingdom) resisted the downturn of the new economy were the ones that avoided investing heavily up front, were influenced by the conservative views of their established offline parent organizations, and kept the size of their online departments reasonably small.

Finally, this study demonstrates that the main differences between the Greek and the U.K. market lie in the bureaucratic nature of the online news media of the former (ERT.gr) and the tendency of the Greek market as a whole to mimic developments that take place abroad.

Future research in this exciting and ever-expanding field of online media business and economics may involve the exploration of the implementation of pricing schemes by online news providers, from a technical point of view. Alongside that, the response of Internet users to these pricing policies and the impact this response may have on the future prospects of the industry as a whole pose some genuine challenges for future studies.

Alexandros Arampatzis

(arampata@edgehill.ac.uk)

is a Lecturer in Media and Communication at Edge Hill University College, Ormskirk, UK. His research interests focus on the business models and the journalistic techniques behind news Web sites. He has worked in various research and industry projects on media management and media economics.

Endnotes

1. According to the latest (January 31, 2004) statistics from Internet World Stats (http://www.internetworldstats.com/), which comprise findings from sources such as Nielsen/NetRatings, the International Telecommunications Union, and local Internet service providers, the penetration of the Internet in south European countries averages around 24% of the population (Greece, 15.2%; Portugal, 19%; Spain, 33%; Italy, 31%), whereas the same figures for northern European countries rise close to 55% (indicatively: United Kingdom, 58.8%; Germany, 54.5%; Austria, 42%; Denmark, 62%; Netherlands, 66%; and Sweden, 76.9%)

2. According to January 31, 2004 statistics by Internet World Stats (http://www.internetworldstats.com/), the penetration of the Internet in Greece amounts to 15.3% of the population, whereas in the United Kingdom the same figure climbs to 58.8%.

3. This is out of an estimated 1 million unique users for the Independent Online.

4. According to a study published by Vodafone, the leading Greek mobile service provider, there are currently 6.5 million mobile handsets in use, in a population of roughly 11 million.

References

Afuah, A., & Tucci, C. (2001). *Internet business models and strategies.* Boston: McGraw-Hill.

Christensen, M. C. (1997). *The innovator's dilemma: When new technologies cause great firms to fail.* Cambridge, MA: Harvard Business School Press.

Chyi, I. H., & Sylvie, G. (2000). Online newspapers in the U.S. *International Journal on Media Management, 2*(2), 70–78.

Coats, R. (2002). *To charge or not to charge? Online business models.* Retrieved April 11, 2003, from http://www.poynter.org/content/content_view.asp?id=11174

Goldhaber, M. (1997). *The attention economy and the Net.* Retrieved February 22, 2002, from http://www.firstmonday.dk/

Gordijin, J., & Akkermans, J. (2001). Designing and evaluating e-business models. *IEEE Intelligent Systems, 16*(4), 23–37.

Hamel, G. (2000). *Leading the revolution.* Boston: Harvard Business School Press.

Karlof, B. (1989). *Business strategy: A guide to concepts and models.* London: Macmillan.

Kelly, K. (1998). *New rules for the new economy: 10 radical strategies for a connected world.* New York: Viking.

Kung, L. (2001, November). How to ensure that ugly ducklings grow into swans: BBC News Online and the challenge of incumbent response to disruptive technologies. Paper presented at the 5th World Media Economics Conference, St. Gallen, Switzerland.

Mings, M. S., & White, B. P. (2000). Profiting from online news: The search for viable business models (pp. 62–97). In B. Kahin & R. H. Varian (Eds.), Internet publishing and beyond: The economics of digital information and intellectual property. Cambridge, MA: MIT Press.

Peterovic, O., Kittl, C., & Teksten, R. D. (2001, October). *Developing business models for e-business.* Paper presented at the International Conference on Electronic Commerce, Vienna, Austria.

Picard, R. G. (1989). *Media economics: Concepts and issues.* Thousand Oaks, CA: Sage.

Picard, R. (2000). Changing business models of online content services: The implications for multimedia and other content producers. *International Journal on Media Management, 2*(2), 60–68.

Picard, R. (Ed.). (2002). *Media firms: Structures, operation, and performance.* Mahwah, NJ: Lawrence Erlbaum Associates, Inc.

Porter, M. (1985). *Competitive advantage.* New York: Free Press.

Poynter Institute. (2002). *Online news business models series.* Retrieved November 4, 2003, from http://www.poynter.org/dg.lts/id.11204/content.content_view.htm

Rappa, M. (2001). *Business models on the Web.* Retrieved November 4, 2003, from http://digitalenterprise.org/models/

Rayport, J. F., & Jaworski, B. J. (2001). *E-commerce.* New York: McGraw-Hill/Irwin.

Saksena, S., & Hollifield, C. A. (2002). U.S. newspapers and the development of online editions. *International Journal on Media Management, 4*(2), 54–61.

Smith, J. (1990). *Business strategy.* Cambridge, MA: Blackwell.

Tapscott, D. (1996). *The digital economy: Promise and peril in the age of networked intelligence.* New York: McGraw-Hill.

Timmers, P. (1998). Business models for electronic markets. *The Electronic Markets, 8*(2), 58–64.

Weill, P. (2001). *Place to space: Migrating to e-business models.* Boston: Harvard Business School Press.

Yin, R. (1984). Case study research: Design and methods. *Applied Social Research Series, 5*(1).

Second Generation Net News: Interactivity and Information Accessibility in the Online Environment

Erik P. Bucy
Indiana University, USA

This study assesses the ways in which local television news operations and major metropolitan newspapers in the top 40 U.S. media markets are making information accessible and structuring interactive experiences online as the industry transitions into a third generation of Internet news. As Net news approaches its first decade of existence, online news sites are assumed to be evolving from a noninteractive, passive model of information delivery into an environment of increased immediacy, content richness, and user control. To investigate this question, a content analysis was performed in 2 waves, once during fall 1998 and again during fall 2000. For comparative purposes, differences across years are examined. In addition, the efforts of local television news sites are contrasted with the online activities of dominant newspaper sites, which have assumed a commanding lead in building a local online audience. The analysis argues for valuing Net news sites less from a profit–loss standpoint and more for the nonmonetary contributions they make in relation to the broader news mission, namely, enhanced coverage, brand loyalty, and news credibility.

Unlike the broadcast spectrum, the World Wide Web presents an almost unlimited amount of transmission and storage capacity. With that comes the potential for even local news stations and newspapers to reach a global audience. Despite some initial reluctance to embrace the online medium, local television network affiliates in the United States have established a firm presence in cyberspace, sometimes through strategic partnerships with other content providers, and a few standout sites are now generating considerable traffic.[1] However, being slow to embrace the online environment has not helped television news. Just 13% of local TV news sites are profitable (Papper, 2003) and most lack the depth and informational appeal of the nearest major metropolitan newspaper site. Major newspaper sites dominate the local Net news market, outperforming all other local media in a majority of media markets nationally (Stone, 2001). Amidst this competitive backdrop, broadcasters are confronted with justifying the existence of their online operations as the industry transitions into a third generation of Net news marked by new methods of storytelling and ways of engaging audiences in public affairs information (Brown, 2000).

The challenges facing local broadcasters, who have not established reliable online revenue models (Anzur, 2001; Papper, 2003), are far more daunting than those confronting major newspapers, whose digital editions are much more likely to be profitable or breaking even (Gipson, 2002). Given the association of news-related online content with market ranking (Chan-Olmsted, & Park, 2000), this analysis examines the informational and promotional packaging of Net news sites and compares the efforts of local television news with the online activities of metropolitan newspapers, which have assumed a commanding lead in building a local online audience (Anzur, 2001). To investigate how these two forms of Net news are making information accessible and structuring interactive experiences online, a content analysis of home page features was performed in two waves, once during fall 1998 and again during fall 2000. The analysis examines differences across years as well as between the broadcast and print media. The article concludes by making a case for valuing Net news sites less from a profit–loss standpoint and more for the nonmonetary contributions they make in relation to the broader news mission.

Three Generations of Net News

With Net news approaching its first decade of existence, online news sites are assumed to be evolving from a noninteractive, passive model of information delivery into

Address correspondence to Erik P. Bucy, Department of Telecommunications, Indiana University, 1229 E. 7th Street, Bloomington, IN 47405-5501. E-mail: ebucy@indiana.edu

an environment of increased immediacy, content richness, and user control. In the view of Merrill Brown, a senior vice president at Real Networks and former editor-in-chief of MSNBC.com, the year 2000 marked the beginning of the third generation of Net news, characterized by enhanced features "that use technology to bring people *closer* to the news to educate, inform, and entertain them" (Brown, 2000, p. 26). During the first generation of Net news, in the early to mid-1990s, online services and news organizations produced simple hypertext pages that redistributed wire copy and other third-party content, and print media learned how to take their efforts online. This first generation of Net news corresponded with the waning days of the "old computing" (Shneiderman, 2002), characterized by cumbersome connections, poor interface designs, unnecessary animations and "GUI widgets," and uninspiring content (see Nielsen, 1996, 1999).

The second generation of Net news, from the mid-1990s to decade's end, moved online journalism to a more independent footing, engaging in original newsgathering and production. Continuous updates became more common, streaming audio and video appeared, Net news became more visual and in-depth, and interactive chats and online discussions emerged, creating news communities. Television news sites were increasingly promoted on air as the place to go for more depth and context, and program schedules were posted online; indeed, by the late 1990s the Web had emerged as an important source of station promotion (Ferguson, 2000). Meanwhile, online newspapers began to explore longer, more complex forms of storytelling with lasting appeal (Harper, 1998) and print journalists began adopting electronic techniques for gathering information and interacting with sources consistent with the emergence of the Internet as an important news medium (Barnhurst, 2002).

Third generation Net news sites are projected to leverage "improved interactive applications [that] will create an entirely new integrated news experience that will serve to engage consumers" (Brown, 2000, p. 26). Taped and live streams will proliferate, in Brown's view, allowing audiences with specialized interests to watch newsmaker interviews, press conferences, hearings, and other events at their convenience. Handheld information devices and broadband access are important enabling technologies of the next generation of news. "The passive newscast and the hours-old newspaper are being replaced" (p. 26) by new practices and technologies, Brown (2000) contended. "But the third generation of Internet news is not just about reinvigorating journalism. It's also an opportunity to engage the next generation of news consumers in the worlds of news and public affairs" (p. 26).

Engaging younger audiences through new technology and immersive presentational techniques is one way of building their interest in the news. Only 28% of those under age 30 report watching local TV news the previous night and even fewer, 26%, report having read a newspaper the day before (Pew Research Center for the People and the Press, 2002). Young audiences are, however, turning to the Web for information, with 44% going online for news at least once a week. Indeed, a Pew Research Center study conducted during the 2000 election asserted that the Internet was "sapping" the broadcast news audience (Pew Research Center for the People and the Press, 2000). Rather than viewing online media from a displacement perspective, the Internet may instead be regarded "as a supplemental medium for developing a relationship with the audience of an offline core product" (Chan-Olmsted & Ha, 2003, p. 612). From a relationship-building standpoint, understanding the nature and extent of Web page features that facilitate user involvement—and return visits—thus becomes paramount.

Reconfiguring the News–Audience Relationship

With the rise of interactivity as the Holy Grail of audience outreach efforts, media organizations have been confronted with the task of keeping users engaged in news content while harnessing the unique capabilities of the Web. Because of its two-way communication architecture (Newhagen & Levy, 1998), the Internet presents media organizations with an opportunity to reconfigure the news–audience relationship in a way that brings users into the editorial loop by "allowing individuals to control their definition of news instead of depending on what producers or editors have predefined as news" (Murrie, 2001, pp. 10–11). At major news and portal sites, this control increasingly occurs through personalization settings that enable users to create custom profiles, track topics of interest, and even modify the interface layout. Gradually, personalization is becoming a local Net news phenomenon, affording some user control over news content.

Conceptually, the key mechanism of personalization is interactivity, defined by Steuer (1995) as "the extent to which users can participate in modifying the form and content of a mediated environment in real time" (p. 46). The different types of interactivity that may occur online have been categorized by researchers into two general dimensions. The first, more common type is *content* (or *user-to-system*) interactivity, which involves the control that news consumers exercise over the selection and presentation of editorial content, whether story text, sound files, audiovisuals, multimedia, or some combination thereof (Massey & Levy, 1999; McMillan, 2000, 2002). Unlike traditional media platforms, the online environment allows users to more fully interact with the medium itself by clicking on hyperlinks, taking part in viewer polls and surveys, downloading information, calling up streaming media, searching archives, customizing information delivery, and making electronic purchases, all "without ever directly communicating with another person" (Stromer-Galley, 2000, p. 118).

The second, less common type of interactivity that may occur online is *interpersonal* (or *user-to-user*) interactivity, involving person-to-person conversations mediated by the network. Such computer-mediated communication includes both synchronous (real-time) and asynchronous (delayed) exchanges, whether in the form of e-mail or its various permutations such as instant messages, chat room discussions, message boards, user forums, Internet telephony and videoconferencing (e.g., Microsoft NetMeeting), and, on entertainment sites, distributed game playing or multiplayer role-playing adventures. Stromer-Galley (2000) drew a similar distinction between media and human interaction on candidate Web pages. Both types of interactivity may be facilitated by the same Web site, depending on the features offered.

Research on traditional media use suggests that both the narrative content and structural features of messages may compel audience attention, increase viewer arousal, enhance memory, and impact subjective evaluations (see Bucy, Lang, Potter, & Grabe, 1999). Consequently, this analysis assumes that Web users are attracted to Net news on account of its informational appeal as well as participatory depth.

Previous Research on Net News

The following review focuses on structural, or site description, studies of Net news content (see Ferguson, 2000; Schneider, Foot, & Harnett, 2001) to motivate a coding instrument for assessing how the online operations of major market television stations and metropolitan newspapers are facilitating access to news and information and configuring interactive experiences in cyberspace. From the literature, two broad categories of home page elements are highlighted: features involving some sort of interactivity and elements related more directly to traditional news content. Whereas early published research analyzing the characteristics of news sites focused on the online efforts of newspapers, increasing attention is now being paid to broadcasting and the Web.

Structural Studies of Online News

Several studies of online news have found forms of content interactivity to be much more prevalent than user-to-user interactivity. An analysis of the content and services of 80 online daily newspapers from 1997 found that, whereas almost all of the newspaper sites in the sample provided hyperlinks to nonnews sites and more than

two thirds provided readers with access to their electronic archives, only a third of the sites facilitated interactive communication either between users or among readers and editorial staff in a live chat environment (Peng, Tham, & Xiaoming, 1999). In a related survey, half of online editors contacted indicated that they placed a high value on timeliness, updating their Web edition more than once a day (Peng et al., 1999).

An examination of the interactive features of English-language Web newspapers in 14 Asian countries by Massey and Levy (1999) found that options for interpersonal interactivity were similarly limited, but that content interactivity persisted. Nearly three fourths of the sites analyzed provided user-searchable archives and nearly all of the sites provided a feedback link for the general delivery of reader e-mail to the newsroom. Scant use was made of the Net's capacity for immediacy—only a third of the sites indicated publication dates or utilized news tickers. Streaming media and hyperlinks within stories were also rare, as were customization features that enhance the accessibility of online information (Massey & Levy, 1999).

Li (1998, 2002) conducted a small-scale design analysis of selected online newspapers in 1996 and again in 1999. Not surprisingly, during the first generation of Net news, in 1996, the online editions of the *New York Times, Washington Post,* and *USA Today* gave more priority to providing textual information than graphical information. When graphics were posted, they appeared primarily on home pages, whereas the sites' internal news pages were dominated by text (Li, 1998). Over the 10-day sample period there was an average of one photograph on each paper's home page. Neither the *Washington Post* nor *USA Today* used photos to illustrate any of their online stories at that time. News content in general was highly interconnected by way of hyperlinks, however, and on the *New York Times* site 95% of online articles were linked to related stories and information.

A second design analysis of online newspapers by Li (2002), this time of the *Washington Post, USA Today, Chicago Tribune, Los Angeles Times,* and *Boston Globe,* determined that home page content, including graphics, news items, and hyperlinks, was both diversifying and becoming more visually appealing but not uniformly enhancing the audience's immediate access to news and information. Importantly, Li (2002) noted, although some news sites may look more visually appealing than others, they may not be more efficient for readers to use.

Studies of the online efforts of local broadcasters commenced soon after the first TV station news sites started appearing on the World Wide Web. A baseline examination of the home pages and internal content of 61 station news sites in 1995—virtually every station with a Web presence then—found a substantial amount of news and programming information on station Web sites, but very little was current (Bates & King, 1996). Stations seemed to be using the Web more for place marking and promotional purposes than for its capabilities as an independent communication medium. A follow-up analysis of 416 TV news sites showed that broadcasters were becoming more sophisticated in their approach to the Web, evidenced by greater use of graphic and visual elements, shorter page lengths, a greater number of external links, and the incorporation of such navigational tools as site indexes and search engines (Bates et al., 1997). Features enabling a certain level of content interactivity, including online forms and archived audio and video, appeared as well. Even so, some basic provisions were overlooked; only 16.4% of station home pages contained any specific mention of local news stories and even fewer posted specific weather or sports information.

Using a sample of 62 television Web sites from 1997, Kiernan and Levy (1999) examined whether the characteristics of individual station sites were related to the amount of competition faced by the station. Their analysis focused on two types of Web site differentiation—information content, operationalized as 13 news categories, and format diversity, operationalized as eight interactive features. Although the site characteristics varied widely, there was more content diversity than format diversity. As for content, half of the sites in the sample offered nine or more different types of news; as for format, half of the sites presented two or more interactive features. The analysis found little relation between station competition and individual site characteristics, suggesting that the content of local TV Net news sites was unrelated to stations' financial resources, market rank, or network affiliation.

A year later Chan-Olmsted and Park (2000) examined the content and structure of 300 local station Web sites across a range of network affiliations, including the three major over-the-air networks as well as FOX, PBS, WB, and UPN. With the exception of e-mail links to station staff, the analysis found more news content and programming-related information than interactive features. A scant 4.3% of stations offered an online newscast, indicating that, as of 1998, the era of broadband content delivery had not yet arrived. Statistically, market ranking was more likely to be associated with news-related content on the front pages of TV station sites than market rank or ownership size; and leading stations were most likely to offer local news and weather, ads, programming information, and links to affiliated network sites.

By comparing the results of previous studies with a sample of 179 local television sites drawn in 1999, Ferguson (2000) confirmed a general trend of station sites becoming more visual and interactive over time while reducing clutter and enhancing program promotion. "Web pages will soon become of equal (or greater) importance than more traditional venues for station promotion," Ferguson (2000) predicted, "especially for attracting the young viewer so desired by advertisers (and thus stations). The key element is interactivity" (p. 345).

Research Questions

The foregoing review of Net news research raises several questions about the nature of information accessibility and interactive experiences afforded by local print and broadcast news organizations in the online environment. To structure the analysis, the following research questions are posed:

RQ1: Are there notable differences between the content accessibility and interactivity features of major metropolitan newspaper sites and major market broadcast sites?

RQ2: How much priority do Net news sites give to infusing their home pages with a sense of timeliness and immediacy?

RQ3: To what extent do Net news sites give control to users through personalization features and customization choices?

RQ4: Are Net news sites becoming more sophisticated over time, as indicated by an increase in content interaction, information accessibility, interpersonal communication features, and network presence items?

Data and Method

To answer these questions a comparative content analysis of local television news and newspaper Web sites was performed. The data for this study were obtained through a purposive sample of local television news affiliates and major metropolitan newspaper sites in the top 36 U.S. media markets in mid-October 1998 and again in the top 40 media markets in mid-October 2000. In each market, the Net news sites for each of the four major network affiliates (ABC, CBS, NBC, and FOX) were identified for coding, along with the dominant newspaper for the corresponding city or region. Web sites were identified through a variety of sources. The uniform resource locators (URLs) for television news and newspaper sites were obtained by searching the local media listings in the Yahoo! search engine by city, consulting network pages for their list of affiliates, and referring to the "major metro" newspaper links listed on the NewsLink Web site (http://newslink.org). The *Broadcasting & Cable Yearbook* was also consulted and supplemental searches were made using the Google search engine.

Except for the dominant newspapers in the New York, Washington, DC, and Los Angeles media markets (the *New York Times, Washington Post,* and *Los Angeles Times*), no national media sites (e.g., ABCNews.com, CBSNews.com, MSNBC.com, CNN.com, *USA Today,* the *Wall Street Journal*) were included in the analysis. This sampling procedure resulted in the identification of 173 Net news sites in 1998 and 200 in 2000. Due to coder error and the lack of some FOX affiliate sites in certain markets in 1998, a total of 167 sites were included in the 1998 data set and 193 sites in 2000. For both years combined, the number of unique sites analyzed for this study was 360, including 75 newspaper sites and 285 local television news affiliates.

Coding Instrument

A coding instrument was devised to measure the content elements and interactive features of Net news home pages. Table 1 presents a list of each home page element measured in this study, grouped by category.

Content elements. Net news content was operationalized in terms of four broad categories of information: text elements, photographs, features that lent a sense of timeliness and immediacy to the page, and network presence items. These categories generally correspond to the content factor discussed by Abels, White, and Hahn (1997) in their user-based study of effective Web page design. Influential content is defined by these authors as online information that is useful, current, concise, and unique, that is, not easily or readily found elsewhere (Abels et al., 1997, p.

256). Other important factors affecting continued use of a site include ease of use and navigability and the presence of an intelligible, well-organized page structure. Ease of use is a key issue for Net news operations interested in attracting crossover audiences, as usability studies typically find that a large percentage of new users have difficulty navigating online environments (see Nielsen, 1999).

Network presence, measured by Bates et al. (1997) and Chan-Olmsted and Park (2000), was deemed important for assessing the branding strategies of both station sites and newspaper pages (see also Bellamy & Traudt, 2000). In the coding instrument, network presence was measured by coding for the presence on the home page of a network or corporate parent logo, the station call letters or newspaper name, and the community served. In addition, each site's home page address (verified from actual page printouts) was scrutinized for the station call letters or newspaper name, and the network call letters or corporate parent name.

Interactive features. Net news interactivity was operationalized in terms of four categories of potential user interaction: commercial transactions, interpersonal communication, content interactivity (multimedia), and information accessibility.

■ Commercial transactions were measured by coding for the ability of site visitors to buy commemorative editions and other organization memorabilia online or through a phone number provided on the home page.

Table 1. Home Page Content Categories

Content elements	
Network presence items	Network or corporate parent logo; station call letters; community served; network or organization name in the Web address
Textual content	E-mail links to and full news stories, press releases, newsperson biographies, and campaign issue positions
Photographs	Photos of news reporters, anchors, and personalities; news sources; news events; political candidates; and other people and events
Immediacy items	Date or time-stamped news stories; news ticker with current headlines; indication of new content; date or time of last update
Interactive features	
Transactional items	Forms to buy memorabilia, make a donation, or register to vote online; mechanisms for volunteering, community activism
Interpersonal communication	Feedback forms; e-mail links to reporters and staff; presence of chat rooms, forums, bulletin boards, and other online discussions
Multimedia items	Instant polls or surveys; games, puzzles, and contests; photos or graphics used as links; links to audio and video (archived or live), related sites, newsletters, news digests, and listservs; links in news stories; e-mail postcards and stories; searchable databases; downloadable graphics, and wallpapers; other forms and links
Information accessibility items	Search engine; index or list of helpful links; help page or forum; FAQ list; site map; content in different languages; schedule or programming information; condensed information or story summaries; ability to customize information display and delivery

Note. All features were coded as being either present or absent (not for the total number of times they appeared on the home page). FAQ = frequently asked questions.

- Interpersonal communication, involving person-to-person conversations or message exchanges mediated by technology, was measured by coding for the presence of bulletin boards, online discussions, and chat rooms as well as e-mail links to reporters, editors, and news directors, and feedback forms for communicating with the news organization or Webmaster.
- Content interactivity measured a range of items designed to bring users closer to the news, including clickable graphics; links to audio and video clips or feeds; forms for newsletters, listservs, or news updates; links to related sites; online opinion polls; the presence of games or contests; e-mail postcards and news story forwarding; and searchable databases.
- Finally, information accessibility was operationalized as features that enhanced usability, including the ability to customize news delivery, find information in condensed or long form, and successfully navigate around a site.

Specific items thought to facilitate information access included the presence of a search engine, site map or index, frequently asked questions (FAQ) list, programming or scheduling information, links to different departments within the site, news story summaries, the capacity to modify information delivery or display, and the capacity to request information specific to a geographic location or in a different language.[2]

Coding Procedure

The unit of analysis was the home page. For station sites the home page generally summarizes and promotes the newscast, whereas for newspaper sites the home page more or less emulates the printed product's front page, which serves as "a measure of what the newspaper believes is important" (Davis, 1999, p. 174). Limiting the analysis to the home page eliminates the need to adjust for the varying size and resources of Net news operations. Larger and more profitable news sites, with a larger budget and staff, contain more elaborate branching structures and substantially more pages than smaller sites. Focusing on the home page treats each site equally and thereby standardizes the coding process; it also minimizes the possibility of coder error associated with searching an entire site for a particular feature or content element.

The coding for both years was conducted as part of a class assignment for an upper level media and politics course at a large midwestern university. In mid-October 1998 and again in mid-October 2000 individual coders were given the URLs for five Net news sites (four station sites and one newspaper site) in each media market and

were instructed to analyze home pages for each category of interest. Coders were instructed to follow links off the home page only if they needed to verify what information or feature was available through that option. For both years the different ways that home page features might be implemented were reviewed during a training session. Before proceeding coders were instructed to open their browser window to full size. For archival and verification purposes, each home page was printed and a hard copy kept for reference.[3]

Depending on the variable, the coding categories yielded either interval- or nominal- (present–absent) level data. Most content elements, such as news stories, links to news stories, and story summaries, produced interval-level data, whereas many interactive features, such as the ability to purchase organization memorabilia, forward a news story, modify information delivery, take part in an online poll, or use a search engine, produced nominal-level data. To simplify the analysis and augment intercoder reliability, which was unacceptably low using the raw data, all interval-level variables were collapsed to nominal level: Different content elements or interactive features are thus reported as being either present or absent. For the analysis, indexes were then constructed by adding together related elements for each content and interactive category. Scale reliability analysis showed the highest reliability coefficients in the 1998 data for media interaction and interpersonal communication ($\alpha = .53$ and .48, respectively), and in the 2000 data for text elements, information accessibility, and media interaction ($\alpha = .45$).[4]

For both years of the analysis 10% of the sample was double-coded to test intercoder reliability, measured using Holsti's reliability formula. For 1998, reliabilities were calculated on a total of 42 variables. The average reliability across all variables was .76. For 2000, reliabilities were calculated on a total of 51 variables. The average reliability across all variables was .72. The average intercoder reliability across both years was thus .74, which was deemed an acceptable measure of agreement for the analysis to proceed. During each data collection, the coding period extended over the last 2 weeks of October. A certain amount of variance in intercoder reliability was thus anticipated, given the regular updating of Net news sites. A distinction should be made, however, between information updates and wholesale page makeovers. The nominal level at which these data were analyzed may have been slightly affected by updating. However, given the timing of the coding process—immediately before an election when audience reliance on online news intensifies—neither the television station nor newspaper sites examined were likely to make substantial changes to their home page designs.

Results

Figures 1 and 2 show that station home pages featured much more content-driven interactivity (multimedia), such as clickable graphics, audio and video feeds, online polls, and searchable databases, than opportunities for interpersonal communication, including bulletin boards, chat rooms, e-mail links to editorial staff, and feedback forms. Differences in the amount of content interactivity were especially pronounced between the "big three" network affiliates and FOX stations, which featured fewer multimedia elements per home page in both 1998 ($M = 2.59, SD = 1.24$) and 2000 ($M = 4.24, SD = 2.2$) than ABC, CBS, and NBC ($M = 3.98, SD = 1.86$ in 1998; $M = 5.87, SD = 1.99$ in 2000). Newspaper sites were also consistently more interactive than FOX sites ($M = 3.85, SD = 1.91$ for 1998; $M = 6.07, SD = 2.23$ for 2000). These differences were significant for both years of the analysis, $F(4, 162) = 3.67, p < .01$ for 1998, and $F(4, 187) = 20.74$,

$p < .001$ for 2000.[5] FOX sites had roughly the same number of interpersonal communication features as other network affiliate sites for both years of the analysis, but TV stations overall facilitated less user-to-user interaction ($M = 1.15, SD = 1.20; M = 1.60, SD = 1.04$) than newspapers ($M = 1.68, SD = 1.22; M = 2.10, SD = 1.26$), $t(165) = -2.27, p < .05$ for 1998, and $t(191) = -2.61, p < .01$ for 2000.

The first research question asked whether there were notable differences between the content accessibility and interactivity of major metropolitan newspaper sites and major market broadcast sites. On average, differences between newspaper and TV sites were small but became slightly more pronounced in 2000 compared to 1998. The following results thus focus on 2000 only. In terms of content accessibility, TV pages incorporated slightly fewer immediacy elements ($M = .93, SD = .96$) than newspaper sites ($M = 1.22, SD = .91$), $t(190) = -1.79, p < .10$, but featured more photographs ($M = 1.62, SD = 1.18$ compared to $M = 1.29, SD =$

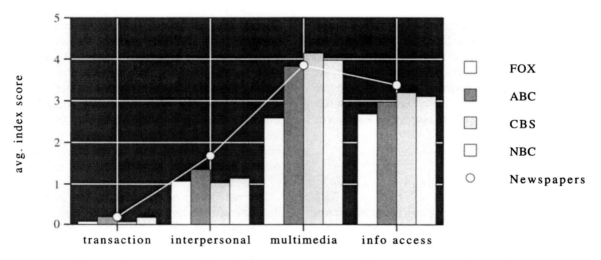

Figure 1.   Interactive features of Net news home pages top 36 media markets, 1998.

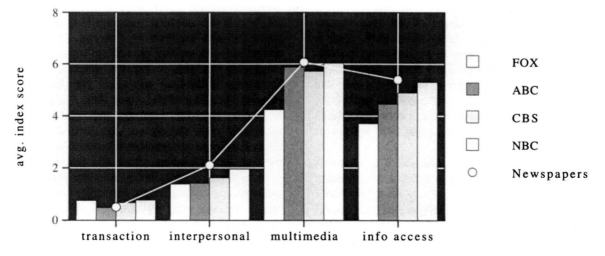

Figure 2.   Interactive features of Net news home pages top 40 media markets, 2000.

.93), $t(191) = 1.64$, $p < .10$. Both newspaper and station sites featured about the same number of stories and links, or textual content. In terms of interactivity, newspaper sites featured more interpersonal communication features ($M = 2.10$, $SD = 1.26$) and information accessibility items ($M = 5.39$, $SD = 1.87$) than TV sites ($M = 1.60$, $SD = 1.04$; $M = 4.62$, $SD = 1.64$, respectively), $ts(191) = -2.61$ and -2.58, $ps < .01$, respectively, but roughly the same amount of content interactivity as the network affiliate sites, excluding FOX (see Figures 1 and 2). For both years there was little difference in the small amount of commercial transaction opportunities on newspaper and TV station sites.

The second research question asked how much priority second generation Net news sites gave to infusing their home pages with a sense of timeliness and immediacy. Immediacy was operationalized as a set features that lent a sense of "nowness" and real-time urgency to the home page. Included were such features as news tickers, a date and time stamp on posted stories, and whether the news organization indicated if the page received regular updates. In relation to other composite variables, the number of immediacy items was comparatively low. Figures 3 and 4 show that Net news pages contained, on average, less than one of these items per page in 1998 ($M = .53$, $SD = .62$), with a notable increase between 1998 and 2000 ($M = .98$, $SD = .95$). In 1998 ABC stations stood out compared to both newspaper and other station sites, with almost one immediacy element per page ($M = .85$, $SD = .74$), $F(4, 162) = 3.69$, $p < .01$. Between-network differences mostly receded by 2000, although newspaper sites began to maintain slightly more immediacy elements on their home pages than TV station sites, as noted earlier.

To answer the third research question, the analysis next considers the extent to which Net news sites gave control to users through personalization features and customization choices, conceptualized here as a site's infor-

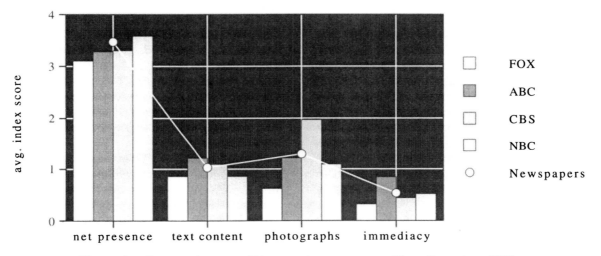

Figure 3. Content elements of Net news home pages top 36 media markets, 1998.

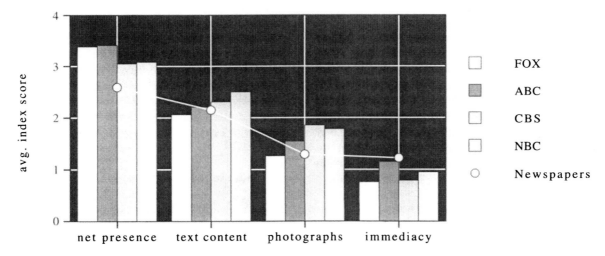

Figure 4. Content elements of Net news home pages top 40 media markets, 2000.

mation accessibility. Compared to other page features, elements that enhanced information accessibility, including site maps, a FAQ list, programming information, news story summaries, and the ability to modify information delivery or display, were fairly abundant. For 1998, there were approximately three accessibility elements ($M = 3.01$, $SD = 1.00$) per home page on all network-affiliated TV sites, and more than three ($M = 3.38$, $SD = .92$) per page on newspaper sites, $t(165) = -1.97$, $p < .05$ (see Figures 1 and 2). By 2000, this number had increased to an average of more than four elements per page on station sites ($M = 4.62$, $SD = 1.64$) and more than five per page on newspaper sites ($M = 5.39$, $SD = 1.87$), $t(190) = -2.58$, $p < .01$. NBC affiliates stood out in the 2000 data, rivaling newspapers for the presence of usability items ($M = 5.30$, $SD = 1.38$). As with the content interactivity index, FOX-affiliated sites lagged somewhat behind the other TV station sites across both years of the analysis with fewer accessibility elements for 1998 ($M = 2.69$, $SD = 1.07$), $F(4, 162) = 2.20$, $p < .10$, and 2000 ($M = 3.71$, $SD = 1.47$), $F(4, 187) = 6.65$, $p < 0001$.

The fourth research question asked whether Net news sites were becoming more sophisticated and interactive over time. As with other index scores, the amount of content-related elements increased between 1998 and 2000, in part because sites were becoming more established and in part because the coding instrument captured a slightly greater range of elements in 2000.[6] The amount of interactive features on home pages overall also rose—by almost 50%—as indicated by the larger index scores on the y axis of Figures 1 through 4. For 1998, network affiliates averaged about four multimedia elements ($M = 3.98$, $SD = 1.86$) and one interpersonal feature ($M = 1.17$, $SD = 1.21$) per home page; by 2000 these numbers grew to almost six multimedia elements ($M = 5.87$, $SD = 1.99$) and closer to two interpersonal features ($M = 1.66$, $SD = 1.06$) per home page. The number of immediacy items, although low, almost doubled between the 2 years studied. Moreover, the amount of information accessibility items increased on both station sites and newspaper sites over the 2-year period.

Finally, in terms of network presence items, a higher percentage of TV sites, 97.4% in 1998 and 93.1% in 2000, more prominently featured their channel number on the home page than their network logo. The percentage of TV sites with a readily identifiable network logo somewhere on the home page actually decreased slightly between 1998 and 2000, from 87% to 84%. Most stations, an average of 70.1% in 1998 and 70.6% in 2000, also chose to post their station call letters as well as the community served on the home page, clearly emphasizing their local identification.

Discussion

Overall, the results of this analysis show that both newspaper and television Net news sites were offering online users a growing amount of interactivity and information accessibility and, at least in the top 40 markets analyzed here, did seem intent on bringing audiences closer to the news. A central component of this effort involved the incorporation of page elements that made content readily available, easily comprehended, and personally tailored. Moreover, Net news sites appeared to be increasing in sophistication over the time period examined here, as indicated by the growth in content interaction, information accessibility, and interpersonal communication features between 1998 and 2000.

Consistent with other Net news research, a greater amount of content interactivity was found on both newspaper and local TV news sites than interpersonal communication mechanisms. The differences between the home pages of major metropolitan newspaper sites and major market broadcast sites appeared small, in part because of the way the indexes were constructed. Interestingly, newspaper sites did feature more interpersonal communication features, information accessibility items, and immediacy elements than station sites, affording more social interaction, personal control, and temporal proximity to events than the home pages of local broadcasters. The skilled use of such design features may drive a certain amount of site traffic, as previous research suggests (Bucy et al., 1999; Chan-Olmsted & Park, 2000), contributing to (but probably not accounting for) the newspaper industry's online lead.

Given the market dominance of online newspapers, the poor initial positioning of many local TV station sites may be difficult to correct, even with television's sizable broadcast reach and cross-promotional advantage. This difficulty stems not just from marketing concerns but from the demanding nature of the online medium itself, which in its present form requires a considerable degree of both textual and technical literacy (see Newhagen & Bucy, 2004). For the Web to attain television's mass appeal, Net news designers will have to overcome these barriers to understanding and use. The information accessibility findings from this study are promising in the sense that local news operations seemed to realize the value of features that enhance usability. Even so, with the lead that newspapers have already established in cyberspace, television stations are confronted with the challenge of developing a more effective cyberstrategy or ceding perhaps permanent control to the print press.

Nonmonetary Contributions of Net News

Competitive and revenue considerations aside, media organizations may stand to benefit by recognizing the nonmonetary contributions of Net news to the broader news mission, of which there are at least three major types—enhanced coverage, brand loyalty, and media credibility.

Each of these are thought to increase audience reliance on the news product.

As for enhanced coverage, Lasica (2002) observed that the Web enables news organizations to deepen the newscast or news hole with information that, for space reasons, cannot be included on the nightly news or in the daily newspaper; facilitates delivery of hyperlocal coverage (e.g., neighborhood weather, crime statistics, and sports) and updates throughout the day; allows news providers to host message boards and discussion forums to build relationships and promote civic discussion of important local issues; and offers more consumer control over the news through access to story archives, customized information delivery, and other features that engage users on an individual level. Even if Net news designers are not outfitting their home pages with all of these features, they were making a growing number available, as this study has shown.

Brand loyalty is another tangible benefit media organizations may derive from online activities that are not revenue or cost based (see Chan-Olmsted & Ha, 2003). In the view of some television industry observers, the primary purpose of an online news site is to increase viewer loyalty to a station and its services, thus counteracting declining audiences for on-air news (see Ferguson, 2000). Among the page elements analyzed here, loyalty may be cultivated through a variety of interactive features that invite involvement and dialogue, as well as content elements that enable site visitors to get the news in the time, manner, and format they want. Brand loyalty across different media platforms is further reinforced through the use of logos, channel numbers, and call letters. From the results, the brand identification efforts of station sites were shown to be primarily local in orientation, with a higher percentage of sites prominently displaying the station's channel number on the home page than their network logo.

Finally, Net news operations can enhance media credibility. Beyond stimulating interest in the news and keeping users captivated, interactive experiences may cultivate impressions of news responsiveness and informativeness, at least for young audiences (see Bucy, 2003, 2004). If this is true, then investments in online news operations are justified not so much for economic reasons but on the basis of enhancing the credibility of the news organization overall. At a time of audience fragmentation and growing concern over news responsibility, perceptions of credibility have important implications for the industry, as audiences tend to pay more attention to and become reliant on media they consider credible (Johnson & Kaye, 1998). Over time, such contributions may come to outweigh immediate concerns about profitability and help retain a news audience increasingly turned off by appointment television and the hours-old, nonpixellated morning newspaper.

Erik P. Bucy

(ebucy@indiana.edu)

is an Associate Professor in the Department of Telecommunications and Adjunct Associate Professor in the School of Informatics at Indiana University, Bloomington, IN. He is the editor, with John Newhagen, of Media Access: Social and Psychological Dimensions of New Technology Use *(2004, Lawrence Erlbaum Associates, Inc.).*

Acknowledgments

This article benefitted from the research assistance of Kimberly S. Gregson and the insightful comments of Maria Elizabeth Grabe and John E. Newhagen. This study was supported by a Grant in Aid of Research from the Office of Research and the University Graduate School, Indiana University, Bloomington. An earlier version of this article was presented at the annual meeting of the Broadcast Education Association in April 2003 in Las Vegas, NV, where it won the top paper award from the Communication Technology Division.

Endnotes

1. In 1995, a milestone year in the Web's development marked by rapid commercialization and technical change (December, 1997), CBS became the first of the four major broadcast networks to establish an online presence. A year later, such pioneering local stations as WRAL-TV in Raleigh, North Carolina, and WCCO-TV in Minneapolis, Minnesota, went online. By 1998, more than two thirds of all TV stations had Web sites (Chan-Olmsted & Park, 2000). A survey of 890 television stations sponsored by the Radio and Television News Directors Association during the fourth quarter of 2002 revealed that 94% of stations airing local news now have a Web site (Papper, 2003).

2. Although every effort was made to standardize the coding instrument for newspaper and TV news sites, and between the two sample years, findings from the first wave of analysis and changes to Net news sites by the time of the second data collection in October 2000 necessitated the addition of several new content and interactive categories. Consequently, a true longitudinal analysis is not possible. However, *within* a given year, differences by coding category, network, and media type (newspaper, TV station) can be observed. The number of items in each category of measure differs between years. A complete list of the individual items constituting each measure is available from the author.

3. To the extent that multiple coders increased the likelihood of error creeping into the coding process, coder error was assumed to be randomly distributed.

4. The scale reliability analysis was performed in a post hoc fashion, after the composite indexes had been conceptually de-

rived. Thus, the validity of the indexes is conceptual rather than statistical. Reliability in content analysis is generally assessed through intercoder reliability measures rather than scale reliability determinations (Singletary, 1994).

5. Although significance tests are reported in the results, they are only intended for comparative purposes within years and for the Web pages analyzed, not for generalizing to the larger population of Net news sites. Because the number of index items varies slightly between the 1998 and 2000 data sets, with more items measured in 2000, no significance tests are reported for between-year analyses.

6. The amount of textual content seems small in these figures because of the nominal level at which the data were coded. Even if the home page of a site had multiple news stories, or links to stories, each category was coded just once as being either present or absent. This approach enhanced intercoder reliability, but at the expense of accurately reflecting the number of items on a page. The analysis is intended to reveal trends in online interactivity and information accessibility rather than descriptively report the exact content of Net news home pages.

References

Abels, E. G., White, M. D., & Hahn, K. (1997). Criteria for Web pages. *Internet Research: Electronic Networking Applications and Policy, 7,* 252–262.

Anzur, T. (2001, January 10). TV news Websites: The myth of convergence. *Online Journalism Review.* Retrieved April 20, 2001 from http://www.ojr.org/ojr/workplace/1017962127.php

Barnhurst, K. G. (2002). News geography & monopoly: The form of reports on U.S. newspaper Internet sites. *Journalism Studies, 3,* 477–489.

Bates, B. J., Chambers, L. T., Emery, M., Jones, M., McClung, S., & Park, J. (1997, August). *Television on the Web, 1996: Local television stations' use of the World Wide Web.* Paper presented to the Association for Education in Journalism and Mass Communication, Communication Technology and Policy Division. Chicago.

Bates, B. J., & King, R. E. (1996, April). *Television and the Web: How local television broadcasters are using the World Wide Web.* Paper presented to the Broadcast Education Association, Management and Sales Division, Las Vegas, NV.

Bellamy, R. V., Jr., & Traudt, P. J. (2000). Television branding as promotion. In S. T. Eastman (Ed.), *Research in media promotion* (pp. 127–159). Mahwah, NJ: Lawrence Erlbaum Associates, Inc.

Brown, M. (2000, October 2). Bringing people closer to the news. *Brandweek,* p. 26.

Bucy, E. P. (2003). Media credibility reconsidered: Synergy effects between on-air and online news. *Journalism & Mass Communication Quarterly, 80,* 247–264.

Bucy, E. P. (2004). The interactivity paradox: Closer to the news but confused. In E. P. Bucy & J. E. Newhagen (Eds.), *Media access: Social and psychological dimensions of new technology use* (pp. 47–72). Mahwah, NJ: Lawrence Erlbaum Associates, Inc.

Bucy, E. P., Lang, A., Potter, R., & Grabe, M. (1999). Formal features of cyberspace: Relationships between Web page complexity and site traffic. *Journal of the American Society for Information Science, 50,* 1246–1256.

Chan-Olmsted, S. M., & Ha, L. S. (2003). Internet business models for broadcasters: How television stations perceive and integrate the Internet. *Journal of Broadcasting & Electronic Media, 47,* 597–617.

Chan-Olmsted, S. M., & Park, J. S. (2000). From on-air to online world: Examining the content and structures of broadcast TV stations' Web sites. *Journalism & Mass Communication Quarterly, 77,* 321–339.

Davis, R. (1999). *The Web of politics: The Internet's impact on the American political system.* New York: Oxford University Press.

December, J. (1997). *The World Wide Web unleashed* (rev. ed.). Indianapolis, IN: Sams.net.

Ferguson, D. A. (2000). Online program promotion. In S. T. Eastman (Ed.), *Research in media promotion* (pp. 323–347). Mahwah, NJ: Lawrence Erlbaum Associates, Inc.

Gipson, M. (2002, July–August). Playing the online game to win! *Presstime,* p. 26. Retrieved December 16, 2003, from http://www.naa.org/presstime/PTArtPage.cfm?AID=4409

Harper, C. (1998). *And that's the way it will be: News and information in a digital world.* New York: NYU Press.

Johnson, T. J., & Kaye, B. K. (1998). Cruising is believing? Comparing Internet and traditional sources on media credibility measures. *Journalism & Mass Communication Quarterly, 75,* 325–340.

Kiernan, V., & Levy, M. R. (1999). Competition among broadcast-related Web sites. *Journal of Broadcasting & Electronic Media, 43,* 271–279.

Lasica, J. D. (2002, April 2). The promise of the Daily Me: From my news to digital butlers. An in-depth look at the different flavors of personalization. *Online Journalism Review.* Retrieved April 1, 2003, from http://www.ojr.org/ojr/technology/1017778824.php

Li, X. (1998). Web page design and graphic use of three U.S. newspapers. *Journalism & Mass Communication Quarterly, 75,* 353–365.

Li, X. (2002). Web page design affects news retrieval efficiency. *Newspaper Research Journal, 23*(1), 38–49.

Massey, B. L., & Levy, M. R. (1999). Interactivity, online journalism, and English-language Web newspapers in Asia. *Journalism & Mass Communication Quarterly, 76,* 138–151.

McMillan, S. J. (2000). The microscope and the moving target: The challenge of applying content analysis to the World Wide Web. *Journalism & Mass Communication Quarterly, 77,* 80–98.

McMillan, S. J. (2002). Exploring models of interactivity from multiple research traditions: Users, documents, and systems. In L. Lievrouw & S. Livingston (Eds.), *Handbook of new media* (pp. 162–182). London: Sage.

Murrie, M. (2001). *Local Web news: Case study of nine local broadcast Internet news operations.* Washington, DC: Radio and Television News Directors Foundation.

Newhagen, J. E., & Bucy, E. P. (2004). Routes to media access. In E. P. Bucy & J. E. Newhagen (Eds.), *Media access: Social and psychological dimensions of new technology use* (pp. 3–23). Mahwah, NJ: Lawrence Erlbaum Associates, Inc.

Newhagen, J. E., & Levy, M. R. (1998). The future of journalism in a distributed communication architecture. In D. L. Borden & K. Harvey (Eds.), *The electronic grapevine: Rumor, reputation, and reporting in the new online environment* (pp. 9–21). Mahwah, NJ: Lawrence Erlbaum Associates, Inc.

Nielsen, J. (1996, May). Top ten mistakes in Web design. *Alertbox.* Retrieved April 1, 2003, from http://www.useit.com/alertbox/9605.html

Nielsen, J. (1999). *Designing Web usability: The practice of simplicity.* Indianapolis, IN: New Riders.

Papper, B. (2003, April). A tangled Web. *RTNDA Communicator.* Retrieved December 16, 2003, from http://www.rtnda.org/research/research.shtml

Peng, F. Y., Tham, N. I., & Xiaoming, H. (1999). Trends in online newspapers: A look at the U.S. Web. *Newspaper Research Journal, 20*(2), 52–63.

Pew Research Center for the People and the Press. (2000, June 11). *Internet sapping broadcast news audience.* Retrieved July 23, 2000, from http://people-press.org/reports/display.php3?ReportID=36

Pew Research Center for the People and the Press. (2002, June 9). *Public's news habits little changed by September 11.* Retrieved July 23, 2002, from http://people-press.org/reports/display.php3?ReportID=156

Schneider, S. M., Foot, K. A., & Harnett, B. W. (2001, May). *Catch and code: A method for mapping and analyzing complex Web spheres.* Paper presented to the International Communication Association, Communication and Technology Division, Washington, DC.

Shneiderman, B. (2002). *Leonardo's laptop: Human needs and the new computing technologies.* Cambridge, MA: MIT Press.

Singletary, M. (1994). *Mass communication research: Contemporary methods and applications.* New York: Longman.

Steuer, J. (1995). Defining virtual reality: Dimensions determining telepresence. In F. Biocca & M. R. Levy (Eds.), *Communication in the age of virtual reality* (pp. 33–56). Hillsdale, NJ: Lawrence Erlbaum Associates, Inc.

Stone, M. (2001, February 22). Local TV Web sites getting more aggressive: Study. *Newsbytes.* Retrieved April 20, 2001, from http://www.newsbytes.com/news/01/162277.html

Stromer-Galley, J. (2000). Online interaction and why candidates avoid it. *Journal of Communication, 50*(4), 111–132.

The Failure of *Project Eyeball*: A Case of Product Overpricing or Market Overcrowding?

Marc Edge
University of Texas at Arlington, USA

The closure in mid-2001 by Singapore Press Holdings (SPH) of its experimental tabloid newspaper, Project Eyeball, after less than 1 year of publication, was popularly attributed to a pair of market factors: its 80-cent cover price and competition from a pair of free tabloids that entered the market hot on its heels. Although pricing and competition were doubtless important contributing factors to Project Eyeball's rapid demise, a pair of additional economic concepts emerges on closer examination of the newspaper's brief history and may provide additional clues to its failure. One is the principle of relative constancy, which held, until it was disproved in the 1980s, that the level of expenditures on media remained fairly constant as a percentage of the overall economy. The other is the influence on management practices of share prices of publicly traded newspaper companies, into which category SPH falls. Considering these factors in addition to price and competition helps to better explain the rapid demise of Project Eyeball.

Project Eyeball was announced in February 2000 by Singapore Press Holdings (SPH) as "Singapore's first integrated print and cyberspace news publication" for "the Net-savvy and opinionated young Singaporean" (Ong, 2000, p. 1). It was an experimental project, taking a "hybrid" form as both an upscale tabloid newspaper and a continually updated Web site, complete with not only text reports but also audio and video postings. Its Sunday edition would be an Internet-only offering. Ambitious projections foresaw circulation of 100,000 and profitability within 3 years (Chua, 2000). SPH gave away 120,000 copies of *Project Eyeball* daily for a week following its launch on August 12, 2000.

The experiment lasted for less than a year, with disastrous results. Less than halfway through its brief life, *Project Eyeball* was described as a "flop" by *Asiaweek* magazine, which reported, "Advertisers shun it, readers can't find it, and not even the SPH hierarchy likes it" (Mitton, 2001, p. 8). When SPH announced on June 27, 2001 that it was pulling the plug and folding the newspaper, a company spokesman admitted *Project Eyeball* had lost S $13.3 million (U.S. $7.3 million) while achieving a circulation of less than 20,000 (Rajeev, 2001). A postmortem consensus

attributed the failure of *Project Eyeball* to a pair of market factors ("Media War and Pricing Hurt *Eyeball*," 2001):

1. Overpricing. The cover price of *Project Eyeball* had been set at 80 cents, compared with 60 cents for the thick *Straits Times*, the broadsheet flagship of market-dominant SPH.

2. Increased competition. Shortly after the launch of *Project Eyeball*, Singapore witnessed an explosion in the number of newspapers published following a liberalization of government media regulation. As a result, government-owned broadcaster MediaCorp began publication in November 2000 of a giveaway tabloid titled *Today*, in partnership with local transit companies. In response, SPH started up yet another new daily, a commuter tabloid giveaway cryptically called *Streats*.[1]

These explanations for the demise of *Project Eyeball* suggest some theoretical implications. Prevailing economic wisdom posits that demand for newspapers by readers is relatively price inelastic, and that higher cover prices should not affect sales significantly (Lacy & Simon, 1993, pp. 30–31). This seems to be contradicted by the Singapore experience. Competition theory is also relevant to this case study, as colorful tabloid newspapers have proven a successful challenge to market-leading broadsheets in contradiction of the natural monopoly theory of newspapers that has traditionally been ad-

Address correspondence to Marc Edge, Department of Communication, University of Texas at Arlington, Box 19107, Office 118 Fine Arts Building, Arlington, TX 76019–0107. E-mail: mail@marcedge.com

vanced to explain newspaper markets. Although Singapore may indeed prove fertile ground for a tabloid competitor to the *Straits Times,* the fact that three of them began publishing in such a short period may have proved too much, too soon. This article chronicles the brief history of *Project Eyeball* and examines economic and regulatory factors for clues to its rapid demise. The preceding explanations and any others that present themselves are then examined for plausibility.

Background

Singapore is an island city-state approaching 4 million in population located near the equator in Southeast Asia, at the tip of the Malay Peninsula, from which it is separated by the narrow Strait of Johor. Enjoying virtually no natural resources—even its domestic water supply has to be imported by pipeline from Malaysia—Singapore has nonetheless built itself through trade into one of the leading "tiger economies" of Asia since gaining its independence from Britain in 1959. A recent specialization in the high-tech industry brought an enviable standard of living by the end of the past century, but the recent worldwide economic downturn has seen a slowing of the rapid economic growth Singapore experienced in the 1980s and 1990s. Much of Singapore's success can be attributed to centralized management of its economy under the leadership of founding Prime Minister Lee Kuan Yew. Now retired from that position but still involved in government as Senior Minister, Lee built Singapore into an economic powerhouse at the same time as he earned an international reputation for strict press restrictions, including licensing of newspapers (Seow, 1998). A series of government-mandated press mergers in the early 1980s resulted in a nationwide newspaper monopoly for SPH, publisher of the venerable *Straits Times,* which was founded in 1845 and currently boasts a daily circulation of more than 350,000.

Project Eyeball took life in 2000 as the 11th newspaper published by SPH, which is a diversified conglomerate with interests in book publishing and real estate. SPH publishes newspapers in all four official languages of multicultural Singapore—English, Chinese (Mandarin), Malay, and Tamil Indian. Its English-language publications, in addition to the *Straits Times,* include the broadsheet *Business Times,* and *The New Paper,* an afternoon tabloid that began publication in 1988 and initiated a tradition of innovative titles for startup dailies at SPH, which was continued by *Project Eyeball* and *Streats.*[2]

The granting of a newspaper license to MediaCorp and of broadcasting licences to SPH in June 2000 was designed to introduce "controlled competition" to Singapore's media (Ang, 2002, p. 246). In announcing the moves, Minister for Information and the Arts Lee Yock

Suan said they were necessary to allow SPH and MediaCorp to take advantage of the synergies provided by the worldwide trend toward media convergence while preserving the government's long-held policy of keeping the reporting of Singapore affairs under local control (Ong, 2000). Within hours of deregulation, MediaCorp announced it had formed a consortium to publish *Today* with Singapore Mass Rapid Transit (SMRT), which operates the island's subway system (30%), the local bus company (15%), and phone company Singapore Telecom, also known as Singtel (10%). The latter had, through its Yellow Pages subsidiary, published a weekly all-advertising "shopper" for more than 2 years before recently folding it. MediaCorp, which held the balance of 45% of shares in the new publishing company, said it projected circulation of its new tabloid, which would contain "bite-sized" news stories for busy commuters, to hit 200,000 in its first year, with an annual revenue target of S $75 million within 5 years (Ong, 2000). MediaCorp Chief Executive Officer Lim Hup Seng said the aim was not to capture readers with typical tabloid fare of sex and crime, however. "We're not going to be sleazy," said Lim. "We don't have the stomach for it" (Ong, 2000, p. 1). Reported the *Business Times:*

> By partnering the transport companies, MediaCorp hopes to overcome the problem of distribution that had crippled past competitors to *The Straits Times* including *The Singapore Monitor* and *Singapore Herald.* Mr Lim denied that the consortium is copying the business plan of Swedish group, Modern Times but dropping it as a partner. Modern Times was earlier engaged in talks with SMRT to launch a metro newspaper. (Ong, 2000, p. 1)

A commuter tabloid for Singapore had been rumored for some time following the success of giveaway publications in Europe and North America. An explosion of such newspapers had been seen in 20 countries since their successful 1995 introduction in Stockholm by Swedish company Modern Times Group (MTG), which was later renamed Metro International. According to Bakker, MTG alone boasted a circulation of 8.5 million among 21 titles in 15 countries by 2002, when it entered the newspaper market in a 16th country, Hong Kong (Bakker, 2002). In 1999, MTG was reported to be in negotiation with Singaporean transit companies to duplicate there its formula that had proven so popular across Europe and North America ("All the News That Fits," 1999) According to the *Business Times,* however, the talks broke down because of MTG's failure, as a foreign firm, to secure a newspaper license (Ong, 2000).

To head the competing *Project Eyeball* team, SPH appointed 35-year-old *Straits Times* Deputy News Editor Bertha Henson, a former political reporter. She promised the new print and Internet publication would be "provocative and controversial" in its quest for an eventual readership of 600,000 (Teh, 2000, p. 1). Provocative and controversial were two qualities for which the press in Singapore had not been known since the government-forced consolidation of ownership in the early 1980s. "I think it is about time for some of these views to surface," said Henson of simmering antigovernment sentiments. "Because if we don't, then they will simply go underground and we'll simply lose credibility as a publishing company" (Teh, 2000, p. 1). Henson promised *Project Eyeball* would seek readers' views through its online version, with forums, chat rooms, and interaction with newsmakers and journalists. "We don't want a bunch of indifferent readers passively accepting our interpretation of news" (Chua, 2000, p. 1). In short, Henson promised a reversal of the existing press paradigm in Singapore, where the *Straits Times* was widely seen as the mouthpiece of the ruling People's Action Party (PAP), which had held power in a de facto one-party political system throughout the four decades since independence. "It won't be a lecturer–student relationship," insisted Henson of *Project Eyeball*. "It will be like we're sitting on barstool and drinking a vodka with you" (Olynec, 2000). Some PAP politicians expressed skepticism. "There is an unfortunate trend in the competitive media to play up the bad cases," said Lim Boon Heng, minister without portfolio. "If you want to do investigative reporting, there must be something that is wrong which has not been attended to. I think there are not many issues in Singapore that fall under that category" (Webb, 2000, p. 9).

By the end of 2000, Singaporeans had more newspapers to choose from than ever, and competition among them was fierce. Headlines in *Project Eyeball* and *The New Paper* atop coverage of the annual Miss Singapore Universe beauty pageant—such as "They Couldn't Even Speak Good English," "Beauty Without Brains," and "Survival of the Dumbest"—drew official government criticism. Information and the Arts Minister Lee called the tabloid coverage "ungracious and unfair to the contestants" and cautioned the rival media companies against biased reporting "in their drive to outdo each other" ("Telling It Like It Is," 2001, p. H15). Lurid and racy news photographs in some of the newly competitive dailies also drew criticism in the conservative city-state.

Soon bad news came in the form of SPH financial figures. Startup costs for both *Project Eyeball* and *Streats*, along with millions of dollars spent to begin broadcasting at English- and Chinese-language television and radio stations, had cut sharply into SPH's previously high profit margin. Contributing to a more than $19-million decline in profits during the first 6 months of the fiscal year had been $4.8 million spent on the launch of *Project Eyeball* ("SPH's Net Dropped," 2001). Worse yet, a long-overdue economic downturn worldwide caused the company to warn that its financial performance for the balance of the fiscal year would be "weak" ("SPH's Net Dropped," 2001). SPH managers had put a brave face on the regulatory changes that had robbed it of its monopoly the previous year. By stimulating competition, the changes would bring more prosperity for all, the company reasoned. "This is not a zero sum game," argued SPH's Executive Vice President for Marketing, Tham Khai Wor. "The pie is going to get bigger. Even if we lose 3–4 per cent, it will be a bigger pie" (Ong, 2000, p. 1). SPH's share of the S $1.4 billion advertising market in Singapore was then 53%, compared with 32% for MediaCorp, but one rationale advanced for media liberalization was that the total advertising market would grow with more publications. Proponents of this view pointed to the fact that Singapore's advertisement expenditures amounted to less than 0.9% of gross domestic product (GDP), compared with 1.8% to 2.0% in countries such as the United States and Japan (Teh, 2000). Nevertheless, news that SPH would lose its newspaper monopoly triggered "nervous" selling of its shares, according to the *Business Times,* to a low of S $25.70 (Teh, 2000). Ten months later, news of SPH's profit decline in the first half of its 2000–2001 fiscal year dropped its shares 70 cents to a 52-week low of $20.10 (Sivanithy, 2001). By the time of the announcement in June 2001 that SPH would close *Project Eyeball,* the price of its shares had fallen to S $18.40, its lowest point since February 1999 ("SPH to Close Project Eyeball Thursday," 2001). News of the closure, however, sent the share price up a full dollar within a day ("S'pore Stocks Creep Higher at Close," 2001).

Additional Theoretical Considerations

The preceding review suggests two additional economic factors worth taking into account in explaining the failure of *Project Eyeball.*

1. The principle of relative constancy (PRC). First enunciated in 1972 by McCombs, the PRC stated that media expenditures by consumers and advertisers will remain fairly fixed over time as a percentage of the economy. More recent research, however, has found that this does not hold true in an era of new technology (Lacy & Ghee-Young, 1997).

2. Stock market influence. Bagdikian (1980) claimed that widespread public ownership of newspaper chains has led to competition in a third market—the stock market—in addition to the markets for information and advertising, in which newspapers have traditionally been acknowledged to compete (p. 64). Recent research in the United States suggests that newspaper company stock prices can indeed play a considerable role in management

decision making, often rendering long-range strategy subservient to the short-term urgencies of share price (Cranberg, Bezanson, & Soloski, 2001).

The remainder of the article discusses the experience of *Project Eyeball* in relation to the enunciated four theoretical factors.

Discussion

Each of the four factors discussed assists to some extent in explaining why and how *Project Eyeball* was launched and suffered such a rapid demise. The experience of *Project Eyeball*, in turn, provides a valuable case study to assist in assessing the validity of each of these theoretical considerations, several of which have been controversial. Each will be considered in the light of *Project Eyeball*, with the assistance of published data.

Pricing

According to Blankenburg (1995), the inelastic nature of demand for newspapers means that when readers find no acceptable substitute, they endure aggressive pricing. However, when acceptable substitutes are available, readers have proven quite sensitive to price adjustments. History has shown the effects of pricing on demand for newspapers from the days of the penny press, when drastic reductions in cover prices caused demand to skyrocket. In the modern era, the real-world effects of newspaper pricing were seen clearly in mid-1990s England, where Rupert Murdoch reduced the cover price of his *Times* of London from 45 pence to 20 pence in 1993. The resulting 10-year price war saw the *Times* more than double its circulation of 360,000 for a time (Doyle, 2002, p. 131). The million-selling *Daily Telegraph* was forced to match Murdoch's price cut, but by the end of 1996 circulation of the *Times* had climbed to a record 861,931 (Snoddy, 1996). A decade later, the *Times* had given back some of its gains, however, with its circulation receding to 631,653 whereas the *Telegraph's* stood at 916,208 (Preston, 2003). The price war finally ended when the *Times* boosted its price back to normal levels in September 2003, pricing its editions at 50 pence on weekdays compared to the *Telegraph's* 55 pence (Glover, 2003). The long-running battle of attrition provided ample evidence for many that price was indeed an important variable in newspaper demand, however. "The newspaper battle in Britain surprised industry observers who predicted when it began that quality newspapers were not price-sensitive like cans of beans in a supermarket," noted one observer.

"The *Times'* soaring circulation proved them wrong" (Drohan, 1998, p. B1).

As Doyle (2002) noted, "The main determinant of elasticity is the availability of substitutes or of products that are perceived as substitutes" (p. 129). When SPH first published *Project Eyeball* and priced it at 80 cents, there were not yet any free tabloids published in Singapore. That situation promised to quickly change as SPH lost its newspaper monopoly in the city-state and MediaCorp announced it would begin publication of *Today* as a free tabloid in competition with *Project Eyeball*. That prompted SPH to trump its new competition with a giveaway tabloid of its own. The following timeline of events in 2000 compiled by Lim (2003) conveniently illustrates the sequence of events:

June 5: MediaCorp unveils *Today*, a free commuter tabloid.

June 7: SPH announces September launch date for *Streats*.

August 12: Singapore sees *Project Eyeball* for first time.

September 2: *Streats* hits the streets.

November 10: *Today* begins circulation.

The sudden advent of newspaper competition in Singapore on June 5, both as announced by the government and as made into a reality by MediaCorp with its unveiling of *Today*, put SPH in the unfamiliar position of responding to changes in the market that were not of its own doing. It chose to respond decisively to MediaCorp's entry, but in trumping its new competition, SPH effectively sacrificed its previously conceived *Project Eyeball*, which at that point was doomed by its 80-cent cover price. "A monopolist can get away with charging very high prices whereas the existence of rival suppliers in the market in the market will encourage firms to compete" (Doyle, 2002, p. 127). The importance of time as a variable in newspaper competition is also seen clearly in the case of deregulation in Singapore. According to Sylvie and Witherspoon (2002) time and change have been underappreciated factors in understanding competition in the newspaper business: "Publications that do not change also do not adequately monitor their markets. ... Simple economics dictates that newspapers must meet market challenges or die" (p. 7). SPH failed to anticipate changes to the newspaper market in Singapore when it conceived *Project Eyeball*, and as a result it withered from infancy.

Lacy and Simon (1993) suggested that quality is a more useful factor to consider in understanding newspaper demand than price (pp. 30–31) Martin's (1998) resource-based model adds to the demand equation such standard economic concepts as utility, opportunity cost, and consumer surplus. A newspaper's "price" includes the cost of opportunities foregone while reading it, according to Martin, and providing utility in excess of the price paid by the reader results in a consumer surplus to the buyer. "Increasing quality increases the utility consumers receive, thereby decreasing the opportunity cost of consuming a given firm's content. Media firms that create quality content reduce consumer elasticity of demand, and should enjoy a competitive advantage" (Martin, 1998). The unique quality provided by *Project Eyeball* during its brief life included two aspects: a "tech-savvy" writing style aimed at capturing a younger readership attractive to advertisers for its disposable income, and an irreverent attitude toward politics designed to engage readers who had long been offered only bland commentary. Neither was apparently sufficient to raise utility above the 80-cent publication price and thus attract enough readers to survive. The fact that most of *Project Eyeball*'s editorial content was available to read at no cost on the Internet may also have played a part in the failure to stimulate demand for this product.

According to former *Project Eyeball* editor Bertha Henson, journalists involved with the fledgling daily resisted pricing the new newspaper so steeply. "Frankly, from the start, I thought it was too high," said Henson. "In fact, I would say that the editorial [department] fought against it because it was too much, too high" (B. Henson, personal communication, December 22, 2000). SPH Marketing Director Tham Kai Wor said the decision to price *Project Eyeball* at 80 cents was "a deliberate experiment on our part to try to raise newspaper prices in Singapore" (K. Tham, personal communication, February 25, 2003). The experiment obviously failed, but according to Tham it was deemed a necessary gamble by SPH.

> We took a chance. We just had to do it, because there was also competition. We wanted to find a new market. It goes back to the 1980s, when we started to design *The New Paper*. There was one category which *The New Paper* was supposed to target—those English literates who are not reading any newspaper at all. We failed. ... *Eyeball* had many, many factors working against it. The main one is this group is not newspaper readers. (K. Tham, personal communication, February 25, 2003)

SPH wrote a new chapter on newspaper pricing in Singapore in early 2004, when it raised the cover prices of all its titles, including a 33% hike for the *Straits Times*, from 60 cents to 80 cents (Sai, 2004). The steep and unexpected price rise brought criticism from the Consumers Association of Singapore, but SPH cited rising costs of production and the fact that cover prices of its newspapers had not been raised since 1995 ("Case Takes Issue," 2004).

Competition

Control of newspaper publishing in Singapore is a legacy of the British colonial era, when publications were required to be licensed under the classic authoritarian model of the press. Controls were tightened further after Singapore achieved independence from Britain in 1959, as simmering ethnic tensions became ignited by press coverage in several notable instances. A brief merger with Malaysia ended in dissolution in the mid-1960s, after which circulation of newspapers from that country was prohibited (Ang, 2002, p. 244). A series of government-mandated press mergers in the early 1980s led to the establishment in 1984 of SPH as a newspaper monopoly publishing morning and afternoon editions of dailies in all four official languages of Singapore. That situation prevailed until deregulation in 2000, when limited competition was reintroduced.

The creation of SPH can be seen as codification by government fiat of the natural monopoly theory of newspapers. This theory explained the gradual disappearance of competing daily newspapers in many cities around the world due to the "circulation spiral," under which the larger of two competing dailies would come to be preferred by advertisers for its greater reach. The trailing daily would gradually lose advertisers and, as a result, readers, until it became unprofitable and was forced to close. The solution to the problem of dwindling newspaper competition in the United States and some other countries became the joint operating agreement, under which two or more dailies share expenses and split profits. However, by the 1980s a new paradigm of product differentiation came to be preferred to the natural monopoly theory of newspapers, as morning tabloids emerged as viable second dailies in many cities that had been left as one-newspaper towns by the closure of second-place broadsheets. By dint of appealing to a younger readership demographic, these colorful tabloids often became profitable for the volume of advertising they attracted for consumer goods. Attracting a younger demographic has always been a problem for newspapers, but it has become increasingly pronounced in an era of new technology (Picard & Brody, 1997, p. 134).

Perhaps as a result of the demonstrated success of morning tabloids in attracting a younger readership in other parts of the world, SPH introduced *The New Paper* as a tabloid in 1988 in an attempt to attract a younger readership. The attempt was largely a failure, perhaps in part due to the curious decision to make *The New Paper* an afternoon daily. In any event, according to SPH Marketing Director Tham Kai Wor, "The gain was very, very small" (K. Tham, personal communication, February 25, 2003). The problem of attracting younger readers to newspapers has been well documented in other countries, with "public journalism" movement of the 1990s largely aimed at reducing the "disconnect" that citizens increasingly feel from civic life. This disconnect is perhaps even more pronounced in Singapore due to cultural peculiarities in the city-state. Censorship and political controls instituted in an attempt to increase economic performance and stabilize ethnic relations have resulted in a lowered level of political interest, particularly among young people (Banerjee & Yeo, 2003, p. 281). A survey of 432 Singaporeans aged 15 to 29 taken by SPH in late 2000 showed a marked indifference to politics, with 9 of 10 saying they would never consider entering political life. This political apathy, according to a published analysis, extended to the point where young Singaporeans were even described as "contemptuous" of politics ("Youths Shun Politics," 2000).

The launch of *Project Eyeball* as a morning tabloid followed the more successful model of morning publication, but it was quickly emulated by MediaCorp with *Today,* which benefitted from the added attraction of free distribution. SPH countered with a similar morning giveaway in *Streats,* and the field was suddenly crowded. The approach taken by *Project Eyeball* in differentiating its product from this competition was in its content and mode of address. It promised in its initial edition that it would poke fun at Singapore's "strait-laced ways Christmas carol-style" and dig up the kind of stories that were not traditionally covered by the press in Singapore:

> Reporters won't pen their prose from any ivory tower. They will crawl through the trenches at ground zero and surf the back alleys of the Net to deliver news you need to know. ... It will question. It will push you to think. It will give you a voice, even if it's not popular or politically correct. Most of all, it'll stick to what matters to you—the Internet-savvy young professional crowd. (Henson, 2000, p. 1)

Project Eyeball did indeed cover the offbeat, including Singapore's only sex change clinic, and its writing style was more informal than what Singaporeans had been used to reading. It insouciance persisted up until its final issue, in which it summed up its own demise as owing to the mistakes of "hitching ourselves onto the dotcom bandwagon" and "looking too much like a technology/Internet only newspaper." The bottom line, however, was the bottom line, as the newspaper itself admitted in its own front-page obituary. "But at the end of day, money talks. And we're not bringing in the moolah. But that's the way the world works" (Henson, 2001, p. 1). This irreverent attitude indeed "endeared itself to the young and Internet-savvy," according to an online obituary, which also reiterated the fundamental conundrum that spelled the newspaper's demise. "The ordinary Singaporean had to choose between paying 80 cents for *Project Eyeball* and getting the other newspapers free. I guess it wasn't a difficult decision" ("Project Eyeball Says Goodbye," 2001). Other cyberactive Singaporeans, however, were more cyni-

cal and questioned whether *Project Eyeball*'s irreverent questioning of authority had hastened its demise. "Is the closing down of *Project Eyeball* merely because of business reasons?" asked the short-lived group Singapore Media Watch, in a letter to the Web site Singaporeans for Democracy. "Could another reason be that it has overstepped the boundaries of politics in Singapore? *Project Eyeball* has been reporting a lot of articles on the opposition. ... It has comprehensive reports of Workers Party handover as well as NSP's [National Solidarity Party] too" (Singapore Media Watch, 2001).

However, whatever competitive advantage the editors of *Project Eyeball* tried to gain, SPH management provided even more competition to its own offspring by providing yet another free choice for Singapore newspaper readers in *Streats.* This practically ensured the failure of *Project Eyeball* by dooming it from its steep cover price in face of the free competition. Although *Streats* was a more viable competitor for *Today* than *Project Eyeball,* and both enjoyed major economies of scale under SPH, enduring the inevitable startup losses of two new dailies was obviously more of a drain on the bottom line than management was prepared to allow to continue. After *Project Eyeball* folded, *Streats* more than held its own against *Today,* capturing about 13% of Singapore newspaper readership in its first year, compared with about 11% for *Today* (and only 1% for *Project Eyeball*). In 2002, the positions of the dueling giveaways reversed, with *Today* being read by 16.3% of Singaporeans, whereas *Streats* was read by only 10.3% (Loo, 2002). The loosening of regulations restricting competition in the Singapore newspaper market undoubtedly altered the playing field on which *Project Eyeball* competed. From enjoying a monopoly in newspaper publishing, SPH was suddenly in unfamiliar territory with competition from a new morning tabloid. The rapid demise of *Project Eyeball* can perhaps be thus seen as a kind of false start to competition.

Relative Constancy

The PRC (also known as the relative constancy hypothesis) has proven one of the more controversial mass communication theories over the past three decades, and has been criticized for its lack of grounding in economic theory. McCombs (1972) first examined data from 1929 to 1968 in concluding that the level of spending on media purchases by advertisers and consumers over that period had remained relatively constant as a percentage of gross national product (GNP), despite technological advances and variations in competition. Although the amount of advertising on television had increased markedly during the latter decades of his study, McCombs found that when adjusted for inflation, population growth, and increases in personal income, media expenditures as a whole had remained fairly constant as a percentage of GNP over the period, and had even declined from 3.46% in 1929 to 3.04% in 1968 (p. 24). This led to media economics being seen as a kind of "zero sum" game, with a decline in newspaper industry fortunes explained by an increase in advertising expenditures on television.

Subsequent research, however, found spending on media buying by advertisers to be not as fixed as first assumed by the PRC. Then with the advent of cable television and VCR technology in the 1980s, consumer spending on media was also found to rise in relative terms. As advertising expenditures are the focus of this section of the article, findings on that aspect of media buying are dealt with here. Research found that only about half of all television advertising revenue was "stolen" from other media, and that an increase in the number of radio stations also increased total advertising revenue (Lacy & Noh, 1997, pp. 9–10). The resulting contradiction of the PRC in advertising expenditures perhaps became instead inspiration for media executives hoping to increase these revenues by exploiting advances in technology and competitive niches.

Thus, when SPH Marketing Director Tham Kai Wor stated on launching *Project Eyeball*, even in the face of increased competition from *Today*, that "this is not a zero sum game," and that "the pie is going to get bigger," he was relying, at least implicitly, on the disproving of the PRC. The increased media competition in Singapore seen at the turn of the millennium therefore provides an opportunity for further testing of the PRC. Data on advertising expenditures across media are easily available, as is that on GDP, and breaks down as shown in Table 1.

The verdict on whether increased competition in Singapore media has served to increase the size of the advertising revenue pie there over the long run will have to be reserved until several more years of data have been collected. However, given the slowdown in both the global and local economy, these increases could indicate that advertising revenue may well rise with increased competition. However, although this may serve as an explanation for the genesis of *Project Eyeball*, along with the host of other new publications that sprang up in Singapore in 2000, it does not help to account for its closure, as more competition would seem to be preferred to less under this

finding. For more clues we turn to our fourth and final area of theoretical consideration.

Share Prices

Ownership of newspaper companies by firms that are publicly traded on stock exchanges has been seen in other countries as a possible factor of significance in management decision making. The impact of financial markets on media management practices was first brought to the attention of many by Bagdikian, who identified it in the late 1970s as a factor that had been overlooked in understanding the impact of increased concentration of press ownership. He identified stock markets as a "third market" whose forces newspaper managers must account for, in addition to their acknowledged markets for readers and advertising.

> The impact of trading newspaper corporate stock on the stock market has meant that news companies must constantly expand in size and rate of profits in order to maintain their position on stock exchanges. ... Instead of the single master so celebrated in the rhetoric of the industry—the reader—there are in fact three masters. (Bagdikian, 1980, p. 64)

According to Underwood (1993), increased corporate ownership of dailies resulted in two trends during the 1970s and 1980s: professional management of newspapers, often by executives with little or no background in journalism; and an increasingly bottom-line, market-driven orientation. He argued that both trends were largely the result of stock market influences. "Wall Street, as publishers have learned, can be insatiable in the demand for earnings growth and unmerciful in hammering a stock if earnings drop" (p. 41). One recent study in the United States found such a marked effect on newspaper management of publicly traded share ownership that it urged the enactment of federal regulations to reverse the trend, despite First Amendment guarantees in that country against government interference in the operations of the press (Cranberg et al., 2001, pp. 147–148).

Table 1. Advertising Revenues in Singapore, 1997–2002

Year	SPH ($'m)	Today ($'m)	All Media	GDP ($'b)	% of GDP
1997	647.4		1,275.3	149.5	.85
1998	574.8		1,186.5	145.9	.81
1999	609.5		1,219.9	143.5	.85
2000	750.6	3.0	1,504.2	160.9	.93
2001	643.2	36.7	1,541.0	154.6	1.00
2002	629.0	62.6	1,685.9	155.7	1.08

Note. Source AC Nielsen, SPH, Singapore Dept. of Statistics. Used with permission from AC Nielsen.

Although SPH shares trade on the local Singapore stock exchange and not on Wall Street, the principle is the same—share prices can be increased with short-term strategies that may not be in the firm's best long-term interest. Thus, pressure from shareholders could theoretically influence management decision making. The effect would become even more direct when executives of the newspaper company are themselves shareholders, or can take advantage of stock options. A review of share prices reveals that the trend line for SPH stock was definitely downward throughout the life span of *Project Eyeball*. However, this was due in large part to the fact that the Singapore stock market index, charted through the performance of 45 key stocks and published in the city-state's largest daily newspaper as the Straits Times Index (STI), began a long slide almost as *Project Eyeball* was conceived. The STI topped 2,500 briefly at the end of 1999, but as soon as 2000 dawned it began to trend downward, as did other world markets. By the time *Project Eyeball* hit the streets, the STI was hovering around 2,000. By the time its closure was announced, the stock index had fallen below 1,700. However, as drastic as the fall in share prices in Singapore was in 2000, the drop in SPH stock value was even more pronounced. Table 2 lists a summary of SPH share prices, calculated as a ratio of the STI from the spring of 2000 until the summer of 2001, when *Project Eyeball* was closed.

The price of SPH stock significantly underperformed the market in Singapore throughout the period, and according to press reports this may have been due in large part to the losses being incurred by *Project Eyeball*. In the absence of boardroom transparency, managerial strategy can only be inferred, but it is a logical assumption that the poor performance of SPH share prices due to its proliferation of unprofitable ventures may have led to the closure of *Project Eyeball*.

Table 2. SPH Share Price Versus Straits Times Index

Month End	SPH	STI	Ratio
April 2000	33.4	2164	1.00
May 2000	25.7	1795	.93
June 2000	27	2037	.86
July 2000	29.5	2051	.93
August 2000	27.7	2147	.83
September 2000	26.1	1997	.85
October 2000	25.1	1976	.82
November 2000	27.3	1952	.90
December 2000	25.6	1926	.86
January 2001	23	1991	.75
February 2001	22	1947	.73
March 2000	19.8	1674	.76
April 2000	20.9	1722	.78
May 2000	19.5	1657	.76
June 2001	20	1726	.75
July 2001	19.3	1666	.75

Note. SPH = Singapore Press Holdings; STT = Straits Times Index. Source *Straits Times.*

Conclusions

The failure of *Project Eyeball* was probably not attributable to any one single factor, but instead to a combination of factors. Pricing the newspaper at 80 cents may have attracted enough readers eager for an alternative to the staid *Straits Times* if two new free alternatives had not been added to the mix. In light of changed circumstances, SPH management's decision to fold *Project Eyeball* and cut its losses is entirely understandable. Although the increased advertising revenue seen marketwide due to the proliferation of publications starting in 2000 is apparent in the data, albeit tentatively, not much of it seemed to flow to *Project Eyeball*, likely due to its lack of popularity with readers. Its negative effect on SPH share prices was the final nail in *Project Eyeball*'s coffin. In the end, coming as it did at the onset of both an economic slowdown and an explosion of competing publications, *Project Eyeball*'s rapid demise can probably best be explained in two words: bad timing.

Marc Edge

(tmarc@ntu.edu.sg)

is a Visiting Assistant Professor in the Communication Department at the University of Texas at Arlington, Arlington, TX. He is the author of Pacific Press: The Unauthorized Story of Vancouver's Newspaper Monopoly *(New Star Books, 2001).*

Endnotes

1. The title was explained as "an amalgam of Streets—where it's distributed, and Treats—because it's free" (Mitton, 2001, p. 8).
2. *Project Eyeball* started out as a "code name" for the prototype publication, but according to one progress report it proved "so suited to what the team aims to produce that it has been adopted as the product name. ... The word 'project' is apt because it connotes something experimental and on-going" (Khalik, 2000, p. 2).

References

All the news that fits, they print. (1999, December 3). *Asiaweek,* p. 13.

Ang, P. H. (2002). Media and the flow of information. In D. Da Cunha (Ed.), *Singapore in the new millennium: Challenges facing the city-state* (pp. 243–268). Singapore: Institute of Southeast Asian Studies.

Bagdikian, B. (1980). Conglomeration, concentration and the media. *Journal of Communication, 30,* 59–54.

Bakker, P. (2002). Reinventing newspapers: Free dailies—Readers and markets. In R. G. Picard (Ed.), *Media firms: Structures, operations and performance* (pp. 77–86). Mahwah, NJ: Lawrence Erlbaum Associates, Inc.

Banerjee, I., & Yeo, B. (2003). Internet and democracy in Singapore: A critical appraisal. In I. Banerjee (Ed.), *Rhetoric and reality: The Internet challenge for democracy in Asia* (pp. 259–287). Singapore: Eastern Universities Press.

Blankenburg, W. B. (1995). Hard times and the news hole. *Journalism and Mass Communication Quarterly, 72,* 634–641.

Case takes issue with higher news-stand prices of SPH papers. (2004, January 17). *Straits Times,* p. H2.

Chua, M. H. (2000, June 7). SPH to launch newspaper for the hip and opinionated. *Straits Times,* p. 1.

Cranberg, G., Bezanson, R., & Soloski, J. (2001). *Taking stock: Journalism and the publicly traded newspaper company.* Ames: Iowa State University Press.

Doyle, G. (2002). *Understanding media economics.* London: Sage.

Drohan, M. (1998, April 20). Black geared for fight. *Toronto Globe and Mail,* p. B1.

Glover, S. (2003, September 13). The price war is over, and it is time to ask who won. *The Spectator* (London), p. 32.

Henson B. (2000, August 12). Prepare to be provoked—*Project Eyeball* is spoiling for a fight. *Project Eyeball,* p. 1.

Henson, B. (2001, June 29). A last look. *Project Eyeball,* p. 1.

Khalik, S. (2000, February 6). New SPH paper gets its licence. *Straits Times,* p. 2.

Lacy, S., & Noh, G.-Y. (1997). Theory, economics, measurement, and the principle of relative constancy. *Journal of Media Economics, 10*(3), 3–16.

Lacy, S., & Simon, T. (1993). *The economics and regulation of United States newspapers.* Norwood, NJ: Ablex.

Lim, K. (2003, November 13). High hopes. *Business Times* (Singapore), p. 2.

Loo, D. (2002, December 23). Battle of the free-sheets. *The Edge* (Singapore), p. 16.

Martin, H. (1998, August). *Modeling strategy for mass media: A resource-based approach.* Paper presented at the Association for Education in Journalism and Mass Communication Annual Convention, Baltimore, MD.

McCombs, M. (1972). Mass media in the marketplace. *Journalism Monographs, 24,* 1–102.

Media war and pricing hurt Eyeball. (2001, July 3). *Straits Times,* p. H7.

Mitton, R. (2001, January 8). A media scuffle to the death. *Asiaweek,* p. 8.

Olynec, N. (2000, June 6). SPH to start new paper in August as it loses industry monopoly. *Bloomberg News.*

Ong, C. (2000, June 6). Broadcast licences for SPH, newspaper licence for MediaCorp. *Business Times* (Singapore), p. 1.

Picard, R. G., & Brody, J. H. (1997). *The newspaper publishing industry.* Needham Heights, MA: Allyn & Bacon.

Preston, P. (2003, July 13). Ten years of price warfare and what have we got? Not an awful lot. *The Observer* (London), p. 6.

Project Eyeball says goodbye, for now. (2001, June 29). Retrieved December 9, 2002, from http://www.getforme.com/previous 290601_ProjectEyeballSaysGoodbyeForNow.htm

Rajeev, P. (2001, June 28). SPH to suspend operations of Project Eyeball newspaper—Singapore media firm cites market conditions. *Asian Wall Street Journal,* p. M2.

Sai, M. (2004 , January 14). Singapore press raises its prices. *Asian Wall Street Journal,* p. M3.

Seow, F. T. (1998). *The media enthralled: Singapore revisited.* London: Lynne Reiner.

Singapore Media Watch. (2001, June 29). Closing down of Project Eyeball: Letter to Singaporeans for Democracy. Retrieved December 9, 2002, from http://www.sfdonline.org/Link%20Pages/ Link%20Folders/01Ds/290601.html

Sivanithy, R. (2001, March 28). SingTel's collapse sends STI reeling below 1,700 points. *Business Times* (Singapore), p. 8.

Snoddy, R. (1996, December 17). Murdoch says cut-price Times will last forever. *Financial Times* (London), p. 12.

SPH's net dropped 8.5% in first half on losses at units. (2001, March 27). *Asian Wall Street Journal,* p. M3.

SPH to close Project Eyeball Thursday. (2001, June 27). *Reuters News.*

S'pore stocks creep higher at close, M&A rules. (2001, June 28). *Reuters News.*

Sylvie, G., & Witherspoon, P. D. (2002). *Time, change, and the American newspaper.* Mahwah, NJ: Lawrence Erlbaum Associates, Inc.

Teh, H. L. (2000, June 7). Singapore's latest paper to readers—Tell us what you want. *Business Times* (Singapore), p. 1.

Telling it like it is—What the editors say. (2001, March 24). *Straits Times,* p. H15.

Underwood, D. (1993). *When MBAs rule the newsroom.* New York: Columbia University Press.

Webb, S. (2000, August 11). New Singapore paper aims to woo younger, tech-savvy readers. *Asian Wall Street Journal,* p. 9.

Youths shun politics, involvement. (2000, December 20). *Straits Times,* p. H2.

GENERAL RESEARCH ARTICLES

Qualitative Media Measures: Newspaper Experiences

Bobby J. Calder and Edward C. Malthouse
Northwestern University, USA

We seek to understand the experience of reading a newspaper. Qualitative and quantitative research methods identify 44 distinct dimensions of the newspaper reading experience. Using statistical models, these experiences are compared across a random sample of 101 daily U.S. newspapers to examine the extent that the experiences vary both across newspapers and among readers of a specific newspaper. Also, hierarchical linear models are used to study the association between readership and each of the 44 experiences. This shows which experiences have the strongest associations with readership and whether the strength of association varies across newspapers. By measuring experiences, media management can improve both content and advertising, ultimately increasing readership.

Media research typically focuses on quantitative measures of usage. In the case of print media, readership is often measured as recent reading. In the United States, for example, newspaper readers are asked whether they read a newspaper yesterday. Media *usage* is a relatively straightforward construct. Just as one can conceive of, say, orange juice usage, one can also conceive of media usage. Usage is about actual behavior. It is not about how people subjectively think and feel about that behavior. Therein lies an important distinction.

People do not just use media, they experience it. There is a subjective, qualitative side to their usage. The most obvious facet of this is involvement. Two people could each read a newspaper on three occasions for about 15 min each time. Person A might be engaged in what she is reading, and even be trying to remember the material. Yet Person B might be reading merely to pass time with no thought of wanting to remember anything. The two peoples' usage is the same, but their experiences are very different.

Our view is that usage and experience are different constructs and must be conceptualized and measured differently. Measures of experience must capture the subjective side of usage. A good measure needs to capture the "qualitative" side of reading in the fullest sense of the word. Another way of putting this is that media products are "experience brands." This article attempts to conceptualize and measure the distinct experiences that define the brand and ultimately lead to usage (Calder & Malthouse, 2003b).

Many words can be used for this construct. *Involvement* is an obvious one. *Enjoyment* is another. In some industry circles words like *wantedness* are used. We use the term *experience* because it captures the idea of what people think and feel when they read, and this is not a unidimensional continuum (as implied by involvement). We postulate that there are many (multidimensional) experiences associated with media use.

The ultimate goal is to identify specific, measurable experiences that characterize involvement with newspapers. Our approach is to avoid defining experiences in terms of survey questions such as "Is this newspaper involving?" or "Is this newspaper one of your favorites?" We want to measure specific, multiple experiences rather than some overall composite reaction. Moreover, a specific experience should have multiple indicators (survey questions) that serve both to measure the construct and (on the assumption that the experience of any medium is inherently multidimensional) to separate it from other experience constructs. Our approach is thus to begin with many potential survey questions that may or may not indicate a variety of experience constructs. These questions

Address correspondence to Edward C. Malthouse, Northwestern University, 1870 Campus Drive, Evanston, IL 60208. E-mail: ecm@northwestern.edu

are analyzed (via exploratory factor analysis) to locate separate experience constructs. Following this, reliability is examined to refine the measurement of each construct in terms of its best survey question indicators. Experiences are then related to usage.

Literature Review

Media measurement has focused mainly on usage, usually measured with a single critical question. Brown (1999) discussed the "read yesterday" question used to measure newspaper readership. Frequency measures such as the number of times per week that people read the newspaper are commonly used in academic studies (e.g., Burgoon & Burgoon, 1980). Time spent reading a newspaper has also been used (e.g., Loges & Ball-Rokeach, 1993).

Recently, Calder and Malthouse (2003a) argued that quantitative measures such as these are inferior to multiquestion measures that treat usage as an underlying construct that must be inferred from data. We developed a latent-variable approach to measuring newspaper readership employing questions spanning frequency of reading, amount of time spent reading, and completeness of reading for weekdays and Sunday. It yields a reader behavior score (RBS) reflecting all six indicators.

Malthouse and Calder (2002) presented a "qualitative-variable" version of this approach using latent class analysis. This version yields nine types of readers, termed reader behavior types (RBTs). One RBT is heavy readers, who read frequently, spend considerable time, and read most of the newspaper on both weekdays and Sunday. Another RBT is selective heavy readers who read frequently and spend considerable time but read less than half of the newspaper. Another is Sunday-only light readers, who rarely read on weekdays but who read a fraction of the paper on Sundays. The RBT measure is found to complement the RBS measures. Heavy readers are found at the high end of the RBS distribution and Sunday-only lights are at the low end. Other types occur in between. Thus RBTs provide additional "qualitative" information, making the RBS scores more interpretable.

Malthouse, Calder, and Eadie (2003) applied a methodology similar to the one used here to identify experiences associated with magazines. Berry, Hercock, and Beard (2003) described a study designed to understand the motivations for reading newspapers in New Zealand.

Methodology

We study a random sample of newspapers so that inference can be extended to newspapers as a medium; the first subsection describes the sample of newspapers. Qualitative research is used to gain insight into experiences, which is then extended through quantitative analysis.

Sampling Publications

The conclusions of this research should generalize to newspapers as a medium. Any one newspaper may no doubt involve unique experiences. However, this research postulates and attempts to show empirically that many experiences exist across newspapers.

This research is part of a longitudinal study of a random sample of 101 U.S. newspapers. The details of the first wave of the sampling plan are provided in Calder and Malthouse (2003a) and summarized briefly as follows. We first drew a stratified random sample of 101 U.S. daily newspapers, stratifying on newspaper and market characteristics including circulation, competition, geographical extent of distribution, and market urbanicity. All types of newspapers are represented in our sample, ranging from small-town local papers to large papers serving urban centers and surrounding areas.

Qualitative Phase

The quantitative phase includes a survey asking respondents the extent to which they agree with questions such as, "Reading this newspaper makes me feel like I am drowning in the flood of news that comes out each day." It is analyzed along with many other items to determine if they indicate a separate experience construct. Two key issues arise with this approach. One is how to obtain the pool of items that are thought to be potential indicators of constructs. We argue that the items should be grounded in data from readers. Accordingly, our item pool is based on in-depth qualitative interviews with readers during which they described their experiences.

We conducted more than 300 personal interviews across seven different newspaper markets. An illustrative quote from one of the interviews is as follows:

> You are inundated by the news on a constant basis ... news updates on TV ... you see it in the paper ... you stand in the aisles at grocery stores and you read it and you're plagued by the news and there's just a point where I don't want to know any more.

Data from these interviews were analyzed to find patterns across individuals. Similar sentiments to the one just quoted were voiced by many others. This led to the drowning-in-the-news item cited earlier. The goal of this stage of the research was thus not quantitative generalization of frequencies, but an enhanced understanding of consumer thoughts and emotions (Calder, 2001).

Details on the format of the interviews, the discussion guides, and the complete set of items are available on our Web site.[1]

Quantitative Surveys

As indicated earlier, this work is part of a longitudinal study and surveys respondents to the first study a second time. In the first study, we mailed 115,890 surveys to consumers in the 101 newspaper markets and 37,036 responded; the response rate was 37%, after dropping undeliverables. For this second wave, we drew a random sample of 15,664 readers from the 37,036 responders to the first wave and received 4,444 responses.

The survey contained the items generated in the qualitative interviews. We seek experience constructs that apply across newspapers. All items refer to a specific newspaper for the survey respondent. Because the same items are used for each newspaper, the data can be analyzed without regard to the specific publication. Our intention is for the aggregated data to describe the newspaper medium.

Quantitative Results

Quantitative analysis consists of three parts: developing experience scales with exploratory factor analysis, quantifying experience levels for newspapers as a medium and variation across individual newspapers with random-effect analysis of variance (ANOVA) models, and measuring the strength of the relation between each experience and readership.

Measuring Consumer Experiences and Readership

The survey included 275 items, constructed from the qualitative research, measuring the experience of reading a specific newspaper. We used exploratory factor analysis and coefficient alpha to develop 44 experience scales. We first factor analyzed all 275 items using the principal components method of estimation and a varimax rotation. There were 68 eigenvalues greater than 1, and a scree plot suggested that 35 to 70 factors would be reasonable. Some factors had many items. The first had 46 items loading most heavily on it with 20 of the loadings greater than 0.5 and the remaining items with loadings greater than 0.3. We factor analyzed these 46 items separately and found 6 eigenvalues greater than 1. Our general approach for developing factors from this large set of items was:

1. Factor analyze all items.
2. Run separate factor analyses on each factor from Step 1.

3. If factor analysis from Step 2 indicates a unidimensional scale based on inspection of a scree plot, purify the scale by dropping items with loadings less than 0.5 and items that cause coefficient alpha to increase.
4. If the factor analysis in Step 2 was not unidimensional, continue factoring the factors until scales are unidimensional.

The analysis resulted in 44 experience scores. See our Web site for a list of items included in each scale, factor loadings, and coefficient alphas. Estimates of experiences are the simple averages of the items. Note that by using the simple averages of the items as factor scores, it is possible for experiences to be correlated, as one would expect. A few of the experience scales have moderately low values of alpha, indicating poor reliability. In most cases, the low values of alpha are due to having too few indicators of the underlying construct on the survey. As future research, we recommend developing additional items.

We measure newspaper readership using RBS (Calder & Malthouse, 2003a). RBS includes six manifestations of readership including the time, frequency, and completion for weekday and Sunday papers. The previous study showed that these six items form a highly reliable scale (α = .92). For the data set analyzed here, α = .77, and improves to .78 if the Sunday frequency item is dropped. To be consistent with previous publications using RBS, we include all six items.

Average Experience Levels

Because we have a random sample of daily U.S. newspapers, our conclusions generalize to newspapers as a medium (at least in the United States). Newspapers, as a medium, might provide some experiences better than other media. Strongly felt experiences by readers might characterize the medium and potentially differentiate it from other media. Likewise, some individual newspapers undoubtedly deliver higher experience levels on, for example, Experience Score 42 (Political bias), than others. This analysis quantifies these notions.

We study average experience levels and variation across newspapers with the following random-effects ANOVA model:

$$x_{ij} = \mu + m_i + e_{ij}$$

where x_{ij} is the experience score for one of the factors for reader j of newspaper i; μ is the overall mean across newspapers; m_i is the random effect, having mean 0 and standard deviation σ_m, on the mean for newspaper i; and e_{ij} is the error term having mean 0 and variance σ^2. Random variables m_i and e_{ij} are assumed to be normally distributed and independent of one another.

Table 1 gives estimates of overall means (μ) and variation across newspaper (σ_m). Recall that experiences are measured on 5-point scales, where 5 indicates a high level of the experience. The experience with the highest average across newspapers is Experience 6 (Regular part of my day), with $\mu = 3.57$, indicating that readers, on average, rate newspapers between 3 (*neither agree nor disagree*) and 4 (*agree*) on being brief and easy to read. Being a regular part of the reader's day, in part, characterizes newspapers as a medium. Experience 35 (Unwilling to share) has the lowest average of $\mu = 2.13$, indicating that across newspapers, readers nearly *disagree* (scale point 2) with statements regarding their unwillingness to share the newspapers with others in the household.

Table 1 also provides *p* values (sixth column) testing the null hypothesis that there is no variation in the means across newspapers (H_0: s $\sigma_m^2 = 0$), implying that readers of all newspapers have the same experience. For example, if the variance of Experience 42 were 0, we would conclude that all newspapers are perceived as equally politically biased. For all but 1 of the 44 experience factors, we reject the null hypothesis at the .01 level that there is no variation in mean experience level across newspapers, and con-

Table 1. Mean of Experience Levels Across Newspapers Estimated With a Random-Effects ANOVA Model

Experience	Label	μ	SE(μ)	σ_m	p	σ
13	Makes me smarter	3.47	0.013	.109	.000	.471
31	Drowning in news	2.26	0.009	.054	.005	.471
43	Ad credibility	3.21	0.010	.070	.001	.502
9	Too much	2.42	0.011	.082	.000	.504
40	Lacks distinction	2.51	0.012	.087	.000	.510
37	Uninformative ads	3.16	0.009	.039	.088	.519
5	Something to talk about	3.47	0.013	.103	.000	.522
21	Lack of local focus	2.57	0.011	.081	.000	.528
11	High quality, unique content	3.11	0.016	.142	.000	.541
14	Wasting my time	2.46	0.013	.106	.000	.543
38	Makes me want to read	3.07	0.011	.066	.003	.547
12	All sides of the story	2.99	0.014	.110	.000	.548
4	Touches and inspires me	3.07	0.014	.111	.000	.552
2	My personal timeout	3.01	0.013	.103	.000	.553
18	Makes me more interesting	2.61	0.012	.087	.000	.553
36	Taking a stand	3.40	0.015	.122	.000	.562
17	Annoyed and unimpressed by ads	2.76	0.011	.071	.002	.569
16	Ad usefulness	3.16	0.013	.093	.000	.577
20	People I know	3.42	0.027	.251	.000	.582
22	Skim and scan	3.07	0.011	.072	.002	.583
34	Unappealing stories	2.77	0.013	.097	.000	.588
1	Looks out for my interests	3.15	0.015	.118	.000	.590
25	Turned on by surprise and humor	3.00	0.012	.079	.001	.598
19	Makes me anxious	2.99	0.013	.089	.000	.599
27	Gender bias	2.56	0.012	.075	.002	.603
8	Grabs me visually	3.17	0.015	.114	.000	.608
15	Shows me diversity	3.49	0.020	.180	.000	.626
7	Clip and save	2.70	0.014	.104	.000	.647
33	News junkie	2.71	0.015	.112	.000	.650
24	Commands my attention	2.72	0.014	.102	.000	.658
23	Poor service	2.45	0.015	.108	.000	.663
29	Awkward to handle	2.32	0.015	.108	.000	.665
42	Political bias	2.93	0.018	.145	.000	.699
32	My dining companion	3.00	0.029	.265	.000	.717
6	Regular part of my day	3.57	0.014	.085	.004	.720
44	Pick up or take with me	2.68	0.017	.129	.000	.720
10	I connect with writers	3.03	0.018	.145	.000	.721
41	Guide me	2.76	0.015	.095	.001	.734
35	Unwilling to share	2.13	0.015	.100	.002	.765
3	Reading on the Web	2.21	0.017	.122	.000	.772
30	Value for my money	2.50	0.016	.104	.001	.790
39	Pass it around	3.29	0.017	.120	.000	.794
26	Like to critique	3.04	0.016	.107	.001	.807
28	Media multitasking	3.00	0.023	.182	.000	.967

clude newspapers differ in the level or degree for each experience.

Even though these standard deviations are highly significant, many are rather small in absolute magnitude due to the large sample size. Values of σ_m (fifth column) indicate how much experiences vary across newspapers. For example, the standard deviation of Experience Score 6 (Regular part of my day) is $\sigma_m = 0.085$; under the assumption that the means across newspapers are at least reasonably normally distributed, approximately 68% of newspapers will have means within ±0.085 scale points, 95% within ±0.17, and so on. Experience 20 (People I know) has one of the largest standard deviations ($\sigma_m = 0.265$). This scale measures how often people see stories about people they know in the paper. This makes sense because one would expect some newspapers to have more of a local flavor than others. Newspapers differentiate themselves from other newspapers on the amount of local coverage.

It is of interest to examine the variation in experience in a different way. Values of σ (column 7) indicate the extent to which readers of a newspaper agree on the experience. Experiences such as 28 (Media multitasking) with $\sigma = 0.97$, 26 (Like to critique) with $\sigma = 0.81$, and 39 (Pass it around) with $\sigma = 0.79$ have particularly large values, indicating large within-newspaper variation. Some readers simultaneously consume other media, critique the writing, and give the paper to others, but many do not have these experiences. Experiences with the most agreement are 13 (Makes me smarter) and 31 (Drowning in the news), both with $\sigma \approx 0.47$. Experiences 43 (Ad credibility) and 9 (Too much) also have small error variance. Within a newspaper, readers agree more on the extent to which the paper makes them smarter and that they are drowning in news.

Relation Between Newspaper Readership and Experience Scores

We hypothesized that experiences drive usage. This section quantifies the concomitant variation between experiences and readership to provide support for this hypothesis. If an experience correlates significantly with usage (the overt behavior of readers) across the newspapers, this is clear evidence that the experience is common across newspapers. Further, experiences that are uncorrelated with readership for some newspapers but correlated for others are said to be *idiosyncratic*. Idiosyncratic experiences are thus indicated when the variance of the correlation between the experience and usage across newspapers is positive. When experience is uncorrelated with readership for all newspapers and the variance not different from 0, then the experience is uninteresting. The level or degree of experience can thus be examined for newspapers in general (as a medium) or for a specific newspaper and compared to others.

More generally, the extent to which experiences relate to media usage provides evidence about the relative importance of different experiences. At least in terms of current media practices, more important experiences should be the ones most associated with usage.

We relate each experience to readership for each of the 101 newspapers analyzed simultaneously with hierarchical linear models (HLM; Kreft & DeLeeuw, 1998) of the form:

$$y_{ij} = (\alpha + a_i) + (\beta + b_i)x_{ij} + e_{ij},$$

where y_{ij} is the RBS of person j of newspaper i, x_{ij} is the measure of an experience, α is the overall intercept, a_i is the random effect on the intercept for newspaper i having mean 0 and variance σ_a^2, β is the overall slope, b_i is the random effect on the slope with mean 0 and variance σ_b^2, and e_{ij} is the error term having mean 0 and variance σ^2. Random variables a_i, b_i, and e_{ij} are assumed to be normally distributed and independent of one another. All models are estimated with the mixed procedure in SAS, Release 8.2.

Table 2 gives estimates from 44 models, sorted in descending order of the overall slopes estimates. Experience 5 (Something to talk about) has the largest positive slope. Across newspapers, its average slope is $\beta = 0.88$. Every unit increase in this scale is associated with an RBS increase of 0.88 scale points, on average. Some slopes are negative. The slope for Experience 5 (Wasting my time) is $\beta = -0.92$, indicating the more people agree with this statement, the less they read the newspaper. Some experiences have slopes that are approximately 0. The p values in the next column evaluate the null hypothesis $H_0: \beta = 0$, that the experience has no linear effect on readership, versus a two-sided alternative. For example, we cannot reject this null hypothesis for Experience 28 (Media multitasking). At least with these data, we cannot conclude these experiences are associated with RBS.

Values of σ_b tell how much slopes vary across newspapers; $\sigma_b = 0$ indicates the slopes have no variance, implying all newspapers have the same slope. For Experience 2 (My personal timeout), SAS is unable to detect variance across newspapers ($\sigma_b = 0$), indicating the slopes for Experience 2 do not vary across newspapers. Providing readers with a timeout has the same effect on readership for all newspapers. This is the case with most newspaper experiences. In some cases SAS is able to estimate positive variation across newspapers, but the variance is not significantly different from 0. For example, Experience 5 (Something to talk about) has a standard deviation in slopes across newspapers of $\sigma_b = 0.014$, but the p value testing the null hypothesis that this standard deviation is 0 is .469.

Table 2. Slope Estimates Using HLM

Experience	Label	β	p	σ_b	p	σ
5	Something to talk about	0.88	.000	.014	.469	1.13
13	Makes me smarter	0.81	.000	.000		1.16
1	Looks out for my interests	0.80	.000	.000		1.13
6	Regular part of my day	0.77	.000	.000		1.09
20	People I know	0.72	.000	.000		1.14
4	Touches and inspires me	0.54	.000	.049	.245	1.19
2	My personal timeout	0.50	.000	.000		1.18
11	High quality, unique content	0.45	.000	.000		1.20
18	Makes me more interesting	0.44	.000	.083	.053	1.19
36	Taking a stand	0.42	.000	.000		1.20
7	Clip and save	0.39	.000	.092	.010	1.19
10	I connect with writers	0.39	.000	.041	.263	1.18
8	Grabs me visually	0.36	.000	.018	.459	1.20
24	Commands my attention	0.34	.000	.078	.049	1.20
25	Turned on by surprise and humor	0.32	.000	.035	.359	1.21
15	Shows me diversity	0.32	.000	.034	.313	1.21
12	All sides of the story	0.31	.000	.000		1.21
32	My dining companion	0.28	.000	.000		1.21
43	Ad credibility	0.27	.000	.000		1.22
39	Pass it around	0.17	.000	.000		1.21
16	Ad usefulness	0.16	.000	.067	.059	1.22
30	Value for my money	0.15	.000	.090	.012	1.21
19	Makes me anxious	0.09	.004	.020	.450	1.22
35	Unwilling to share	0.06	.045	.111	.004	1.22
26	Like to critique	0.05	.060	.093	.005	1.22
42	Political bias	0.04	.148	.062	.128	1.21
28	Media multitasking	0.04	.050	.000		1.22
33	News junkie	0.01	.690	.107	.002	1.22
44	Pick up or take with me	0.00	.947	.106	.003	1.22
37	Uninformative ads	−0.03	.468	.000		1.22
41	Guide me	−0.05	.088	.054	.188	1.22
3	Reading on the Web	−0.15	.000	.081	.046	1.21
34	Unappealing stories	−0.20	.000	.107	.001	1.21
17	Annoyed and unimpressed by ads	−0.22	.000	.090	.036	1.21
38	Makes me want to read	−0.23	.000	.032	.394	1.21
27	Gender bias	−0.23	.000	.118	.001	1.21
23	Poor service	−0.27	.000	.122	.000	1.21
21	Lack of local focus	−0.27	.000	.100	.019	1.21
29	Awkward to handle	−0.34	.000	.081	.050	1.19
40	Lacks distinction	−0.43	.000	.106	.012	1.20
9	Too much	−0.54	.000	.101	.025	1.19
22	Skim and scan	−0.56	.000	.070	.101	1.18
31	Drowning in news	−0.70	.000	.143	.000	1.17
14	Wasting my time	−0.92	.000	.117	.001	1.11

However, there is significant, or nearly significant, variation in slopes across newspapers for some experiences. Experience 31 (Drowning in the news) has σ_b = 0.143, which is highly significant (p = .000). This indicates that for some newspapers, feeling drowned by the news is less correlated with readership than for others. Based on the assumption that the slopes have a normal distribution across newspapers, 99.7% of newspapers should have drowning-in-the-news slopes between −0.70±3 × 0.143, all of which are negative. Therefore, drowning in the news has a negative association with readership for all newspapers, but it is more negative for some. Experience 33 (News

junkie) has highly significant variance in slopes, yet the grand slope β is not significantly different from 0, indicating this factor is idiosyncratic. For some newspapers, being a news junkie is associated with readership but not for others. Neither the slope nor the variance of Experience 37 (Uninformative ads) is significant, making this factor uninteresting.

In view of the across-newspaper relations between the experiences and usage behavior obtained here, the data are sufficient to establish that almost all of the newspaper experiences relate to RBS. There are four uninteresting experiences and four idiosyncratic ones. The other experiences relate to usage behavior across newspapers in a manner that implies that they are potentially useful metrics for any newspaper and certainly for newspapers as a medium.

Conclusions

This research confirms that reading newspapers is a rich, multidimensional experience. The qualitative phase and factor analysis of the quantitative data identify experiences that are common across a random sample of 101 U.S. daily newspapers. Our analysis indicates that these experiences apply to newspapers as a medium and to individual newspapers. By regressing usage on experiences with HLMs, we show that across newspapers, greater usage is associated with higher experience levels for most experiences. To reiterate, the results indicate a robust relation such that it is worthwhile to consider these experiences in connection with newspapers as a medium or with any individual newspaper.

Once the existence of common experiences is established, it is of most interest to note that newspapers as a medium are certainly higher on some experiences than others and individual newspapers vary in their level or degree of an experience. Tables 1 and 2 show the overall pattern of how the industry and individual newspapers stand on the experiences identified in this research. Newspapers as a medium are high on experiences such as: Regular part of my day, Shows me diversity, and Something to talk about. Our conclusion from these results is that these experiences represent the strengths of the medium. There may be strategic reasons for any individual newspaper to discount one or more of them, but otherwise individual newspapers ignore them at their peril. They represent a new, more complete way of looking at the value that newspapers provide.

Beyond this, the broader implications of this research are, in our view, fivefold. First, newspaper readership cannot be entirely understood or evaluated only in terms of usage behavior (and given our previously reported results, especially not in terms of single, narrow measures of usage such as whether a person read yesterday). There is a subjective, qualitative side of readership, as measured by the experiences proposed here, that must be considered as well. Second, newspaper reading experiences are highly multidimensional. We have identified at least 44 newspaper experiences that appear to be sufficiently separate enough constructs to warrant consideration in further research and practice.

The third implication is that for each of the experiences identified, this research provides survey measures that could be incorporated into industry-level research and into benchmarking research by individual newspapers. This would have the incidental benefit of refining the present experience measures and adding new ones. Fourth, these results also bear on the issue of media-neutral media planning. To the extent that newspaper experiences are found to be different from the experience of other media, this could provide a way of evaluating each medium more fully on its own merits. Finally, a better understanding of experiences may also be beneficial in designing and evaluating newspaper advertising as creative. There is a need to view the media environment not just in terms of exposure but of context as well.

Bobby J. Calder

(calder@northwestern.edu)

is the Charles H. Kellstadt Distinguished Professor of Marketing, Psychology, and Journalism, Director of Research at the Media Management Center, and Director of the Center for Cultural Marketing, all at the Kellogg School of Management, Northwestern University, Evanston, IL. Calder's research focuses on marketing research, marketing planning, and consumer behavior.

Edward C. Malthouse

(ecm@northwestern.edu)

is an Associate Professor in the Integrated Marketing Communications Department at the Medill School of Journalism and the Senior Research Statistician of Medill and the Kellogg School of Management, Northwestern University, Evanston, IL. His research focuses on media and database marketing.

Endnotes

1. http://www.medill.nwu.edu/faculty/malthouse/ftp/npexp.html

References

Berry, S., Hercock, C., & Beard, L. (2003). "If they need it they'll read it"—Understanding readers' needs. In *Proceedings of the Worldwide Readership Symposium* (pp. 253–267). Ipsos-RSL, Harrow, England.

Brown, M. (1999). *Effective print media measurement.* Harrow, England: Ipsos-RSLLimited.

Burgoon, J., & Burgoon, M. (1980). Predictors of newspaper readership. *Journalism Quarterly, 57,* 489–596.

Calder, B. J. (2001). Understanding consumers. In D. Iacobucci (Ed.), *Kellogg on marketing* (pp. 151–164). New York: Wiley.

Calder, B. J., & Malthouse, E. C. (2003a). The behavioral score approach to dependent variables. *Journal of Consumer Psychology, 13,* 387–394.

Calder, B. J., & Malthouse, E. C. (2003b). What is integrated marketing. In D. Iacobucci & B. J. Calder (Eds.), *Kellogg on integrated marketing* (pp. 6–15). New York: Wiley.

Kreft, I., & DeLeeuw, J. (1998). *Introducing multilevel modeling*. Beverly Hills, CA: Sage.

Loges, W., & Ball-Rokeach, S. (1993). Dependency relations and newspaper readership, *Journalism Quarterly, 70,* 602–614.

Malthouse, E. C., & Calder, B. J. (2002). Patterns of readership: A qualitative variable approach. *International Journal on Media Management, 4*(4), 248–260.

Malthouse, E. C., Calder, B. J., & Eadie, W. (2003). Conceptualizing and measuring magazine reader experiences. In *Proceedings of the Worldwide Readership Symposium* (pp. 285–306). Ipsos-RSL, Harrow, England.

Regulatory Changes and Impacts on Media Management in the United States: A Look at Early Research

Alan B. Albarran and Kenneth D. Loomis
The University of North Texas, USA

The increasing consolidation of radio and television stations in the United States as a result of changing regulatory policies is having a direct impact on the role of the media manager. This article reviews the regulatory changes that have taken place regarding media ownership, and how it brought about changes in management practices. A summary of 2 research studies undertaken to examine the impact of regulatory changes on media management of radio and television stations is presented. Managers of radio clusters (at least 3 stations) and television duopolies were surveyed to ascertain how consolidation was affecting the way stations are managed. The data and findings in this article are discussed in terms of broader implications for media management outside the United States in an era of increasing globalization.

Broadcast (audiovisual) media management in the United States continues to experience massive change as a result of shifting regulatory policies and philosophies concerning media ownership. This article presents an analysis of the primary regulatory changes impacting media management, and summarizes key data from two independent research studies conducted with actual managers of radio and television stations in the United States that illustrate how these changing regulatory policies have affected media management.

The findings clearly have implications for other countries experiencing or anticipating regulatory changes within their own media system from two standpoints. First, the U.S. system is often looked on as a potential bellwether for management practices. Second, U.S.-based companies continue to seek opportunities outside their domestic borders, adding to the globalization of media companies reflecting a capitalistic orientation (McPhail, 2002).

U.S. Broadcast Ownership Policy: Shifting Patterns and Philosophies

The most direct way that regulatory policy impacts media management in the United States lies in the ownership provisions allowed by the government through the Fed-

Address correspondence to Alan B. Albarran, Department of Radio, Television and Film, The University of North Texas, P. O. Box 310589, Denton, TX 76203. E-mail: albarran@unt.edu

eral Communications Commission (FCC). Since the advent of broadcasting the U.S. system was established independent of government ownership, save for some frequencies reserved for military use. In the United States, broadcasting has existed primarily as a commercial enterprise since radio began selling advertising in 1922 (Sterling & Kittross, 2002).

There is a limited body of literature that examines broadcast ownership in the United States. Among the most important works are Compaine and Gomery's *Who Owns the Media* (2000), the multiple editions of Bagdikian's *The Media Monopoly* (1997), McChesney's works on consolidation (Herman & McChesney, 1997; McChesney, 1999), and a number of studies in scholarly journals that address trends in ownership (see Howard, 1995, 1998; Sterling, 1975) and economic aspects of ownership (see Bates, 1988, 1993). However, none of these studies examines the impact of ownership changes on media management, the subject of this investigation. The following sections provide a look at key regulatory changes impacting media ownership.

Regulatory Efforts: Pre-1990s

U.S. broadcasting was established on the principle of scarcity, reflecting the philosophy that more individuals would want to broadcast than permitted by available frequencies (Kahn, 1984). Thus, the FCC adopted a public interest standard in determining who would be allowed the privilege of owning a broadcast license. The scarcity concept served to limit the number of stations a single individual or corporate entity could own for many decades (see Logan, 1997).

The first formal ownership guidelines established by the FCC occurred in 1941 following a series of investigations into concerns over the practices of the broadcast networks (Kahn, 1984). In 1964, the FCC officially codified what became known as the rule of sevens, stating that no individual or corporation could own more than 7 stations in any class, limiting the maximum number of owned stations to 21, or 7 AM, 7 FM, and 7 TV. There was one exception with broadcast television: An owner could own no more than 5 stations in the lucrative VHF class (channels 2–13); the other two stations had to be in the UHF range (channels 14 and higher).

The rule of sevens remained intact until 1984, when the FCC became fully engaged in a deregulation mode that had started in the late 1970s. At the time the FCC was eliminating many rules that were deemed outdated and inefficient (Fowler & Brenner, 1982). By 1984 cable television was rapidly growing across the country, and the networks were starting to lose viewers. Owners had lobbied Congress and the FCC for years to allow relaxation of the ownership limits.

The FCC adopted new rules that began in 1985, increasing the ownership limits to 12–12–12, with additional criteria for television owners. TV owners could own no more than 7 stations in a particular class, and their total reach of the national audience could not exceed 25%. For many television companies, the reach cap prevented groups from reaching their maximum number of stations.

Despite these dramatic regulatory changes, there is no empirical evidence or identifiable studies indicating how media management was impacted prior to the 1990s. During the 1990s, further liberalization would result in shifting managerial styles, first in radio, and later in television.

Regulatory Efforts: The 1990s and Beyond

It was in the 1990s that deregulatory momentum combined with healthy market conditions to enable broadcast companies to rapidly accelerate consolidation. The impact on management was dramatic. No longer could preexisting organization structures accommodate the changes, because now numerous stations were operating together under one roof. It is on the consequent changes in managers' responsibilities and orientations that this study is focused.

In 1992, the FCC increased the limits on radio ownership to 18 stations in each class, and modified the duopoly

rule, which prevented an owner from controlling more than one station of the same class in a market.[1] Under the new rules, a radio owner could now own up to 2 stations in the same class in a market. In most cases, a single individual would serve as the general manager (GM) for all stations. In 1994, the FCC again liberalized the ownership limits for radio, increasing the amount of stations owned by a single owner to 20 in each class of service, or a total of 40 stations. Both the 1992 and 1994 rulings reflected the fact that the radio industry consisted of more than 10,000 stations, and even with the ownership changes there would still be literally hundreds of radio owners across the industry.

More changes occurred just 2 years later with the passage of the 1996 Telecommunications Act. For decades Congress amended various provisions of the Communications Act of 1934, but the 1996 Act is recognized as bringing sweeping changes to both the radio and television industries (Owen, 1999; Shane, 1998).

In radio, national ownership caps were eliminated, but local caps were adopted to prevent undue concentration in individual markets (Albarran & Pitts, 2001). The FCC used a tiered approach; in markets with at least 45 stations one owner could control up to 8 stations, with no more than 5 in the same class. In markets with 30 to 44 stations, the limit was 7 stations, with no more than 4 in the same class, and so forth.

In television, national ownership limits were eliminated, and the reach cap rose to 35%. Together, these changes to radio and television ownership set off a massive wave of mergers, acquisitions, and deal making as companies consolidated their media operations to achieve greater operational efficiencies and economies of scale. Further, the new Act required the FCC to conduct a biennial review of ownership criteria to evaluate changing industry conditions.

Television ownership was further liberalized in 1999 with the FCC approving TV duopolies—ownership of two stations in a market—provided the combinations were not among the top-rated stations in the market and were limited to VHF–UHF combinations. As with radio, the move to create TV duopolies had a significant ripple effect on media management, in that a single individual could now manage these new duopolies.

In June 2003, the FCC made further changes to television ownership as a result of its biennial review. The reach cap increased from 35% to 45%. The FCC also allowed for the creation of television triopolies[2], or clusters of 3 stations in a market owned by the same individual or company provided there were at least 18 stations in the market and only one of the stations was among the top four in terms of audience ratings ("FCC Sets Limits," 2003). Uproar over the new 45% limit led to Congress acting later in the summer of 2003 to maintain the 35% cap, but negotia-

Table 1. Major Philosophy and Policy Decisions Impacting U.S. Broadcast Ownership

Date(s)	Philosophy	Major Decisions
1927–1979	Scarcity	Limits on network ownership (1941).
		Rule of sevens adopted on ownership (1964).
1979–1995	Deregulation	Ownership limits increased to 12-12-12, with television audience reach cap of 25% (1985).
		Changes to duopoly rules in radio (1992, 1994).
1996–Present	Competition	Telecommunications Act removes national limits on radio and television ownership; establishes local caps on radio ownership; television audience reach increases to 35% (1996).
		TV duopolies allowed (1999).
		Audience reach cap increased to 45% TV, later revised to 39%; Triopolies allowed in markets with 18 stations (2003).

Note. Compiled from various sources by the authors.

tions eventually resulted in an increase to 39% (see Ahrens, 2003).

Table 1 summarizes the major decisions and the resulting action affecting broadcast ownership. These changes in media ownership have radically altered the radio and television landscape in the United States. Concomitantly, these changes have dramatically impacted the role of the broadcast manager, who must not only function in an intensely competitive environment, but also manage multiple properties—some of which may even compete with one another for audiences and advertisers. Trying to understand this new managerial environment led to two national studies of U.S. media managers, the findings of which are presented in the next section.

The New Managerial Environment

Two separate studies were initiated beginning in the summer of 2001 to attempt to gauge how the changes in the regulatory environment since the early 1990s had directly impacted managers of radio and television stations in the United States. Specifically, the studies targeted managers who were now responsible for managing multiple stations—at least three in the case of radio, or a duopoly in television. Table 2 illustrates exactly how the managerial environment was set following major policy changes in

Table 2. Potential Number of Stations Managed in Local Markets Before and After Regulatory Changes

	Before 1996	After 1996
Radio	1–2 depending on duopoly	Up to 8 stations

	Before 1999	After 1999
Television	1	2

1996 in radio (establishment of local ownership caps) and 1999 in television (duopolies established).

Both studies began with qualitative in-depth interviews with a group of GMs (10 for radio, 6 for television) involved in managing more than one station to identify how they were adapting to the new environment, challenges they had encountered, time management, and attitudes toward managing more than one station. The interviews were recorded, transcribed, and content analyzed to find common themes and patterns. From these interviews, a detailed mail survey was prepared for each industry. Both surveys were pretested with a small sample of managers to remove any ambiguities or confusion with the instrument.[3]

Radio Study

The radio study was limited to the top 25 radio groups. A database was created using each company's radio holdings to identify where they operated clusters of stations. Using Web sites and other reference information, we identified 318 radio GMs eligible to receive the survey among the top 25 companies.[4] Potential respondents were first contacted by phone to inform them that they would receive a survey, and asked for their participation. Following Dillman (2000), the participants received the survey and a cover letter in December 2001, along with two follow-up mailings if they failed to respond. These efforts resulted in a response rate of 48%, or 154 usable surveys.[5]

Television Study

The television study also began with in-depth interviews, which were initiated in the spring of 2002. In developing a database of TV duopoly general managers, the Internet directory *100,000 Watts* was used to identify potential respondents (100kwatts.tmi.net). This process identified 101 television GMs managing television duopolies in the United States at the time of the survey. Using the same contact protocols as in the radio study, television GMs were first mailed surveys in June 2002, with each respondent receiving two follow-up mailings. Of the 101 eligible respondents, 69 returned a usable survey for a return rate of 68%.

Results of the Studies

Most of the radio and television managers were male (radio = 85%; television = 81%) and had several years of managerial experience (radio = 11 years; television = 7+ years). In terms of descriptive information, highlights of the two studies follow.

Radio

Approximately 78% of the radio managers said they were spending more time at their job than ever before, of which 41% of their time was devoted to their stations' sales efforts (see Table 3). The rest of their work time was divided fairly equally among programming (17%), budgeting (13%), marketing (12%), and generating nontraditional revenue (6%). When combined, the three financial-oriented responsibilities (sales, budgeting, and nontraditional revenue) account for 60% of the GMs' workday activities. Table 3 also shows the GMs reported spending almost twice the amount of time with their department heads (40%) than with staff (24%), themselves (17%), or corporate individuals (12%). In citing which area was most important to their success as a manager, 51% of

Table 3. Radio GMs Self-Reported Time Allocation for a Typical Week

Percentage of time working with different responsibilities	
Sales	41%
Programming	17%
Budgets	13%
Marketing	12%
Nontraditional revenue	6%
News	2%
Various other	9%
Percentage of time working with different individuals	
Department heads	40%
Staff-level employees	24%
Themselves/alone	17%
Corporate management	12%
Consultants	2%
Various other	5%

Note. N = 154.

the radio GMs identified the quality of their respective department heads as the single most important criterion. The GMs with the greater number of employees, and the larger number of stations in their clusters, were more likely to rank department heads as their most important asset. When assembling management teams, owners might want to more carefully consider the abilities of those hired or promoted to middle management. Those individuals, above anyone else, are likely to be the most valuable players of their franchise.

Attitudes toward management. In the study, 30 Likert scale questions derived from the qualitative interviews were used to measure managerial attitudes toward their jobs (Loomis & Albarran, 2003). Respondents answered using a 5-point scale ranging from 5 (*strongly agree*) to 1 (*strongly disagree*).

To identify the underlying orientations at work among managers, an exploratory factor analysis was ordered. A priori decisions regarding the factor solution required that each factor have an eigenvalue of 1.0, contain at least two variables, and have loadings of at least .50. The solution identified four factors explaining 38.45% of the variance.[6]

The first factor, labeled people oriented, reflected the managers' concern for staff and themselves. The second factor, priority oriented, included variables that have to deal with juggling priorities for work and family. The third factor, procedure oriented, reflected items related to managerial decision making and dealing with department heads. The fourth factor, performance oriented, focuses on performance in regards to financial and budgetary obligations.

To identify any differences among these four orientation dimensions, correlations were ordered using the factor scores as variables run against key demographic characteristics of the study. These correlations found GMs with 16 or more years of experience were more likely than those with 1 to 5 years to express concerns with short decision making time frames, the amount of time they spent working with financials, and the responsibilities they have delegated to middle managers. Managers in the two largest radio groups—Clear Channel and Infinity—also reported greater levels of discomfort with those elements, as did the GMs with greater numbers of department heads and total number of employees. It is likely the GMs with the most experience, and those working in the larger environments with more people, have had to make the biggest adjustments in terms of how they do their jobs.

Even though the procedure orientation showed the greatest differences among demographic breakouts, the performance factor—measuring elements of financial management—proved to be the strongest factor overall.

In nearly every demographic breakout the performance focus scored the highest mean average of the four factors, indicating the statements in that factor were the ones with which the GMs most agreed. This seems to indicate the GMs clearly agreed on their job priorities. Regardless of market size, years of experience, sex, or anything else, GMs understood their highest priority was making as much money for their company as they were able.

Television

Results were similar for the television duopoly managers. Approximately 75% of the TV managers indicated they were spending more time on the job managing two stations as opposed to a single station, again at the expense of time with family and outside activities. Notably, television GMs ranked the importance of department heads even higher then their radio counterparts. Sixty-five percent of TV GMs said the quality of the department heads was the single most important element of their own success.

Managers indicated they spent the majority of the time working with sales, followed by news (see Table 4). The managers of duopolies with less than 100 full-time employees spent more time on sales than the managers of duopolies with more than 100 employees (36% vs. 22%). This difference was mostly compensated for by time spent on news, with managers of larger duopolies spending twice as much time on their stations' news products (20% vs. 10%). Undoubtedly, the more competitive nature of local news in the larger markets influenced this difference.

The characteristics of the workforces employed at the television stations have changed since the creation of duopolies. Almost half (49%) of the GMs reported a reduction in the number of full-time employees at their duopolies, whereas 80% of the respondents indicated the size of their part-time staffs had either stayed the same or decreased since the stations merged. However, even as the total staff

Table 4. Television GMs Self-Reported Time Allocation for a Typical Week

Percentage of time working with different responsibilities	
Sales	28%
News	15%
Budgets	11%
Marketing	11%
Personnel issues	11%
Programming	8%
Engineering and technical	8%
Nontraditional revenue	7%
Various other	7%

Note. $N = 69$.

size of the duopolies had decreased, 74% of the GMs said their sales forces increased. Clearly, the increase in the size of the sales staffs came at a significant cost to other departments, and illustrates the importance of sales and marketing to the bottom line, and efforts to secure a greater percentage of advertising dollars in the local market.

This workforce shift also impacted employee morale. Most of the GMs (64%) said they detected anxiety among their staffs during the merger process. When asked to describe the nature of this anxiety, the GMs most often mentioned concerns about job security and increased workload. Other concerns involved stress over coordination issues, a general fear of the unknown, and employees' unwillingness to change. Employee anxiety seemed to be most acute in duopolies in larger markets with a greater number of employees. Seventy-nine percent of the GMs in the top 50 markets noted employee anxiety. Only 50% of the GMs in the smaller markets identified such anxiety. Similarly, 73% of the GMs with more than 100 employees sensed employee anxiety, whereas only 52% of the GMs with fewer than 100 employees did so.

Attitudes toward management. There were 23 attitudinal statements constructed based on the qualitative interviews (see Loomis & Albarran, 2003). These items, coded similarly to the radio study, were also subjected to exploratory factor analysis to identify managerial orientations for television. The same criteria for a factor (two variables with loadings of .50; eigenvalue of 1.0) were used in the television study. The procedure produced six factors explaining 62.6% of the variance.

The first factor, autonomy, includes items reflecting the necessity of freedom to operate without undue oversight or micromanaging. The second factor, performance, includes variables dealing with financial aspects of duopoly management. The third factor, purpose, reflects the importance of focusing the staff's efforts—and then adequately compensating employees—for the development of an effective brand identity for the duopoly. The fourth factor, public interest, shows the importance of service to the community through news and public service programming. The fifth factor, human resources, concerns the challenges of effectively communicating the duopoly's new vision while implementing the merger's logistics. The last factor, team building, represents the importance of hiring the right people to accomplish the work and challenges with managing a duopoly. (The factor solutions for both studies are detailed in Appendix A and Appendix B.)

To see if any of the six orientation factors was correlated with demographic characteristics of the respondents, chi-square tests were conducted using the factor scores as variables against the demographic items. Each factor was cross-tabbed with gender, market size, years of general managerial experience, the number of employees in the duopoly, and the number of department heads in the duopoly.

The only significant difference was found in the relation between the team building dimension and the number of department heads, $\chi^2(6, n = 66) = 15.15, p < .019$. A one-way analysis of variance between team building and the number of department heads reinforced the association and the direction of the relationship, $F(6, 69) = 2.805, p < .018$. This suggests the more a GM perceives his or her effectiveness as being dependent on the quality of employees, the greater the tendency to employ more department heads. This finding, coupled with the fact the GMs consider department heads the most important element of their own success, points to the necessity for strong middle management in duopolies.

No significant differences were found in any of the other chi-square comparisons. Therefore, the managerial orientations of duopoly GMs are consistent across the demographic descriptions.

Discussion

These studies illustrate a rapidly changing managerial environment in U.S. radio and television where managers are responsible for multiple stations with increasing pressure to produce profitable operations. The intense competitive market for advertisers and audiences in U.S. markets becomes even more challenging in a consolidated environment, as multiple stations are expected by owners to generate expanded revenues.

This high-stakes environment has led to two observable changes among radio and television managers. First, managers in both studies indicated they are passionate about the challenges of their jobs, but they also indicated they are working longer hours than before, often at the expense of time for family, friends, and other activities. Second, managers identified greater reliance on middle managers to help with the multiple responsibilities encountered in managing multiple stations.

This second point deserves further elaboration. While middle managers (e.g., sales, programming, operations, promotions, etc.) have always held important roles in broadcast management, they have absorbed many tasks formerly performed by the GM. Such tasks include budget, personnel, strategic planning, and alliances with other units. This change has allowed GMs to focus on generating greater cash flows for the various operations under their control, and serving as liaisons to the owners.

In the United States, the consolidation of both radio and television has led to the decline in the number of GM positions; in fact, at many stations one will likely find former GMs serving in middle management roles. No doubt others have left the industry altogether through retirement or attrition, perhaps some to the newly emerging satellite radio industry. This suggests that the paths to becoming a middle manager, often a logical goal for new employees to the industry, will likely take longer to achieve and be more competitive. In all likelihood, middle managers will have fewer opportunities to move up in a consolidated environment, as fewer GM positions will exist. In fact, 52% of the GMs in this study said the number of their department heads had not changed, even as their clusters grew larger. Only 25% of the managers indicated they had added department heads as the clusters grew in size.

All of this points to a possible shift in the qualifications of radio and television middle managers. No longer will stations be served by simply promoting reliable individuals from within the organizations. Skill sets not previously required of many middle managers of single stations—such as proficiency with financial statements, budget analysis, and motivational skills required for larger staffs—will now become baseline requirements for anyone hoping to achieve management status. It is unlikely that journeymen professionals with practical experience, but with limited business abilities, will any longer be considered qualified for middle management promotions. Although this may not bode well for the current broadcast labor force, it may provide hope for those who have experienced the diversity of training provided by a university-level education, or for those who have business experience in other large industries.

Similar forces are at work in the staff-level positions below the GMs. Consolidation has also eliminated some of those jobs, resulting in increased responsibilities, stress, and competition for even the entry-level positions that remain. This seems especially true in larger market station groups with bigger staffs. In such environments, strategies should be in place to mitigate the negative effects of consolidation on employee morale. Strong management will find ways to maintain positive work environments by effectively communicating the challenges and opportunities of the new marketplace.

There is much we do not know about management in this new environment. These initial studies, the first to provide a national look at radio and television management, will hopefully provide some benchmark data that will be useful in future research. The studies do suffer from a few limitations. The most obvious are the use of self-report data from the respondents, and the fact that most of the data were gathered from managers working primarily with the largest media companies. Still, the high response rate and the timeliness of the data are important in obtaining a picture of the challenges facing managers of radio and television clusters in the United States.

Although the management of broadcast media is clearly evolving in the United States, a larger question for further research is how these practices might also occur in other countries around the globe that find their media systems in transition. U.S.-based companies continue to expand globally (McPhail, 2002). Clear Channel, the largest radio operator in the United States, is also one of the largest radio operators around the globe, owning stations in 60 different countries (see http://international.clearchannel.com/new/). Companies like Viacom, Disney, and Time Warner have numerous international television interests, so the influence of American corporations is widespread. The culture of these large American companies is increasingly requiring diverse skills at the middle management level. These requirements are likely to be expected in countries in which these companies conduct business. To what extent these managerial practices might be emulated or adopted in other countries deserves further inquiry and study.

Although such a question is beyond the scope of these initial investigations, the implications of the changing U.S. market on international media management practices is an area demanding more attention from media management scholars. Likewise, more research will determine how effective these shifts in U.S. managerial practices are in actually producing more profitable radio and television clusters, and the resulting personal impact on managers and their employees.

Alan B. Albarran

(albarran@unt.edu)

is a Professor and Chair of the Department of Radio, Television, and Film at the University of North Texas, Denton, TX. His research interests revolve around the management and economics of the communication industries.

Kenneth D. Loomis

(loomis@unt.edu)

is an Assistant Professor in the Department of Radio, Television, and Film at the University of North Texas, Denton, TX. His research interests include media management, media effects, and religiosity and the media.

Endnotes

1. Prior to 1992, an owner was limited to a single AM and a single FM station in the same market. The changes in the radio duopoly rule allowed for an additional station to be acquired.
2. Only a limited number of major media markets would have enough stations to qualify for triopoly ownership.
3. A copy of the survey instrument for each study is available from the authors.
4. To be eligible for the survey the GM had to manage a minimum of three radio stations.
5. The 154 managers in this study reported that they managed a total of 1,058 stations.
6. The factor solution produced a total of 11 factors, but Factors 5 through 11 either failed to produce a factor with at least two variables or the factors had loadings lower than .50. These single-item factors were deleted from further analysis. Given the exploratory nature of this study this solution seems reasonable.

References

Ahrens, F. (2003, November 25). Compromise puts TV ownership cap at 39%. Retrieved January 8, 2004, from http://www.washingtonpost.com

Albarran, A. B.. & Pitts, G. G. (2001). *The radio broadcasting industry.* Boston: Allyn & Bacon.

Bagdikian, B. (1997). *The media monopoly* (5th ed.). Boston: Beacon Press.

Bates, B. J. (1988). The impact of deregulation on television station prices. *Journal of Media Economics, 1,* 5–12.

Bates, B. J. (1993). Concentration in local television markets. *Journal of Media Economics, 6,* 3–22.

Compaine, B., & Gomery, D. (2000). *Who owns the media?* (3rd ed.). Mahwah, NJ: Lawrence Erlbaum Associates, Inc.

Dillman, D. A. (2000). *Mail and Internet surveys: The tailored design method* (2nd ed.). New York: Wiley.

FCC sets limits on media concentration. (2003, June 2). Retrieved January 15, 2004, from http://www.fcc.gov/Daily_Releases/Daily_Business/2003/db0602/DOC-235047A1.doc

Fowler, M. S., & Brenner, D. L. (1982). A marketplace approach to broadcast regulation. *Texas Law Review, 60,* 207–257.

Herman, E. S., & McChesney, R. W. (1997). *The global media.* London, England: Cassell.

Howard, H. H. (1995). TV station group and cross-media ownership: A 1995 update. *Journalism & Mass Communication Quarterly, 72,* 390–401.

Howard, H. H. (1998). The 1996 Telecommunications Act: One year later. *Journal of Media Economics, 11*(2), 21–32.

Kahn, F. J. (1984). *Documents of American broadcasting* (4th ed.). Englewood Cliffs, NJ: Prentice Hall.

Logan, C. (1997). Getting beyond scarcity: A new paradigm for assessing the constitutionality of broadcast regulation. *California Law Review, 85,* 1687–1707.

Loomis, K. D., & Albarran, A. B. (2003). *Managing television duopolies: A first look.* Unpublished manuscript. The University of North Texas, Denton, TX.

McChesney, R. W. (1999). *Rich media, poor democracy.* Urbana: University of Illinois Press.

McPhail, T. (2002). *Global communication: Theories, stakeholders, and trends.* Needham Heights, MA: Allyn & Bacon.

Owen, B. M. (1999). *The Internet challenge to television.* Boston: Harvard University Press.

Shane, E. (1998). The state of the industry: Radio's shifting paradigm. *The Journal of Radio Studies, 5*(2), 1–7.

Sterling, C. S. (1975). Trends in daily newspaper and broadcast ownership. *Journalism Quarterly, 52,* 247–256.

Sterling, C. S., & Kittross, M. (2002). *Stay tuned: A history of American broadcasting* (3rd ed.). Mahwah, NJ: Lawrence Erlbaum Associates, Inc.

Radio Study Factor Loadings

| | Factors | | | |
Items	People Oriented	Priority Oriented	Procedure Oriented	Performance Oriented
I am concerned about burnout among my staff.	.79	.12	.01	.00
I am concerned about burnout for myself.	.73	.31	.01	.01
I have had to work harder at creating quality time with my family.	.26	.79	.21	.12
I have had to work harder at creating quality time with my spouse.	.01	.76	.01	.01
My workload has significantly increased from when I managed fewer stations.	.01	.51	.33	.30
I have less time to make decisions than I used to.	.23	.26	.60	.01
I spend too much time working with budgets and reports.	.28	.26	.55	.42
Department heads are now doing the work that general managers used to do.	.00	.12	.50	.01
My job is more about management and less about radio than ever before.	.00	.13	.19	.67
Financial and budget considerations are the top priority with me.	.00	.00	.00	.63
Eigenvalue	5.3	2.6	2.0	1.7
% of variance	17.7	8.6	6.6	5.6
Total variance explained		38.45%		

Note. Italic indicates items used to construct factor variables.

Appendix B. Television Study Factor Loadings

Items	Autonomy	Performance	Purpose	Public Interest	Human Resources	Team Building
I receive more supervision than is necessary from those above me.	.83	-.21	-.14.00	.00	.00	
I am feeling more pressure from those above me than before.	.73	.00	-.12	.00	.00	.15
My duopoly is effectively attaining its revenue potential in the advertising marketplace.	-.10	.87	.00	.00	-.18	.28
Advertisers understand how television consolidation can help them.	-.10	.61	-.24	.44	.00	-.15
I spend too much time working with budgets and reports.	.31	-.57	.00	-.12	-.21	.34
It is more important than ever before to have a good promotion department.	.00	-.17	.71	.00	.00	.00
Having a strong local identity is the most important thing for my television stations.	-.15	.00	.66	.11	.00	.22
My company recognizes the need to adequately compensate its employees.	-.41	.32	.58	.00	.00	.00
My employees generally have taken on the additional responsibilities with a positive attitude.	-.13	.00	.55	.16	.23	.00
Consolidation has enabled us to place a greater emphasis on improving our journalism.	.10	.00	.00	.77	.10	.00
Consolidation has enabled us to place a greater emphasis on improving our community involvement.	.00	.00	.32	.71	-.12	.13
Consolidation has increased the amount of inventory we give to public service.	-.16	.23	.00	.60	.00	.00
It was challenging for the staffs to understand the company's vision.	.00	-.13	.14	.00	.77	.00
It was challenging for the staffs to transition into working together, instead of against each other.	.00	.00	.00	.00	.74	.20
My workload has significantly increased from when I managed just one station.	.22	.00	.00	.00	.11	.56
I love the challenge of my job.	-.21	.00	.19	.15	.26	.52
To me, the most important thing I do is hiring the people below me.	-.14	.00	.27	.00	.22	.52
Eigenvalue	3.5	3.1	2.7	2.2	1.5	1.4
% of variance	15.3	13.5	11.8	9.3	6.5	6.1
Total variance explained		62.6%				

Note. Italic indicates items used to construct factor variables.

Theoretical Approach/ Methodology

Has the book a theoretical approach? Is the applied methodology useful for the author's objectives? Is the context of the information clear? Is the publication positioned within existing literature? Are the terms clearly defined? Is the information consistent?

Structure

How does the chosen structure help the reader to understand the information?

Depth of the Analysis

Is the content sufficient to explain the described phenomenon?

Contribution to New Knowledge

How does it contribute to existing knowledge? Does it use up-to-date data?

Applicability

Is the content useful? Does it help in solving practical problems?

Clarity and Style of Writing

Are the ideas presented in a clear and comprehensible way? Are specific and illustrative examples given? Is the information concise?

Blockbusters and Trade Wars: Popular Culture in a Globalized World

by Peter S. Grant and Chris Wood

☐

reviewed by Nicola Simpson

The term *globalization* is very popular these days, particularly with regards to media. We live in a world where popular culture is pervasive and invasive, touching every person from Boston to Bangkok. On some level we recognize the influence of far-reaching media, and understand that as our cultural universe expands, the power structure behind it contracts. However, that recognition will only turn to discomfort once we are made fully aware of the peculiar nature of the "cultural industries"—a term privileged by many countries, and scorned by the one country whose dominance seems unshakeable. In *Blockbusters and Trade Wars: Popular Culture in a Globalized World*, Peter S. Grant and Chris Wood skillfully illuminate the strange world of global media, and although they do not reassure us that our choices will be individual and independent, they do reveal the intricacies that make the media unlike any other economic good.

For the last 30 years, America has been charged by academics with cultural imperialism. Cultural imperialism is not a new phenomenon—consider the British empire in the 19th century—but this new post-colonialism exists at a time when international communication is faster, cheaper, and more direct than ever before. Satellites, cable, and the Internet have created an environment in which entertainment is mass produced and consumed at a speed that seems almost instantaneous. The locus of all this commotion is the United States or, more precisely, Hollywood. So the eternal question is this: In the face of American gigantism, how can other countries defend their cultural borders or provide any kind of domestic alternative to the force of Hollywood products?

Grant and Wood's prime example of this tension between American culture and the rest of the world is Canada. If globalization is defined as "a process in which borders are eliminated and multinational companies can extend their reach across geographical boundaries" (p. 2), then the geographical, economic, and intellectual proximity that Canada has to the United States makes it unique in the fight for cultural sovereignty. After all, Canadians were watching American television before Canadian television existed! The longest unprotected border in the world does not just allow for political osmosis, but the seepage of ideas and values, both common and uncommon. For Americans comfortable in their self-awareness, Canada is "just like us," only more polite and with a preternatural obsession with hockey and irreverent comedy. Canadians, however, tend to be more uncomfortable with their bullish neighbors, rallying to the cause of a national culture that is indistinct at best. When asked to define Canadian-ness, the typical response is mental stuttering, resulting in the only assertion possible under the circumstances: "Not American."

This kind of response, although philosophically intriguing, absolutely stymies government agencies trying to ascribe national identity to a media product. International coproductions are on the rise, and even "American" blockbusters are bound to include creative and technical personnel from beyond just the United States. However, when it comes to determining nationality, Grant and Wood point out that the onus is on the author, not the idea (p. 164). And that system may be what makes the cultural identity of global media products a bit murky.

However, as Grant and Wood astutely point out, the struggle for the Canadian film, television, recording, and publishing industries to play with the big boys is persistently lopsided. It seems nearly impossible to create a media product that will satisfy both Canadian cultural agendas (as set out by funding and government agencies) and be competitive in a global market saturated by pricier, flashier U.S. content. Canadian producers, as well as their global counterparts, are beating their heads against the wall of the "curious economics" that insulate the cultural industries from meaningful trade disputes. On the surface, the math seems simple. An ever expanding channel universe means more venues for media products. However, although nearly every country in the world regards its music, books, and movies as "cultural products" under the General Agreement on Tariffs and Trade, the United States resolutely insists that such goods are simply industrial products, no different than the average widget. Added to this frustration is the fact that Hollywood can produce these goods on a scale unattainable in other economies, and can export them to markets where viable domestic alternatives would undoubtedly be more expensive to produce. It is a lose–lose situation for any competitor, but for the munificence of quotas and subsidies.

So are quotas and subsidies the best competitive strategy? Not necessarily, say Grant and Wood. Quotas can artificially inflate the market for indigenous products, and subsidies "risk rewarding the undeserving" (p. 304). However, the doomsday scenarios they present are revelatory, not discouraging, and their points acutely ironic. The tax incentives that help support Canadian producers have also turned the country into a mecca for American "runaway" production, much to the dismay of California trade unions. Funding systems that bolster production do not necessarily translate into assistance with distribution; the authors note that close to 60% of films made in Britain in 2000 have yet to make it to theaters (p. 67). For many countries, domestic production is a black hole that sucks in money and returns a cultural product that is less tangibly valuable than the investment. Ultimately, quotas and subsidies seem to be less of a competitive strategy, and more of a coping mechanism.

Although Grant and Wood offer little in the way of new analysis of this problem, they combine facts and figures with interviews that academics are hard-pressed to elicit. Seeing the motivations of the men behind the curtain is illuminating. However, *Blockbusters and Trade Wars* is not simply a journalistic account of the industry's dilemmas—the theoretical foundation is solid, building on recent work by Richard Caves, Colin Hoskins et al., and Harold Vogel. The only quibble that academics may have with the journalistic style is the maddening lack of footnotes, for those who want to play follow-the-leader with sources. The "tool kit" they offer—including support for public broadcasting, scheduling and expenditure requirements for private broadcasters and other gatekeepers, subsidies and quotas for underrepresented genres, and stricter enforcement of competition and ownership policies—contains nothing new. However, Grant and Wood try very hard to be encouraging about this uphill battle, suggesting that "any government prepared to support its own creators without limiting their freedom of expression surely then deserves the gratitude of other nations, not their criticism" (p. 317). Canada, stand up and take a bow. Or rather, bend over?

Rating

Rating Criteria	Rating
Theoretical Approach/Methodology	+++
Structure	++++
Depth of the Analysis	++++
Contribution of New Knowledge	+++
Applicability	+++++
Clarity and Style of Writing	+++++
Rating Points: excellent: +++++	poor: +

Douglas & McIntyre, 2004

464 pages

ISBN 1–55365–009–3

www.douglas-mcintyre.com

Review Author

Nicola Simpson
University of Pennsylvania, USA
nsimpson@asc.upenn.edu

Economic and Financial Press: From the Beginnings to the First Oil Crisis

by Ángel Arrese

☐

reviewed by Reimar H. Mueller

The book is divided in three parts. The first part covers the origins of the Economic and Financial Press to the first third of the 19th century. The second part covers the 1830s to the 1929 crisis. The third part covers the time from the Great Depression to the first oil crisis.

The author starts his analysis in the first part of the book by looking at the early developments of the financial press. He cites examples of Germany (the Függer family), Spain (Simón Ruiz), and Great Britain (Thomas Gresham III). He writes about the first stock markets in Amsterdam and London and also makes a reference to the first stock market bubbles in history. Furthermore, he writes about the first "public" debates in the financial press on economic issues such as free trade. Those early newspapers combined the publication of data, the coverage of news, and the expression of an opinion. The latter was a novelty and revolution at that time. Expressions of opinion caused some controversy, as the opinion is biased by nature and reinforced or supported stock market bubbles. The author continues by looking at the early public discussion about the principles of political economy. From 1750 on, the public discussion of the complex process of the industrial revolution was a common activity among the enlightened class. He gives special attention to the birth of economic publications like the reviews that developed in Great Britain in the late 18th and early 19th century, such as the *Edinburgh Review*. Despite these special review publications, economic news and reviews started to appear in the general and political press at that time as well.

In the second part of the book, the author points out that the United States took a leading role in the financial press as it became the great emergent market and the model of the liberal economy. The author discusses the roots of scientific journals on economics as well. He sees the institutionalization of economics as a scientific profession as the major driving force behind the increased publication of scientific journals on economics. Between 1880 and 1890 some of the major academic publications began to appear. In 1881, *Jahrbuch für Gesetzgebung* and *Verwaltung und Volkswirtschaft im*

Deutschen Reich appeared in Germany; in the United States, *Quarterly Journal of Economics* started publication in 1886; in Italy, *Giornale degli Economisti* began in 1886; in France, *Revue d'economie Politique* was launched in 1887; in the United Kingdom, the *Economic Journal* and the *Economic Review* began in 1891. The author continues by looking at the news agencies, which also developed in the early and mid-18th century. Reuters is one he looks at in more detail. He focuses on Reuters because Reuters's first clients were mainly companies and not journalistic clients. He continues this chapter by introducing the daily financial newspapers such as *Financial Times* in the United Kingdom, *Wall Street Journal* in the United States, and *Frankfurter Zeitung* in Germany, among others. The next medium he investigates is the general news press, which started to publish economic and financial news as well. However, it was not before the first decade of the 20th century that one could speak of true financial journalism as opposed to the customary, old transmission of facts, known as financial reporting. The author also looks at the paradigms of the business magazine in this chapter. He introduces the start of U.S. business magazines such as *Forbes, Business Week,* and *Fortune*. The first issue of the North American business magazine, *Business Week,* was published in 1929. He concludes this part of the book by looking at the public debate on economic issues facilitated by the media. This debate was fueled by the articles of such persons as Karl Marx and John Maynard Keynes. Both contributed regularly to the economics sections of newspapers. Other influential writers mentioned in the book are Josef Schumpeter, Francesco Ferrara, Frédéric Bastiat, Robert Giffen, and Walter Bagehot.

In the third part of the book, the author covers the press and the economy in the Keynesian era; that is, from the Great Depression to the first oil crisis. He describes how many of the financial news companies struggled with the aftershocks of the stock market crash in 1929. The stock market slump caused a decline in advertising revenues for the business press. The author describes how publications like the *Wall Street Journal* and *Financial Times* managed to overcome the crisis. In most cases they broadened their journalistic coverage. Politics influenced the business side of life, so those financial publications also started to write about politics and its implications for business. This development continued throughout World War II. After the war and well into the 1960s, the major financial publications like *Financial Times* and *Wall Street Journal* further widened their journalistic coverage. They realized that they had to cover everything that was appealing to its target group, and they have been successful with this approach. Other countries, especially those heavily affected by the war such as Germany, lost most of their publications due to the military government installed in Germany. However, a few years later, some business publications reopened and managed to be successful. The author names two of these, *Handelsblatt* and *Frankfurter Allgemeine Zeitung,* the successor of the early *Frankfurter Zeitung.* The author continues by describing the evolutions media companies underwent from small newspaper or magazine publisher to specialized media groups. These developments were apparent in the United States but similar developments took place in Europe as well. With the expansions of national economies and more disposable income in the hands of consumers, the magazine markets worldwide saw a large expansion. Besides special-interest magazines, one saw also the emergence of pure play news magazines covering important public interest issues instead of only economic ones. One popular example is *Newsweek.* The author describes how the magazines ventured out and looked for other business opportunities. He closes his book by looking again at how economists shaped the public debate about financial issues.

This book is a wonderful contribution to the literature on the development of the financial press in the early 19th and 20th century and highly recommended to re-searchers in need of insights into this time period. The author manages well to integrate multiple aspects of this development and gives a truly international perspective on the topic.

Rating

Rating Criteria	Rating
Theoretical Approach/Methodology	+++
Structure	+++++
Depth of the Analysis	++++
Contribution of New Knowledge	++++
Applicability	++++
Clarity and Style of Writing	+++
Rating Points: excellent: +++++	poor: +

Ediciones Universidad de Navarra, S.A., 2001

196 pages

ISBN 84-313-1893-7

Review Author

Reimar H. Mueller
University of St. Gallen, Switzerland
reimar.mueller@unisg.ch

The Economics of Copyright: Developments in Research and Analysis

edited by Wendy J. Gordon and Richard Watt

□

reviewed by Carl Henning Reschke

The book *Economics of Copyright* by Wendy J. Gordon and Richard Watt contains 10 contributions by authors ranging from PhD students to established and well-known researchers; consequently, quality in terms of breadth and depth and the style of writing vary.

Although it is not mentioned explicitly, there is a Web site of the Society for the Economic Research on Copyright Issues (SERCI; www.serci.org) on which the chapters of the book can be found. As a note, I find it interesting that the authors managed to reserve copyright for their contributions, because usually copyright transfer is required by publishers in order to ensure efficient copyright protection. This makes the book an interesting example for a transition process we will probably observe in many areas where creative people will be able to increase their standing relative to producers and distributors. Copyright plays an important role in this.

The book is therefore itself an interesting example for the underlying situation on which it sheds light. The change of distribution possibilities in information goods begs the question of whether it makes sense to publish such a book. It will probably mainly go to libraries and may well rot there, because researchers have access to and will find those chapters that they are interested in faster and cheaper on the Internet than in the book. As nice as the book looks and as good the print quality may be, eventually we deal with conference contributions with a work-in-progress character and with a comparatively short lifetime of interest. The papers will hopefully advance and get published in journals or other books. Therefore, the question is this: What is the added value—apart from conservation, a problem that the Internet and digital solutions do not yet address satisfactorily—for future historians? Are not publishers, which definitely have a role as selectors and bundlers of quality, shoveling their own grave, by publishing more and more, profiting from resources that are mainly provided by society in Europe, that get stretched more and more in the face of mounting information, resources that could be used better in advancing science in other ways?

Now, this is one of the perverse effects of economic competition pressure in combination with human (group) behavior in organizations, which is characterized by limited foresight, group think, and not being able to think outside of the box, until top management announces a fundamental change in strategy. Thus there is the need to do more and more of the same to be "better" than the competitors. So, there is no quarrel with the editors and the middle managers of this and other publishers. Nevertheless, these are the conditions from which revolutions result, be they economic, social, or political. This subject would have merited attention in the book as well, because it provides the metaperspective to put the issues together and evaluate different copyright regimes. The main social and economic question on the relation between changes in copyright policy, distribution, and industry structure is one of political economy: whether the Internet and digital technologies will be a case for capitalist society, or whether it will develop into a case for communist visions of society.

Principally, cheap production and distribution technologies with a potentially wide reach could make Marx's prediction on the development of capitalist societies toward communism come true—at least partially and at least for those goods that can be distributed digitally. Everybody throws the goods he or she has produced on a heap, for instance, in the form of personal Internet pages and peer-to-peer networks, and everybody takes what he or she needs from that heap. Everybody is happy because users are behaving fairly and taking only what they deserve, and they also get what they need. Of course, economists—and not only those—have claimed gluttony, greed, and generally selfish behavior work against such a vision. They can also ask about transactions (e.g., search and quality assessment) limiting such a model. As mentioned, one may also ask about the cost and possibilities of preservation of scientific and cultural goods produced and distributed digitally. Generally, we will find that a communist vision will not work well in the case of rivalrous physical goods, but it may work in the case of digital goods that can be copied in a nonrivalrous fashion. Wide dissemination of information goods may be preferable to accumulation of wealth and incentives for individuals to engage in production. Social welfare arguments may therefore support public funding of the technical and administrative infrastructure for such a situation. Such is the setting and wider importance of the economic copyright questions that the book covers. In the words of Benkler (2002):

> Since the core of commons-based peer production entails provisioning without direct appropriation, and since indirect appropriation—intrinsic or extrinsic—does not rely on control of the information, but on its widest possible availability, intellectual property offers no gain, and only loss, to peer production. (p. 73)

Stan Liebowitz deals with the question of whether copyright owners can appropriate the returns in the face of the new copying technologies. He starts by discussing the historical cases of videocassette recording, audiotaping, and particularly photocopying, where price discrimination was possible by separating between library and individual subscription, allowing for indirect appropriation of additional value generated by increased diffusion of knowledge through copying. Apart from the economic issues, he gives interesting personal information on his own involvement in the economic assessment of copyright issues. On far too few pages, he then discusses the Napster case, in which indirect appropriation by record companies seems impossible and evidence either for substantial harm through copying as well as evidence for lack of harm is missing, leading to the conclusion that behavior and economic models do not fit. This is not particularly new to me as a heterodox economist, but it is exciting news, as this signals increasing acceptance in mainstream economics. One suggestion to remedy this situation is to think of Napster and peer-to-peer networks as tools that increase attention for particular pieces of work and their creators, thus increasing sales, besides having a potentially negative effect on sales.

Paul Belleflamme discusses the pricing of information goods with low reproduction cost in the presence of illicit copying. The discussion and model are tailored to public goods with exclusion rights, for which the technological protection measures discussed by Frachy and Rochelandet are required. If there are no such measures, because creators donate their works to the public as in the case of freeware software, they are pure public goods. The question is then how can creators, and if need be distributors, make money on such goods, provided they want that at all, which might then be a question of transaction cost. Belleflamme uses the assumption that copies are of inferior quality to originals in a Bertrand–Nash setting. This assumption is likely to be wrong in the case of digital goods. He distinguishes two scenarios and in the first, with constant unit cost of copying, reaches the conclusion

that copying is likely to damage social welfare except for the case when copies are of poor quality or costly to acquire, which might be given users' search cost. However, this might be limited to a small numbers of users taking over the search role and distributing this information as described by Gladwell (2000). The second scenario, with positive fixed cost and no marginal cost of copying, cannot yet be fully treated and still needs further mathematical investigation.

Lisa N. Takeyama deals with piracy, asymmetric information, and product quality. She discusses the case that copies are of inferior quality and are used to assess the quality of experience with goods, which might then lead to a decision to buy the original product. Therefore the presence of even unauthorized copying may benefit the producer or distributor and increase social welfare. Assuming that repeat purchases occur, when quality of first purchases is high, copying can lead to weeding out inferior quality, and inducing producers to reveal information on quality a priori in the form of light or trial versions. For some areas, the assumption that actual quality is repeated is in doubt given the often declining quality of, for example, cinema blockbuster or book sequels, but makes sense as an assumption about consumer beliefs. To a certain degree, this constitutes a market inefficiency that is exploited by producers, which in turn could be checked by a threat of copying, allowing preconsumption inspection. Her conclusion is that standard measures of harm from copying may be overstated and that copyright should be oriented toward encouraging ex-post copying purchase.

Ruth Towse's "Copyright Policy, Cultural Policy and Support for Artists" discusses copyright policy issues and their relation to creativity on the basis of a cultural economics perspective. Interestingly, she refers to an argument against copyright law made by Plant in the 1930s, that there is a conflict of interest between publisher and author, concluding that copyright law would worsen authors' situation by publishers setting higher prices than authors would, which leads to higher competition and overproduction of low-quality products. Based on the relatively weak bargaining position of artists vis-á-vis firms she argues that strengthening copyright may well favor firms more. She finishes with a short assessment of data available and a call for more empirical data on cultural production.

Jorge Alonso and Richard Watt analyze the "efficient distribution of copyright income" using efficient sharing rules in royalty contracts using the Nash bargaining solution. Their results depend on the risk aversion of creators and distributors; for instance, if these differ there cannot be efficient fixed-proportion sharing rules. One advantage of portfolios of risks possibly explaining the continued existence of large producer–distributors is that they can pool the risks from individual projects. This would mean that individual creators will face continued asymmetric bargaining situations, suggesting a need for ensuring competition between distributors and or increased possibilities for creators to show off their quality, which is hinted at in Towse's contribution.

"Innovation of music" and the accompanying market structures in pre- and post-Napster scenarios are discussed by Tobias Reger. The author makes a good summary of the situation but the chapter takes only an economic perspective, which is too limited to account for the social issues that are necessarily involved in innovation. The discussion is too short and a model is mentioned, but it is not explicitly described.

The relation between "Coypright and Antitrust Issues" is discussed by Giovanni B. Ramello, leading to a model of asymmetric competition and a discussion of policy guidelines. He concludes that the characteristics of information goods and incentives by copyright law lead to a dialectic interaction between antitrust and copyright laws as well as inefficient behavior. Technological change alters the structure of markets and pushes those copyright owners violating the law to reveal the nature of their practices.

A discussion of the relation between protection technologies for digital products, which can be and are used as competitive arms, and copyright, whose costs are borne by society at large, making for a more equitable playing field, is provided by "Self-Help Systems: Good Substitutes for Copyright or New Barriers to Competition?" by Joelle Frachy and Fabrice Rochelandet.

Francesco Parisi and Ben Depoorter analyze the market for intellectual property as complementary oligopoly based ultimately on Cournot's duopoly model. They justify this with an (alleged) increasing degree of composite creation of derivative works. Although it can be stipulated that creativity was always of a highly combinatory nature, this does not affect the validity of their argument. They show that—assuming copyright holders do not coordinate their prices for their individual component works—monopoly may produce second best alternatives. Using complementary inputs, in oligopoly situations of two or more producers, each charges the optimal price for his or her complement, which results in higher prices and quantity restrictions than does a monopoly, which charges prices on the combined output.

Finally, Fabrice Rochelandet, in "Are Copyright Collecting Societies Efficient Organizations? An Evaluation of Collective Administration of Copyright in Europe," asks the questions that many payers of radio, TV, and copying fees ask, too. He discusses some theoretical problems and develops a comprehensive set of indicators. Performance is assessed based on values from 1991 through 1998 using decision envelope analysis (DEA) methods. German readers will be delighted to hear that GEMA fares well relative to other societies. His results indicate that levels of intermediary control and restrictive legal systems fare less well than either strict or low legal control. The increased cost of supervision in a strict legal system like Germany may well be balanced by the additional fees compared to legal systems with low legal control.

The book contains a set of chapters tackling the interaction of economics and copyright, which is part of an interesting societal development, making it interesting for those interested in this topic in the face of changing production and distribution technologies. Whether the added value of the book form over Internet downloads justifies the price tag is a question that individual buyers will have to decide. From my point of view, the most interesting chapters are those that deal with the "hot" issues on digital copyright protection and effects of new technologies, like Napster, on users, and less so chapters that press questions in the procrustean bed of more or less well-known mathematical economics.

References

Benkler, Y. (2002). Coase's penguin, or, Linux and the nature of the firm, v.0.4.3. Available at http://www.benkler.org/CoasesPenguin.PDF.

Gladwell, M. (2000). *The tipping point: How little things can make a big difference*. London: Abacus.

Rating

Rating Criteria	Rating
Theoretical Approach/Methodology	+++
Structure	+++
Depth of the Analysis	++
Contribution of New Knowledge	+++
Applicability	++++
Clarity and Style of Writing	+++
Rating Points: excellent: +++++	poor: +

Edward Elgar, 2003

216 pages

ISBN 1-84376-263-3

Review Author

Carl Henning Reschke
University of Witten/Herdecke, Germany
chreschke@yahoo.com

Strategic Responses to Media Market Changes

edited by Robert G. Picard

☐

reviewed by Bozena I. Mierzejewska

Reports on the developments of media markets indicate many changes, but we do not learn much from them about how media companies respond to them and how they adapt their strategies. Those questions are addressed by the 16 authors contributing to this book. Based on selected papers presented at a conference held in October 2003 in Joköping, Sweden, this book explores changes in the media environment and their consequences on existing media structures and firms. This collection is a highly interesting and comprehensive volume in which the world's leading specialists on media management theory and research deliver many answers and pose new questions.

Although the book is not divided into specific sections, its structure is clear. From general issues it proceeds to in-depth discussions of particular strategies, firms, and media industries in various countries. The editor and host of the conference, Robert Picard, starts with a synthesis of the main environmental and market changes affecting strategies of media firms. This is followed by Alfornso Sanchez-Tobernero's discussion about the future of media companies and new forms of management. Those chapters bring us closer to understanding the great variety of managerial and strategic challenges facing media companies.

Perhaps the most exciting contribution to the field is the collection of analyzed cases of successes and failures of various strategies employed: analysis of mergers of AOL Time Warner and Vivendi Universal written by Albarran and Gormly, and an analysis of the development of new newspapers in Europe by Gustafsson. Based on a very interesting statistical analysis, Chan-Olmsted identifies trends in global merger and acquisition activities in the global media industry. Discussions of French and German newspaper industries written by Desmoulins and Kopper, respectively, identify how and why the newspaper market has gone through very dramatic transformations. Those cases show that even very different markets faced very similar challenges. Cases devoted to broadcasting media address the issues of firm performance by Küng utilizing examples of BBC, HBO, and Pixar. Hoyer discusses TV2 in Norway. Hollifield, Vlad, and Becker address problems facing media organizations in emerging economies. For those looking for more theoretical discussions, the obvious choice should be Lacy's exploration of fuzzy markets.

All those articles are very different and support its analysis and conclusions on varied sources, so the whole collection is not as homogenous as it could have been. It is a bit like food: Some suit an individual's tastes more than others, but each of them could be used as very valuable additional reading material or cases for student discussion.

A book containing such a breadth of coverage and current evidence represents a major achievement. It provides a valuable resource for teachers and students and interesting reading for media managers and those interested in understanding the changing media industry.

Rating

Rating Criteria	Rating
Theoretical Approach/Methodology	++++
Structure	+++
Depth of the Analysis	++++
Contribution of New Knowledge	++++
Applicability	++++
Clarity and Style of Writing	++++
Rating Points: excellent: +++++	poor:+

Jököping International Business School, 2004

180 pages

ISBN 91–89164–46–6

www.jibs.se

Review Author

Bozena I. Mierzejewska
University of St. Gallen, Switzerland
izabella.mierzejewska@unisg.ch

Calendar of Events

2004

October

■ 10/01/2004 to 10/02/2004

Corporate Governance of Media Companies
Stockholm, Sweden
http://www.ihh.hj.se/mmt/event1.htm

■ 10/14/2004 to 10/15/2004

Mobile Games—Extending Porfitability across the Entire Value Chain
Barcelona, Spain
http://www.c5-online.com/index.cfm?conference=2850

November

■ 11/03/2004 to 11/04/2004

World Electronic Publishing Conference
Prague, Czech Republic
http://www.wan-press.org/beyond_p_w/index.html

■ 11/12/2004 to 11/13/2004

New Economy Comes of Age: Growth and Dynamics of Maturing New Media Companies
Stockholm, Sweden
http://www.ihh.hj.se/mmt/event2.htm

■ 11/13/2004 to 11/13/2004

Central European Regulatory Seminar
Warsaw, Poland
http://www.ectaportal.com/html/index.php?pgd=events_article&rec=367

■ 11/14/2004 to 11/26/2004

Tourism and Media
Melbourne, Australia
http://www.buseco.monash.edu.au/units/tru/conferences/callpapers.php

■ 11/25/2004 to 11/27/2004

European Television and Film Forum
Vienna, Austria
http://www.wan-press.org/beyond_p_w/index.html

2005

February

■ 02/24/2005 to 02/25/2005

World Newspaper Advertising Conference
Rome, Italy
http://www.wan-press.org/rome2005/

April

■ 04/06/2005 to 04/09/2005

Cinema and Technology Conference
Lancaster, United Kingdom
http://www.lancs.ac.uk/fss/cultres/events/cinematech/cinematech.php

Lightning Source UK Ltd.
Milton Keynes UK
178281UK00002B/5/P